Teaching Race

Master Class
Resources for Teaching Mass Communication
Series Editor: Chris Roush (Quinnipiac University)

Master Class: Teaching Advice for Journalism and Mass Communication Instructors, by the AEJMC Elected Standing Committee on Teaching, edited by Chris Roush

Testing Tolerance: Addressing Controversy in the Journalism and Mass Communication Classroom, by the AEJMC Commission on the Status of Women, edited by Candi Carter Olson and Tracy Everbach

The Graduate Student Guidebook: From Orientation to Tenure Track, by the AEJMC Board of Directors, edited by Katherine A. Foss

Teaching Race: Struggles, Strategies, and Scholarship for the Mass Communication Classroom, by The AEJMC Minorities and Communication Division, edited by George L. Daniels and Robin Blom

About AEJMC

The Association for Education in Journalism and Mass Communication (AEJMC) is a nonprofit organization of more than 3,700 educators, students, and practitioners from around the globe. Founded in 1912 by Willard Grosvenor Bleyer, the first president (1912–1913) of the American Association of Teachers of Journalism, as it was then known, AEJMC is the oldest and largest alliance of journalism and mass communication educators and administrators at the college level. AEJMC's mission is to promote the highest possible standards for journalism and mass communication education, to encourage the widest possible range of communication research, to encourage the implementation of a multicultural society in the classroom and curriculum, and to defend and maintain freedom of communication in an effort to achieve better professional practice, a better informed public, and wider human understanding.

About the Series Editor

Chris Roush is the dean of the School of Communications at Quinnipiac University. He previously spent seventeen years at UNC-Chapel Hill, where he was Walter E. Hussman Sr. Distinguished Professor, senior associate dean, and director of the master's program. He is the author or co-author of ten books, including the business journalism textbook *Show Me the Money: Writing Business and Economics Stories for Mass Communication* and a biography of former *Wall Street Journal* editor Vermont Royster. He has written books about Home Depot, Pacific Coast Feather Co., and Regions Financial. Roush is a board member of the Foundation for Financial Journalism and worked at the *Sarasota Herald-Tribune, Tampa Tribune, Atlanta Journal-Constitution, BusinessWeek,* and Bloomberg News. He was named the Journalism Professor of the Year in 2010 by AEJMC and the Scripps Howard Foundation. The judges noted that Roush "has become the expert in business journalism—not just at Chapel Hill, but throughout the country and even in other parts of the world."

Teaching Race

Struggles, Strategies, and Scholarship for the Mass Communication Classroom

The AEJMC Minorities and Communication Division

Edited by George L. Daniels and Robin Blom

ROWMAN & LITTLEFIELD
Lanham • Boulder • New York • London

Published in partnership with the Association for Education in Journalism and Mass Communication Elected Standing Committee on Teaching

Published by Rowman & Littlefield
An imprint of The Rowman & Littlefield Publishing Group, Inc.
4501 Forbes Boulevard, Suite 200, Lanham, Maryland 20706
www.rowman.com

86-90 Paul Street, London EC2A 4NE, United Kingdom

Copyright © 2021 by the Association for Education in Journalism and Mass Communication

All rights reserved. No part of this book may be reproduced in any form or by any electronic or mechanical means, including information storage and retrieval systems, without written permission from the publisher, except by a reviewer who may quote passages in a review.

British Library Cataloguing in Publication Information Available

Library of Congress Cataloging-in-Publication Data Available

ISBN: 978-1-5381-5455-7 (cloth)
ISBN: 978-1-5381-5456-4 (pbk.)
ISBN: 978-1-5381-5457-1 (electronic)

Contents

Foreword ix
    Melody T. Fisher, Mississippi State University

Introduction xi
    George L. Daniels, University of Alabama, and Robin Blom,
    Ball State University

Part I: Structural Changes 1

1 Radically Transforming Programs and Syllabi 3
    Danielle Brown Kilgo, University of Minnesota

    Perspective: Creating Spaces of Collective Unlearning 15
    Angie Chuang, University of Colorado

2 Incorporating a Critique of Coloniality 21
    Ilia Rodríguez, University of New Mexico

    Perspective: Teaching Race within an
        Intersectionality Framework 35
    Nathian Shae Rodriguez, San Diego State University

3 Committing to Excellence in Diversity and Accreditation 41
    Mia Moody-Ramirez, Baylor University

    Perspective: Teaching Diversity at HBCUs
        Requires a Deeper Dive 53
    Robbie R. Morganfield, North Carolina A&T State University

Part II: Positionality in the Classroom — 57

4 When the Lecturer Is a Minority — 59
   Alfred J. Cotton III, University of Cincinnati

   Perspective: When the Lecturer Is Biracial
      or Multiracial — 70
   Elliott Lewis, Syracuse University

5 When the Faculty Is a Majority — 75
   *Brian J. Bowe, Western Washington University/
   The American University in Cairo*

   Perspective: When the Majority Lecturer Is in
      the Minority — 86
   Gregory Adamo, Morgan State University

6 When the Lecturer Is International — 91
   Masudul K. Biswas, Loyola University Maryland

   Perspective: When the Lecturer Is from a
      Different Culture — 102
   Mariam F. Alkazemi, Virginia Commonwealth University

Part III: Guidance and Mentorship — 107

7 Teaching Diversity in Immersive Learning Courses — 109
   Gabriel B. Tait, Ball State University

   Perspective: Cultural Understanding of Diverse
      Communities — 121
   Aqsa Bashir, University of Florida

8 Diversity Issues in Campus Newsrooms and Agencies — 125
   Tamara Z. Buck, Southeast Missouri State University

   Perspective: Covering Race Panic Stories and Diversity
      Flare-Ups — 136
   Cristina L. Azocar, San Francisco State University

9 Embracing a Pedagogy of Pain — 141
   Meta G. Carstarphen, The University of Oklahoma

   Perspective: Confronting Color-Blindness — 152
   Keonte Coleman, Middle Tennessee State University

10 Guiding Research in Issues of Diversity and Difference — 157
    Troy Elias, University of Oregon

    Perspective: Mentoring Students of Color — 168
    Maria De Moya, DePaul University

Afterword: Of Insurrection, Injustice, and a Racial Reckoning 175
Deb Aikat, University of North Carolina at Chapel Hill

Index 185

About the Editors and Contributors 191

Foreword

Melody T. Fisher, Mississippi State University

The publication of this text could not have happened at a more opportune time. In addition to it providing guidance for current race-related teaching dilemmas, this book is presented during our milestone fiftieth anniversary—in 1961, founder Lionel Barrow Jr. presided over the Minorities and Communication (MAC) Division's first business meeting. The scholarship contributed to this book is a realization of Dr. Barrow's advocacy for the inclusion of education on race and media communication. MAC's founding members included in the constitution "to encourage the teaching and design of courses and textbooks that would present an unbiased view of the role of minority groups in the United States; offer critique of media representations of minorities; and prepare students for professional work in multi-racial environments."

This book is of personal interest to me not because of my current position as head of the MAC Division but due to my calling as an educator. I have taught at both a historically Black college and a predominately White institution, and for the success of myself and my students, had to adjust to each setting. As a public relations instructor, I am keenly aware of my identity as I present material to students. My students and I discuss the role of organizational communication and establishing relationships with audiences, and we always explore the nuances of reclaiming trust when racial discrimination or other mistreatment has taken place. I have learned through the years to build my arsenal of references, knowing that cultural barriers must be overcome to achieve understanding.

MAC is the first AEJMC division to author a book in the Master Class series from Rowman & Littlefield. It is my hope that it will be a great resource for you.

Introduction

George L. Daniels, University of Alabama,
and Robin Blom, Ball State University

Do you remember the first time you were made aware of your skin color and its role in what you might accomplish in life? What did you feel when you first learned this? Who delivered this message to you? Sometimes the reality of race hits us square in the face during a negative confrontation or experience. For others, that reality is revealed only through hearing about or learning about another person's experience. It might be in the form of a highly publicized event that shocks the nation or the world. Because of the high likelihood that those kinds of messages would be delivered in mass mediated or communicated form, those of us who are experts in the field charged with training the preparers and presenters of those messages (that is, journalists, filmmakers, PR practitioners, etc.) need to be optimally equipped to deliver instruction on this reality of race. Such instruction ranges from the history of those from underrepresented racial groups to how to apply that knowledge in crafting a media message and even how to engage in classroom conversations on sensitive subjects.

Equipping the instructor to teach students about race and reporting on race is about more than just learning terms and definitions. It is much more than learning how to use equipment. It even exceeds just providing guidance on what words to write or what to say on camera. The burden we carry as journalism and mass communication educators when it comes to teaching about race is inextricably linked to our own lived experiences. That lived experience may be different if we come from a marginalized group with a history of oppression. Do you happen to fall in one of these marginalized groups? Can you "objectively" teach students how to develop and deliver messages about race without mentioning your own experience? Should you do that? And what about teaching race and diversity when you are not from a marginalized group?

So far we have posed a lot of questions. You may find that this book raises more questions than answers. And that's okay. In the constant process of improving our teaching, questions are opportunities to think further about how we do what we do, and sometimes those questions are not answered until we make individual decisions for a specific lesson or class session on a particular day.

WHY ANOTHER BOOK ON TEACHING RACE

As the members of the AEJMC's oldest and largest unit focused on issues of diversity, equity, and inclusion, the Minorities and Communication (MAC) Division is proud to offer this compilation of writings on teaching that we hope will provoke discussion, dialogue, and even debate. If you, our reader, engage with the material here, there will be many moments of introspection and reflection.

You may wonder why we decided to do another book on the topic of teaching race, especially when at least four other books with similar titles have been published in the past few years. After publishing numerous books on teaching, Stephen Brookfield (2019) offered *Teaching Race: How to Help Students Unmask and Challenge Racism*, an edited volume on how to create teachable moments to unmask racism. His contributors offer guidance on such topics as teaching whiteness in predominantly White classrooms, negotiating conflict in teaching race, creating conditions for racial dialogues, and helping students uncover positionality.

Elsewhere, Cyndi Kernahan's (2019) *Teaching about Race and Racism in the College Classroom* combined her dual background as a psychology professor and the leader of the teaching and learning unit of her college to offer a way of teaching race and racism that is not blaming or shaming. Instead her six-chapter treatment is compassionate while also honest about the realities of racism and White supremacy in the United States. One of her chapters gives guidance for developing a "Secure Teacher Identity," even though you may receive lower teaching evaluations and experience emotional difficulty.

Both of these books were published on the heels of a third volume of case studies and exercises on *Exploring Campus Diversity*. Sherwood Thompson and Pam Parry's (2018) book includes fifteen cases specifically dealing with classroom climate. While we were putting the finishing touches on our project, word came of a fourth volume expected to be released. More recently, Cohen, Raynor, and Mack (2021) assembled fifteen essays from a variety of disciplines in *Teaching Race in Perilous Times.*

So why another volume? The short answer to that is teaching race in a journalism and mass communication context is different. While we applaud the advice of these other books, we know that when you are preparing students not only to deal with their own development in understanding race and racism but also to couple that with their development as preparers of messages for others who consume media, the burden on faculty to "get it right" is enormous.

This project was far along in its development by the time of George Floyd's death at the hands of police in May 2020. Yet the weeks of social unrest that followed produced not only an awakening for people around the world, but also a conundrum for news managers asked to respond to questions about treatment of journalists of color in their own newsrooms where messages about race and racial unrest were being prepared.

The last time a comprehensive book-length treatment for current and future educators specifically focused on teaching about race and ethnicity in the journalism and mass communication classroom was produced was Martindale's *Pluralizing Journalism Education* in 1993. Shortly after the Accrediting Council on Education in Journalism and Mass Communications (ACEJMC) implemented its Diversity Standard (then known as Standard 12), her volume offered twenty-four essays and articles focused on diversity recruitment, curriculum, and student media. Since that time, the ACEJMC accreditation standards have been updated twice, and a third update set to take effect in 2022 contains a more robust diversity standard. Both the revised ACEJMC Values and Competencies and the new Standard 4 on Diversity and Inclusiveness appear in chapter 3.

Our more than two hundred members of the AEJMC MAC Division have programmed dozens of teaching panels for our annual conference each summer and, within the past decade or so, for the AEJMC Midwinter Conference. Multiple MAC members have won teaching contests for their diversity and inclusion innovations in the classroom.

This volume represents the logical next step in diversity efforts that began more than fifty years ago with thanks to Lionel C. Barrow, one of the handful of African American PhDs who was part of the then AEJ (the precursor of AEJMC) and did his part in response to the assassination of Dr. Martin Luther King Jr. (Barrow and King had been classmates and fraternity brothers at Morehouse College.) AEJ established the Ad Hoc Coordinating Committee on Minority Education, which was tasked with ascertaining, stimulating, and coordinating the activities of AEJ members in bringing more Blacks and other minority group members into the journalism (and mass communication) pipeline. The committee eventually morphed into a permanent unit of the association—the MAC Division, which has made the membership of the association and the field more racially diverse. Unlike the other contributions to this volume, this introductory chapter is the product of two authors. As the only coauthored component, it contains food for thought from two faculty members from two completely different backgrounds: a never-married African American cisgender male, raised in the former capital of the Confederacy, who cites his Christian beliefs as far more important than his race in his everyday life; and a White male who is a native of the Netherlands and whose partner is an immigrant herself—both growing up thousands of miles away from the cornfields of Indiana in vastly different cultures. Much of what we use to set up this volume on teaching race is built on our personal experiences. For the sake of clarity, the next two sections are written in first person as they contain our individual thoughts and reflections on our understanding of teaching race.

GEORGE'S EXPERIENCE

To return to a couple of the questions posed at the beginning of the chapter, I would point to "the talk" my late father had with me about the history of how Black Americans and White Americans interact. That was the first time I was made aware of my skin color as a potential indicator for how other human beings would interact with me. He stressed the importance of not allowing what was then thirty years ago influence or impact what would become my future. At the time of "the talk," I was enrolled in a fantastic private school where we went to chapel every Wednesday and opened each day with biblical lessons. But the school was predominantly White. Most of my friends were White Americans, and that was not a problem for me. I described that school as "fantastic" because it gave me the critical spiritual and educational foundation that shaped my worldview and outlook today.

Even as I reached the seventh and eighth grade, I was active in the NAACP Youth Council, and in the process of talking about NAACP events on television appearances, I discovered news media and journalism as a career. This journey in negotiating race as an active member of the NAACP continued into high school when I was introduced to a predominantly Black public high school where I was teased for "talking White." That same high school is where I entered the "honors" track and eventually served as president both for my high school's student senate and the citywide student senate for all high schools in the Richmond (Virginia) Public Schools. These experiences shaped how I approach teaching race and many other subjects.

My dad delivered the message about race, but I discovered the news media as a tool for writing my own race story. As a high school student, I published stories in my hometown's afternoon newspaper, *The Richmond News Leader*. Then, when I arrived at Howard University to start college, I was given a heavy dose of Black history that was so much a part of the culture of "The Capstone of Black Education." Located in Washington, DC, Howard University since its founding in 1867 has played a central role in the African American educational experience. Among historically Black colleges and universities (HBCUs), Howard has produced the greatest number of graduates with advanced degrees. If nothing else, as a Howard University graduate, you were going to graduate as a leader who was fully aware of the accomplishments of Black people and committed to the needs of those in the African diaspora. Indeed, I graduated having served both a year as the vice president of my college's student council and editor-in-chief of Howard's award-winning student newspaper, *The Hilltop*.

Along the way, I had a class with former MAC Division Head Clint Wilson, who was both an associate dean of Howard's School of Communications and the instructor for a course on the "History of Black and White Press." It was not many years later that I learned of Wilson's (1985) influence as coauthor of *Minorities and Media: Diversity and the End of Mass Communication* with Felix Gutierrez. I also did not realize the role of another book, *Split Image: African Americans in the Mass Media*, which Jannette Dates and William Barlow (1993), two Howard professors, authored. Both books by Howard University faculty have been influential in the field of mass communication and the research and teaching on the topic of race and diversity.

After working in television news and producing thousands of newscasts at stations in my hometown of Richmond, Virginia; Cincinnati, Ohio; and Atlanta, Georgia, I discovered a new career as a media researcher and teacher in the Grady College of Journalism and Mass Communication at the University of Georgia. That is where I took a master's course in race, gender, and media. I learned how challenging it can be to teach about race, but I also was enlightened about the potential I could have as a researcher investigating questions related to race.

Today when I teach diversity classes at the University of Alabama, I warn students about three things involved in any course on race or diversity: (a) it is personal, (b) it is political, and (c) it is constantly changing. Usually once a year, I get to teach graduate or undergraduate courses focused on communication and diversity or race, gender, and media. But as focused as those electives are in the delivery of instruction on race, my teaching on race within other skills courses is even more important. For example, in a large lecture core course in electronic reporting, I employed two "interventions" to more robustly teach students how to cover race and racism. In the fall of 2019, I assigned my students a five-page reading from the 2019 *Associated Press Stylebook* and "race-related coverage." Then there was a lecture on the topic that included highlights from the reading and a presentation of Len-Ríos and Perry's (2020) concept of excellence in journalism (include context, complexity, voices, authenticity, and proportionality). These basic concepts were the core ideas in the lecture, which also included examples of race panic stories such as one involving a campus official who resigned after some controversial statements about race were made on Twitter.

On their first test, students did poorly on the two multiple choice items directly linked to the content from this unit. Two-thirds of the class could not correctly identify what the *A.P. Stylebook* says about covering racism. Only twelve out of thirty-eight students could recall that a reporter should have a conversation with senior managers when determining whether to call a statement, action, or policy "racist." Most of the students erroneously thought that one should never call an action "racist." That was a key point of this guidance from the *A.P. Stylebook* that students failed to absorb. That first test also included an item that asked students to recall the definition of a race panic story, which is one where public dialogue about race is suddenly confused, charged, and agitated. Officer-involved shootings that gave rise to the #BlackLivesMatter movement and controversial remarks about race or ethnic groups by political candidates were two examples of such stories. Three-fourths of the students correctly answered that question from Lehrman and Wagner's (2019) book *Reporting Inequality: Tools and Methods for Covering Race and Ethnicity*.

Two months later in the last part of the semester, during the second "dose" on race and racism in that same class, a second unit on "Race, Racism, and Ethics" built on the basic concepts from the first section with a second lecture that included information from Project for Excellence on Journalism as Cartography. The Project for Excellence on Journalism created a map for navigating society that should include people from all communities regardless of race, religion, or socioeconomic status. In the same unit, students were told how the Society of Professional Journalists suggests that journalists examine their own cultural values and avoid imposing those values on others along with avoiding stereotyping by race.

A single item on their third test asked students to recall points from the "Race, Racism, and Ethics" unit. Eighty-nine percent of the students correctly answered the question. The lesson learned from introducing this first-time unit on "Covering Race and Racism" is that such a unit must be integrated multiple times in a course. Second, the approach of showing actual stories where race and racism were presented may be more effective than simply going over the rules in the *A.P. Stylebook*. However, one cannot rule out that the timing of the units can also be a factor in the level of retention of the information. The next time I am teaching our introductory course in electronic reporting, I do intend to have both units again and will initiate some practice exercises.

In sharing this example from my own teaching, I exemplify the approach the other authors take in each of the chapters in this volume. I think about teaching and learning from a scholarly perspective, where I could ask questions about students' learning and collect information to find answers (Bishop-Clark & Dietz-Uhler, 2012). In the scholarship of teaching and learning, we as instructors are constantly trying new approaches to facilitate learning that reflect our responsiveness to a changing environment and our understanding of our critical role as instructors teaching race.

ROBIN'S EXPERIENCE

My first visit to the United States was with my hometown baseball team in 1997 as part of an exchange program with a team in Lansing, Illinois. It was the trip of a lifetime for a bunch of teenagers who finally would visit Wrigley Field and Comiskey Park after watching those iconic stadiums on television for years. You have no idea how thrilled we were when a yellow school bus waited for us outside O'Hare Airport. Why, you ask? While the buses are certainly not known for their luxury comfort, we only knew about them because of *The Simpsons* and other American television shows and movies. (Back home, all of us biked to school every day.) We did not care that a chiropractor was needed after that forty-five-minute drive to Lansing. It was fabulous to be Bart Simpson for a day!

The most interesting aspect of the trip, besides the seven games we played against high schools and other local clubs, was that all team members stayed with host families. This gave us a much richer experience of life in America rather than two weeks semi-unpacked in a standard Holiday Inn room with the same kids I grew up with at home. The Biliks, my host family, came to visit two years later when the Lansing team traveled to my hometown, and they invited me to stay with them again the following year.

Evidently, the exchange program had many upsides as we learned a lot about a different culture, even though in hindsight it was only a very narrow slice that the Chicago suburbs offered. Predominantly *White* suburbs I should add, as there were also murkier moments more relevant to this book on race and diversity. For instance, a resident of Lansing told me (or should I say *warned* me) that the town was in peril because "the

Blacks are moving in." He whispered because no one around us, in what I vaguely remember was some sort of lunch café, was supposed to hear it. I do recall much more clearly that I was nodding somewhat awkwardly while pretending to fully understand what he was saying.

I did not immediately.

English was not my best language. In fact, I was among the worst students in my English, French, German, and Latin high school classes for years. So it took a little bit to process what actually happened, yet the phrase "the Blacks are moving in" is still a vivid memory more than two decades later, as well as that uncomfortable, nauseating feeling of disgust when it sunk in what had happened. I shiver thinking about it, like I did then, even after all these years.

It was not that I was unaware of racism, despite growing up in a predominantly White suburb called Ridderkerk on the outskirts of Rotterdam. The Netherlands may be known for its tolerance, but that is just a façade—the Dutch are as racist, xenophobic, and homophobic as any other country. We are just pretty good at convincing ourselves that we are not—the White majority, that is, first and foremost. People of color have many other experiences when they bring up potential reparations for the Dutch slavery past or the use of blackface as part of St. Nicholas traditions. In those cases, tolerance for dissent is often short lived or nonexistent.

Numerous high school friends frequently blamed Turkish, Moroccan, and Moluccan immigrants—or any people of color for that matter—for increasing crime rates. Of course, there was an exception for their one friend of color because "he was a good one" (which they told him over and over again). These forms of xenophobia were not a surprise at a time when there were openly racist members in the Dutch Congress who found in refugees and other asylum seekers ideal scapegoats for anything that went wrong in society.

Multiculturalism—which was the umbrella term used at that time to discuss any race- and ethnicity-related issue—was an important topic that I covered as a novel newspaper reporter soon after matriculating at the School of Journalism in Utrecht. I wrote numerous diversity-related stories over the years, from tense public meetings protesting the construction of an asylum center in a small rural community to attempts by local governments to decrease racial and ethnic biases in hiring processes. Yet I always had a nagging feeling of being un(der)prepared to deal with such complex issues, while not being able to pinpoint exactly what was wrong or missing. And honestly, at the time I was not even closely aware of the true scale of systemic racism that minority communities had endured for centuries in the Netherlands and elsewhere. (Leave it up to the Dutch educational system to romanticize its colonial past as a bunch of adventurers roaming the high seas looking for honorable trade partners around the globe.)

An opportunity to study at San Francisco State University as an international exchange student in 2002 helped me on a path to learn more about diversity by signing up for "Racism: Cross-Cultural Analysis," an anthropology course by Dr. Linda Tavernier-Almada. She exposed me to many racial and cultural topics that I had no clue about—with, as the most shocking exhibit, the full-length showing of *Birth of a Nation*. Talk about a horrific eye opener . . .

Another course that I took was a media ethics class by Professor Austin Long-Scott, the first African American reporter hired full time by the Associated Press, who told us numerous stories of him covering the Civil Rights Movement in the South. Many of his class materials were developed together with the Maynard Institute, which advocates for accurate representation of minorities in newsrooms and in the news. Additionally, I enrolled in the civic journalism course taught by Professor Venise Wagner, whose coedited volume *Reporting Inequality* was mentioned earlier. Our classroom was essentially Bayview-Hunters Point, two predominantly African American neighborhoods in the southeastern corner of San Francisco that were featured in the 1963 documentary *Take This Hammer*, in which James Baldwin said, "This is the San Francisco America pretends does not exist" (Moore, 1963). That is how many community members still felt almost four decades later when we met them during public forums that Wagner organized for us. This is where we heard the stories of neglect by "City Hall" and the lack of resources in comparison to many affluent communities around the Bay Area.

A year later, I ended up on the East Coast, this time as an international exchange student at the State University of New York at New Paltz, where I took another course about racism. This one was taught by Dr. A. J. Williams-Myers, who deservedly had the African Roots Community Center Library in Kingston, New York, named after him a few years ago. He assigned us readings about the role of mass media in transmitting cultural images of African American women and White racism, including his own work on White violence (Williams-Myers, 1995).

All these educators shaped me tremendously on my own journey in academia. I ended up teaching a one-credit diversity and media course soon after I arrived at Ball State University, and I recently received the opportunity to develop a course called "Eyewitness Misidentification and Social Injustice" in our honors college. It allows me to show students how eyewitness misidentifications, as well as news media coverage of these false accusations, have harmed innocent people and often their vulnerable communities as well. Students read *Picking Cotton*, *The Anatomy of Innocence*, and the tenth anniversary edition of *The New Jim Crow*.

Additionally, they watch Ava DuVernay's *13th*, *The Innocence Files*, *The Confession Tapes*, *Exhibit A*, and other documentaries showing them how eyewitness misidentification, police brutality, and deliberate political ignorance have caused mass incarceration and endless structural violence toward Black, Indigenous, and People of Color.

Most of my students in the class so far have been White. They learn a lot as evidenced by one particular phrase that pops up numerous times during our class discussions: "I had no idea." Some feel betrayed by their high schools for having to unlearn many things they were told erroneously. They become more and more horrified, sad, troubled, and angry every step along the way while reading, watching, and discussing the traumatic experiences of the innocent.

As an educator, it is rewarding to see students learn things about their world they did not know before, similar to my own experiences as an exchange student. Nonetheless, many questions linger. If my White students learn so much from all the traumatic examples of innocent people, how are those examples experienced by the students of color in my class, whether or not they have lived many traumas on their own or know others who did? How do I position myself as an ally for the oppressed? How do I avoid coming across as performative, as in performing wokeness? What if I say *the wrong thing* during a class discussion? How do I recognize that I said *the wrong thing* in the first place? The classes at San Francisco State and SUNY New Paltz have been helpful, but as an educator born and raised outside the United States, I do not pretend to know or understand all the intricacies of discrimination in this country. It took me years to understand that particular words or phrases are racist. What should I assume that all my students know about diversity—majority and minority students alike? How do I avoid accidentally *mansplaining* intersectional issues of race, gender, and diversity when I do not know what they know already?

This stuff is hard, uncomfortable, and emotionally draining at times. It is not a coincidence that this volume's title includes "struggle"—because a struggle it is occasionally—while the stakes feel enormous. If I cannot figure these things out, how could I be sure that my students can in the classroom and, later on, in their careers? They may be communicating with thousands of people at a time. In my mind, there is no room for error.

Therefore it is an understatement to say that there is a lot to learn about teaching race, regardless of anyone's background, which is the main reason why I joined this project. Similar to the feeling of un(der)preparedness to deal with issues of race as a journalist, there are always feelings of un(der)preparedness as an educator in this regard—even beyond the usual imposter syndrome mood swings that thrive in academia. In search of answers (although as said earlier, we may end up with many more questions in the end), this is a tiny contribution to finding strategies that hopefully make us all better educators and encourage scholarship that allows us to document successes and opportunities for future progress in teaching race.

Let us move on and tell you what to expect in this volume.

DIVERSE VOICES

As the editors of this volume, we made some important decisions early on. For instance, as this is a book about teaching race and diversity, we wanted to feature a large variety of voices. One solution was to include many chapters about different subtopics of teaching race, but that meant as a potential downside that none of the chapters would go beyond a superficial discussion of those subjects. Therefore we opted for a design with ten chapters that are each followed by a shorter perspective by another scholar that focuses on a related topic. This allowed us to cover more topics with more depth.

We also deliberately created a list of specific chapters and perspectives that we wanted to see covered in the book. A subsequent choice was to invite scholars to contribute rather than sending out the typical call for chapters—although this was not without challenges either. Many scholars feel lost and are uncomfortable writing about topics beyond their narrow slice of expertise that they usually focus on in academic settings, and this project was no exception. That resulted in quite a lot of soul searching and long yet interesting conversations with many of the contributors before they felt comfortable with the direction we envisioned.

These struggles were worth it eventually, and the result is even more impressive when keeping in mind that this book was written in what felt like a pressure cooker. The authors were confronted by a deteriorating pandemic wreaking havoc on their personal and professional lives, which was also largely overlapped with a nerve-wracking presidential election that followed months of protests by those demanding racial and social justice. Additionally, the contributors to this book often had less than two months to write their first draft to allow this volume to be available before the start of the 2021–2022 academic year. If anything, this showed the dedication of all the contributors to this volume and their priorities toward teaching race and diversity.

Creating a list of topics we wanted to see featured in this volume was far from easy as there are so many aspects of teaching race that are deserving of their own chapter. We decided to focus the core of the book on the positionality of faculty members in relation to their student bodies while teaching race. You will see several chapters and perspectives focusing on classroom dynamics for when a lecturer is a minority or majority. For instance, Alfred J. Cotton III writes about many layers of complications for a racial minority to teach race, and Elliott Lewis explores this from a biracial perspective. On the contrary, Brian J. Bowe talks about his experiences of teaching race as a White majority educator, and Gregory Adamo does the same based on his experiences teaching at primarily White institutions and in his current position at a historically Black university. To complement this positionality core of the book, Masudul K. Biswas and Mariam F. Alkazemi focus on the challenges of teaching race in a different culture as a foreigner in the United States.

All chapters include practical information and teaching tips that educators can utilize in their own classrooms, but we added a few chapters and perspectives that go more in depth in course design and student advising. Gabriel B. Tait focuses on teaching diversity in immersive learning settings within diverse communities, which is followed by Aqsa Bashir's perspective on teaching cultural understanding and communication beyond one's own community. The awareness of racial aspects within communities is also important for students participating in campus media and agencies. Tamara Z. Buck reports on the essential leadership roles of advisers of campus newsrooms and agencies in mentoring students, and Cristina L. Azocar focuses specifically on reporting about race panic stories and diversity flare-ups on campus. Meta G. Carstarphen's chapter details her experiences in creating an interdisciplinary course about the 1921 Tulsa Race Massacre and the complexity of teaching racial trauma, which is followed by Keonte Coleman's perspective on confronting color-blindness. All these chapters and perspectives point to the important need for students to develop research skills specifically focused on understanding race and their need for mentorship, which are the main topics of contributions by Troy Elias and Maria De Moya.

Although the positionality of faculty is the core of this volume, with further emphasis on practical implications to teach race and mentor students to produce messages involving race, all of those aspects rely on the structures of the institutions where this instruction takes place. Whereas much of the social unrest in the summer of 2020 was focused on political and law enforcement structures, institutions of higher education have their own wrecking ahead of them—to put action to their words of valuing diversity, inclusion, equity, and belonging. Therefore this volume has a different starting point before delving into classroom positionalities. In the first chapter, Danielle Brown Kilgo points out how current journalism programs, curricula, and syllabi contribute to the current political and social crises, and she provides a pathway for the radical transformation of media education. Angie Chuang's perspective shows the importance and challenges of decolonizing classrooms in practice. Ilia Rodríguez continues this discussion by focusing on intercultural dialogues and critical communication pedagogy through the lens of coloniality, Critical Race Theory, and the decolonial act in journalism and media studies. Nathian Shae Rodriguez adds to this his intersectionality framework of teaching race. As ACEJMC accreditation influences what and how to teach within program curricula, Mia Moody-Ramirez reflects on the updated diversity standard by ACEJMC and how changes could potentially affect instructors in teaching race. Last, Robbie R. Morganfield adds to this discussion by examining teaching about diversity and race at HBCUs.

While we were in the home stretch to finish this volume, during one of our many virtual meetings to talk through editing logistics, we looked bewildered at our screens while a mob was storming the U.S. Capitol, and we saw guns drawn on the House Floor. At that point, the severity of the insurrection in progress was yet unclear and still beyond belief. Soon after the dust settled and the scale of the brutality became evident, we felt it was important to address racial aspects visible in responses to recent protests by law enforcement and others. Only blocks from where peaceful #BlackLivesMatter protestors were swept away with tear gas and flash-bang grenades for a photo-op a few months earlier, a primarily White crowd walked in and out of the heart of the U.S. government almost undeterred—one of them even smiling for a picture with House Speaker Nancy Pelosi's lectern on his shoulder. In response to this mob at the Capitol, Deb Aikat wrote an afterword about facilitating difficult classroom discussions about race and diversity.

STRUGGLES, STRATEGIES, AND SCHOLARSHIP

To wrap up this introduction, we would like to share an example of one of the "struggles" that is involved in teaching race. Since this volume follows the 7th edition of the Publication Manual of the American Psychological Association, we originally intended to strictly adhere to the recommendation on racial and ethnic identification, which capitalizes the words "Black" and "White" when referring to an individual or group. However, some of the contributors to this volume disagreed with that policy for various reasons. For example, if an instructor is teaching a journalism class where the Associated Press Stylebook is the authoritative reference, he or she would only capitalize "Black," but not "white." The AP announced this change in its usage rules in 2020, weeks after publishing the latest print edition of its stylebook (Bauder, 2020). Other scholars in this volume operate from an ethos where capitalizing "White" is inconsistent with the philosophy that undergirds their work as scholars. Given these differing ideas on the central focus of this book, race, you will find the word "White" appears differently depending on the author of the chapter or perspective. Elsewhere, we have decided to use caps for "Civil Rights Movement" when referring to an era, but lower case in other instances. Similarly, "Critical Race Theory" is also presented with caps as it refers to a given name.

Finally, we want to thank a few people who helped us along the way. Several MAC Division members formed an advisory board to provide us feedback about our initial outline of the book. All five contributed to the volume later as well (Deb Aikat, Danielle Brown Kilgo, Mia Moody-Ramirez, Robbie Morganfield, and Gabriel Tait). We also would like to thank Master Class series editor Chris Roush for all his support and wisdom in guiding us in this process. The same needs to be said about Natalie Mandziuk and her team at Rowman & Littlefield. We also want to thank four graduate assistants, Ida Cage, Gwyn Hultquist, Elena Lazoff, and Becca Schriner, who helped us with some nitty-gritty editing and formatting. Last but not least, we are thankful for the support from both the AEJMC leadership team and the MAC Division.

Overall, we hope that these chapters and perspectives move forward critical discussions on how to transform educational programs among all areas under the umbrella of AEJMC. We also hope that this volume continues to shape these transformations over an extended period. Therefore you will see an emphasis on the scholarship of teaching and learning in multiple areas in this book, which is a deliberate attempt to stimulate instructors to not only reflect on their own teaching moving forward but also to document systematically the things they try in the classroom to teach race. There is no need to reinvent the wheel over and over again, especially when time is of the essence when it comes to adding antiracism pedagogy and making other important and rigorous changes in our curricula and lesson plans that allow all students to flourish in inclusive environments. Although—ironically—the Association of *Education* in Journalism and Mass Communication has no education division, the MAC Division welcomes any scholarship that contributes to the progress of teaching race. Additionally, despite the lack of a dedicated division, there is a flagship publication in *Journalism & Mass Communication Educator* that could feature much more scholarship on teaching and learning about diversity issues. By publishing successes and potential avenues for future success in teaching race, our fields can hopefully continue to advance struggles into strategies and more scholarship.

REFERENCES

Bauder, D. (2020, July 20). AP says it will capitalize Black but not white. *The Associated Press.* Retrieved June 24, 2021, from https://www.ap.org/ap-in-the-news/2020/ap-says-it-will-capitalize-black-but-not-white.

Bishop-Clark, C., & Dietz-Uhler, B. (2012). *Engaging in the scholarship of teaching and learning: A guide to the process and how to develop a project from start to finish.* Stylus.

Brookfield, S. D. (2019). *Teaching race: How to help students unmask and challenge racism.* Jossey-Bass.

Cohen, J. E., Raynor, S. D., & Mack, D. A. (2021). *Teaching race in perilous times.* SUNY Press.

Dates, J. L., & Barlow, W. (1993). *Split image: African Americans in the mass media.* Howard University Press.

Kernahan, C. (2019). *Teaching about race and racism in the college classroom: Notes from a White professor.* West Virginia University Press.

Lehrman, S., & Wagner, S. (2019). *Reporting inequality: Tools and methods for covering race and ethnicity.* Routledge.

Len-Ríos, M., & Perry, E. L. (2020). *Cross-cultural journalism and strategic communication: Storytelling and diversity.* Routledge.

Manarin, K. (2018). Close reading: Paying attention to student artifacts. In N. L. Chick (Ed.), *SoTL in action: Illuminating critical moments of practice* (pp. 100–8). Stylus.

Martindale, C. (1993). *Pluralizing journalism education: A multicultural handbook.* Greenwood Publishing.

Moore, R. O. (Director). (1963). *Take this hammer (the director's cut).* National Educational Television. https://diva.sfsu.edu/collections/sfbatv/bundles/216518

Thompson, S., & Parry, P. (2018). *Exploring campus diversity: Case studies and exercises.* Rowman & Littlefield.

Williams-Myers, A. J. (1995). *Destructive impulses: An examination of an American secret in race relations: White violence.* University Press of America.

Wilson, C. C., & Gutierrez, F. (1985). *Minorities and media: Diversity and the end of mass communication.* Sage Publications.

I
STRUCTURAL CHANGES

1

Radically Transforming Programs and Syllabi

Danielle Brown Kilgo, University of Minnesota

Journalism and mass communication programs have long been critiqued for their slowly adaptive curricula and programmatic changes. Though most major news organizations were fully online by the new millennium and were invested in social media by 2006, journalism programs lagged behind. The rapid progression of technology proved to be challenging, and, for many, instead of learning important skills for the trade in school, degreed media makers were learning in the field. In her commentary on journalism and mass communication programs, Royal (2017) noted that many programs still had not incorporated essential topics and skills like analytics, coding, and design thinking. Royal wrote, "How are these topics covered in your program? If the answer is 'they aren't,' then your curriculum is obsolete" (Royal, 2017, para. 10). She called for programs to engage in redesigns that attract students. "At a time when understanding the role of media in society has become essential, we must continue to invest in and innovate media education to prepare professionals and educate the public" (para. 14).

Royal's (2017) critique and call to reimagine curriculum is a useful model for also thinking about how our programs and curricula address race. Ask yourself: How many lectures incorporate conversations about power, White supremacy, colonialism, and antiracism in their key lessons? If the answer is "not very many," then *your program is a complicit actor to the broader racist system*. Years of scholarship have routinely found that our field is still structured in a way that supports a racist system that marginalizes Black, Indigenous, and People of Color (BIPOC; for example, Chakravartty, 2020; Moody et al., 2013).

This chapter contributes to literature that has diagnosed the rampant problem of underrepresentation and marginalization in our field, programs, and classrooms (for example, Chakravartty, 2020; Moody et al., 2013). I explore how our journalism programs, curricula, and syllabi contribute to the current political and social crises we are facing. I also discuss how the culture, norms, and trends that persist in journalism and mass communication programs have helped protect the status quo, making us accomplices to the uniquely polarizing and overtly racist environment we see in our modern times. Following, the second half of this chapter will provide pathways for the radical transformation of the system of media education: from program to syllabus.

WHERE WE STAND

The 2020 COVID-19 pandemic put all of us in uniquely compromised positions, touching our lives in ways that will likely change our realities for decades to come. During this time, many of us around the world remained in an extended lockdown when, on May 25, 2020, video of police violence and the murder of George Floyd began to circulate in the news cycle. Floyd's death not only reenergized the Black Lives Matter movement, it also served as a turning point in the fight for human rights. Calls for change came from around the world—the following days revealed solidarity campaigns between communities and public announcements from major corporations in support of activists and their causes. Universities around the world held listening sessions, publicly recommitting to increasing diversity and centering racial equity. Referred to as the summer of racial reckoning, this important moment came amid the amplified rallying cries of racists, who have found validation in a world that is seeing the acclivity of the most vicious forms of White supremacy.

Prior to this moment, journalism and mass communication studies had its own poignant moments of racial reckoning. One such moment was in 2018, after Chakravartty et al.'s (2018) article in the *Journal of Communication* sparked an in-print, offline, and online conversation about just how common White-authored communication scholarship was in top journals (#CommunicationSoWhite). Their work advocated for better representation for BIPOC in our top research journals and more conscious inclusion in our citation practices. One of the piercing points that emanates from their discussion is that there is little equitable progress in our discipline. Within the academy, White, male, Western orientations of communication scholarship still dominate our journal citation lists (Chakravartty, 2020) and our journal editorial boards (de Albuquerque et al., 2020). The same orientations guide predominant perspectives that appear in many of our undergraduate textbooks (Alemán, 2014), while graduate school curriculum has been shown to habitually disavow critical theories of race (Chakravartty & Jackson, 2020). The main conclusion from this essential discourse: *mass communication and journalism studies, curricula, and professions are largely dominated by White and Western voices.*

A HISTORICAL ALLEGIANCE TO COMPLICITY

Journalism and mass communication programs have never been the force that disempowers and overrides the habitual and paradigmatic reproduction of marginalizing narratives that criminalize, demonize, and erase people from backgrounds that are not White or Western. In our classrooms, for example, this shows up as the underrepresentation and underperformance of students from disadvantaged backgrounds. It rears its ugly head in elitist positions that elevate only a handful of students in a program and leave the rest to find their way on their own. In our syllabi, it appears in the token inclusion of the discussion about identity—there's a week on racism instead of a curriculum designed to address it. One might brush off the need to regularly discuss our racist system in the context of a class that emphasizes technology or election coverage or journalism history. That would be a mistake, however. These subjects are all shaped by a racist system. For example, scholars like Benjamin (2019), Noble (2018), and Browne (2015) have shown the racialized power system has been replicated in digital spaces. From our alumni, it shows up in their content (for example, Bramlett-Solomon & Carstarphen, 2017; Campbell, 1995; Dates & Barlow, 1990; Deepe Keever et al., 1997; Dixon & Williams, 2015; Mastro et al., 2011; Mourão et al., 2018; Poindexter et al., 2003; Poindexter & Stroman, 1981; Reid-Brinkley, 2012; Roberts, 1975; Sui & Paul, 2017). On the shoulders of giants, my research that critiques press patterns finds little new about the portrayals of BIPOC (for example, Kilgo & Harlow, 2019).

In the nineteenth and early twentieth centuries, the press was successful in instigating racist fears and provoking mobs and massacres around the United States. Journalism institutions (including universities and newsrooms) have, for the most part, only offered superficial remedies for these problems—even though there were thorough investigations and guides for doing more complex work. Take, for example, the Hutchins Commission of 1947. The final report concluded that the press inadequately served the public. The report ultimately recommended that news organizations (a) provide truthful, comprehensive, and intelligent accounts of the day's events, in a context that gives them meaning; (b) serve as a forum for the exchange of comment and criticism; (c) project a representative picture of the constituent groups in the society; (d) include the presentation and clarification of the goals and values of the society; and (e) allow for full access to the day's intelligence. The report provided journalism ethics scholars with a solid foundation and was well received by some journalists. There is no denying the Hutchins report's impact on journalism programs. The report and its foundations appear on many syllabi in programs across the country still today.

However, the Hutchins Commission's active members were considered prolific scholars—all male, all White—bringing to question the commission's ability to assess just how inadequate the service of journalism was, especially for people of color. Twenty years later, a clear deficiency was identified. Following the urban uprisings of the 1960s, the Kerner Commission of 1967 revealed that media coverage remained overwhelmingly problematic, but more so for certain groups over others. The Kerner Commission articulated the overwhelming reliance on whiteness and criticized the White-only perspectives that prevented adequate reporting of the challenges, problems, histories, and culture of Black communities. The commission went so far as to call the entire profession "shockingly backward" in its inclusion and representation of Black people in newsrooms and in media coverage (National Advisory Commission on Civil Disorders, 1968, p. 384).

Incredibly, this biting critique did not lead to the revolution one might expect. Journalistic output continued to fail people of color. Scholars have found that BIPOC were marginalized or misrepresented regularly in coverage through the end of the twentieth century (for example, Campbell, 1995; Dates & Barlow, 1990; Deepe Keever et al., 1997; Entman & Rojecki, 2000; Poindexter et al., 2003; Poindexter & Stroman, 1981; Roberts, 1975) and well into the twenty-first century (for example, Bramlett-Solomon & Carstarphen, 2017; Dixon & Williams, 2015; Kilgo & Harlow, 2019; Mastro et al., 2011; Mourão et al., 2018; Reid-Brinkley, 2012; Sui & Paul, 2017). BIPOC people continue to be underrepresented in newsrooms, with an increasing number of journalists of color publicly denouncing the discrimination and ostracism in their newsrooms (for example, Toll, 2015). As such journalism and mass communication programs are training students of color for a profession that has neither welcomed them with open arms nor represented them in the so-called elite newsrooms (News Leaders Association, 2019). Other communications fields, including public relations and advertising, also struggle with diversity problems. In 2019, the U.S. Bureau of Labor Statistics reported that 82 percent of advertising and public relations professionals were White.

Diversity issues also affect how professionals, scholars, and students navigate the university system. With faculty of color still severely underrepresented in the majority of programs around the world, many students do not have access to mentors who can push forward their careers and help them navigate the challenges of passionately existing in majority-White spaces. Likewise, faculty of color are often overburdened through inequitable expectations, service obligations, mentorship demands, and importantly the emotional toll that follows—a consequence that is not unique to our profession.

A RADICAL MOVE FORWARD

Collectively, this history illustrates a core and persistent truth: the diversity and inclusion platforms and initiatives pushed forward in universities, accrediting systems, and newsrooms have not been enough. How might we transform this dynamic but persistent dominance of White supremacy in our programs, classrooms, and the industries in which we expect our students to thrive?

I argue that the best answer here is *radically*. As a metaphor, this does not mean we are changing our hair from a natural color to glow-in-the-dark neon. However, radical transformation does require that we unravel the foundational structures that host and protect oppressive systems. To do this, we can no longer rely on the normative; we *have* to consider neon as a viable option. Radical change requires that we use out-of-the-box thinking to unsettle roots spread throughout the grounds of broader systems built to oppress certain people. Radical critique and its usefulness in significant change means tackling the systems of power that create injustices and building a blueprint for change that seeks to eradicate this injustice (Jensen, 2010). We have to identify where racism persists in our system, and we have to build an agenda that is directly aimed at relentlessly snuffing it out. Radical change means returning to the accrediting course objectives and critiquing their purpose and worth. Radical change means returning to our journalism histories and rejecting narratives that glorify some people and also minimize the positions and perspectives of marginalized communities. Radical change means that we begin to remember the things that have been forgotten. Lesser known than Ernie Pyle's hailed Pulitzer Prize–winning work was his demonization of Japanese people and prisoners:

> They were wrestling and laughing and talking just like normal human beings. And yet they gave me the creeps, and I wanted a mental bath from looking at them. (Cited in Dower, 1986, p. 78)

We must diffuse the false binaries of good and bad, legendary and controversial. Refusing to do so makes us accomplices in a racist system. Radical change also looks like the Pulitzer Prize–winning work in the *New*

York Times's 1619 Project, which brought to light hidden histories' lasting legacy in a racist system. Its radicalness reached all the way to the White House. Former President Donald Trump said that the project defiled history and that a "radical revolution . . . was taking place in our military, in our schools, all over the place" (Behrmann, 2020, para. 3). Transformation takes more of this radical revolution. We must embrace the possibility that our classrooms can be radical vessels for change. We have to decolonize and diversify everything.

Importantly, the idea of diversifying has been around a long time. Diversification's core goal is to bring in new perspectives. But diversification is most useful when all facets are diversified: student bodies, advisory committees, administrators, and faculty. Diversity statements, diversity committees, and diversity initiatives have never been the answer because they do not offer changes to the foundations of journalism programs but instead act as add-ons. That is why past efforts have not revolutionized our journalism programs as a whole.

While diversification is a buzzword we have heard for a long time, decolonization requests the radical return to the roots of our nation's first transgressions to give back what was stolen from Indigenous people and those sold into slavery. As Tuck and Yang noted, "Decolonization brings about the repatriation of Indigenous land and life" (2012, p. 1). The authors critique social scientists and education systems alike for the incorporation of the term "decolonization" into their social justice and equity goals, which they argue reduces decolonization to a metaphor and erases the violence of colonialism. Decolonization means not only centering equitable approaches that integrate non-Western, non-White narratives as imperative norms for understanding our field, it also requires us to focus on equity—recreating and reimagining curricula and programs that incorporate the practices from, for example, Native American newspapers. A radical turn in journalism programs would also incorporate the practices and triumphs of those who had to plead their own cause outside the parameters of the mainstream because they were not considered whole humans. As we strive to decolonize our curricula, we cannot forget that this goal is rooted in a historical process that cannot be solved by one educator, one administrator, or one school because decolonization is radical and requires a reallocation of resources. Our programs must reconsider their fiscal responsibilities and their programmatic priorities.

WHERE CAN I START?

Decolonization and diversification cannot simply be a politically correct, outward move that does not unravel power structures. Realistically, however, systems resist change, and this will not happen overnight. Until then, as individual instructors, professors, and mentors, we hold a significant amount of power that can chip away at the system. I offer five key places we can all start building a quorum.

Reject Journalistic Objectivity

Though some might nod in agreement about the elusiveness of objectivity, our curriculum remains built on its foundations and continues to be an expectation that our journalism students are expected to adopt and that journalists hold. Objectivity is a great *idea*. The problem, however, is that we carry journalism's lust for the idea of objectivity alongside its unattainable standards and our failed allegiance. We should not cling to our failed relationship with objectivity. In fact, we should break up with it. It is time to move on.

We must reject the idea of objectivity and what we wish journalism *could* be. We cannot just move on to similar terms like "fair" and "accurate" without first acknowledging that journalism has not been fair or accurate in some of the most critical moments. Fairness has also not been journalism's status quo. Accuracy has privileged a specific set of facts and fact makers.

Our radical, decolonized classrooms and programs must first acknowledge these failures. Then we must analyze the deficits these failures have created. Finally, we must commit to a new ethical foundation that centers on equity and moral responsibility. We must let the past influence our future: this is the path to redemption, this is the path for trust building with marginalized communities, and this is the path for diversity in our classrooms. You might think letting the past the past dictate our future is biased. So be it.

In my courses, I begin with this same rejection of objectivity. I acknowledge I am biased. I acknowledge that I have an identity, a life experience, and a history that changes how I see the world. I acknowledge my places of power. I discuss the bias I hold in all its forms: those that I have and am trying to change, those that I hold and defend, and I imagine those that I do not know I hold and push against any settling with ignorance. I tell my students I cannot know everything that everyone is feeling or thinking or experiencing. And neither can they. It is uncomfortable and risky. However, this step is essential for the radical breakup with objectivity. It is the first step at helping future media makers acknowledge and grapple with their own biases, especially those they are blinded to or have been taught to ignore.

Change Your Course Objectives

Radical change takes more than cookie-cutter course objectives. We cannot rely on static course objectives to drive our syllabi planning. Take, for example, the ACEJMC's core competency related to diversity, often found in the course objectives sections of syllabi: *"demonstrate an understanding* of gender, race ethnicity, sexual orientation and, as appropriate, other forms of diversity in domestic society in relation to mass communications" (ACEJMC, n.d., para. 10). What understanding of race and ethnicity prevails in a White-dominated profession? To better serve our students we must commit to the objective of helping them understand racism's systemic function and White supremacy's persistent power in today's society. We must teach our students about the aggressors, not just the victims. We must also change those course objectives every year to address morphing forms of oppression.

Place the Discussion of Systemic Oppression in All Your Reading Lists and Lesson Plans

We are all familiar with the countless, painstaking hours it takes to prepare an original syllabus with the perfect reading list. As updates are made to that curriculum from year to year, we tend to go with what we know, maybe updating a few things here or there. But the radical diversification of our syllabi and curricula requires more.

Decolonizing your syllabus might mean creating new units that center on the perspectives of BIPOC people, but it is also important to remember that the systemic nature of racism and its intersections makes a discussion relevant to every topic. To assume or presume that there is not "enough" research on issues related to race and colonialism to incorporate into some topics is to be complicit in a racist system and contribute to the silencing and citation politics that shape our entire profession (Chakravartty et al., 2018). There *is* room for discussions of systemic oppression in every topic. Yancy's (2008) work can drive regular conversations about the white gaze in a lighting class. Clark's (2018) research can be used to describe technology adoption and utilization variances. Richardson's (2020) findings can become your go-to for conversations about mobile and citizen journalism. Decolonization requires instructors and teachers to reconsider normative assumptions like who are leaders in knowledge production and who has been made invisible.

Several projects have made accessible archives so that instructors are able to find articles from BIPOC communication scholars quickly. For example, in the spring of 2020, I launched a curation project called iCite, an inclusive citation project that highlights the work of Association for Education in Journalism and Mass Communication's Minorities and Communication Division members from past and present that emphasizes race and ethnicity work (bit.ly/iCiteMACDatabase). The same year, the Glen M. Broom Center for Professional Development in Public

Relations at San Diego State University launched a massive database of Black mass communication scholars from around the world (Sweetser, 2020). Social media discourse initiatives are great places to look for new scholarship. For example, #CiteBlackWomen seeks to elevate the work produced by Black women, who are often subject to erasure.

Normalize Difference

Diversification and decolonization resist the regurgitation of static theoretical approaches and methodologies and instead require the introduction of new perspectives, opinions, and ideas into classrooms and programs. Doing so is bound to create differences in opinion. Instead of seeing these differences as controversial, unnecessarily subjective, or polarizing, expect difference. Make it essential. Demand its existence. Difference invites critical thinking skills, critical reading skills, and conversations that open the hearts and minds of others. Briefly put, normalizing difference in our syllabi and in our classrooms can "reimagine our normative ways of doing research" (Gardner, 2018, p. 832), teaching research, and reimagining curricula. The normalization of difference can release people from positions impervious to progress and instead incorporate new ideas.

In many of my classes, I try to normalize differences by asking students to place themselves in the perspectives of others as part of the outcome of an assignment. After completing a portrait assignment in my beginning photography classes, I require students to return to their subjects and present their final work. Students must conduct an interview, and ask the subjects questions like: Were the final images fair? Were those depictions representative? What could have been changed? There are almost always differences in how the student sees their work and the subject does. The student sees the picture one way, the subject sees the picture another. This assignment encourages students to consider those differences, consider the consequence of choosing certain images on the subjects, and utilize this knowledge to make future decisions that go beyond the newsworthiness of one particular photograph. Another semester, students listened to Nikole Hannah-Jones's 1619 podcast about racism in the healthcare system, and we discussed how that experience might change the way people experienced the 2020 pandemic. Students were sent on a hunt to find stories that reflected this history in mainstream news, learning the important lesson that stories about racism's systemic effects were not and are not the norm. Create assignments that help students see differences (or see their own differences) and explore the world through the eyes of those who are privileged to just "be normal."

Do Not Become Complicit (Again)

Changes must be revisited and reevaluated often. The process of diversification and decolonization is reiterative. Because White supremacy and patriarchy permeate every system in our society, we are not done with one pass, one initiative, or one change. Diversification and decolonization efforts must happen constantly. They must be a regular part of our daily routine. We must make them habitual.

The revolutionary change we hope to see in the professional world can start in the classroom. We can center on conversations about social injustice and power and teach ethical, responsible media making that drops the blinders of objectivity, educates about bias, and transforms norms and routines. "*The classroom remains the most radical space of possibility in the academy*" (hooks, 1994, p. 11).

REFERENCES

ACEJMC (n.d.). *Principles of accreditation.* http://www.acejmc.org/policies-process/principles/.

Alemán, S. M. (2014). Locating whiteness in journalism pedagogy. *Critical Studies in Media Communication, 31*(1), 72–88.

Behrmann, S. (2020, September 29). Trump says he moved to end racial sensitivity training in federal agencies "because it's racist." *USA Today.* https://www.usatoday.com/story/news/politics/elections/2020/09/29/presidential-debate-trump-claims-he-moved-end-racial-sensitivity-training-federal-agencies-because-i/3583361001/.

Benjamin, R. (2019). *Race after technology: Abolitionist tools for the new Jim Code.* Polity.

Bramlett-Solomon, S., & Carstarphen, M. (2017) *Race, gender, class and media: Studying mass communication and multiculturalism.* Kendall Hunt.

Browne, S. (2015). *Dark matters: On the surveillance of Blackness.* Duke University Press.

Campbell, C. P. (1995). *Race, myth and the news.* Sage.

Chakravartty, P. (2020). #CommunicationSoWhite in the age of ultra-nationalisms. *Communication, Culture & Critique, 13*(2), 270–74.

Chakravartty, P., & Jackson, S. J. (2020). The disavowal of race in communication theory. *Communication and Critical/Cultural Studies, 17*(2), 210–19.

Chakravartty, P., Kuo, R., Grubbs, V., & McIlwain, C. (2018). #CommunicationSoWhite. *Journal of Communication, 68*(2), 254–66.

Clark, M. (2014). *To tweet our own cause: A mixed-methods study of the online phenomenon of "Black Twitter."* Doctoral dissertation, University of North Carolina at Chapel Hill. Carolina Digital Repository. https://cdr.lib.unc.edu/concern/dissertations/gt54kn18h.

Dates, J. L., & Barlow, W. (1990). *Split image: African Americans in the mass media.* Howard University Press.

de Albuquerque, A., de Oliveira, T. M., dos Santos Junior, M. A., & de Albuquerque, S. O. F. (2020). Structural limits to the de-Westernization of the communication field: The editorial board in clarivate's JCR system. *Communication, Culture and Critique*, 13(2), 185–203.

Deepe Keever, B. A., Martindale, C., & Weston, M. A. (Eds.). (1997). *U.S. news coverage of racial minorities: A sourcebook, 1934–1996*. Greenwood Press.

Dixon, T. L., & Williams, C. L. (2015). The changing misrepresentation of race and crime on network and cable news. *Journal of Communication*, 65(1), 24–39.

Dower, J. W. (1986). *War without mercy*. Pantheon.

Entman, R. M., & Rojecki, A. (2000). *The Black image in the White mind*. University of Chicago Press.

Gardner, P. M. (2018). Diversifying ICA: Identity, difference, and the politics of transformation. *Journal of Communication*, 68(5), 831–41.

hooks, bell. (1994). *Teaching to transgress. Education as the practice of freedom*. Routledge.

Jensen, R. (2010). Beyond race, gender, and class: Reclaiming radical roots of social-justice movements. *Global Dialogue*, 12(2), 1–12. http://www.worlddialogue.org/contentuser.php?id=487.

Kilgo, D. K., & Harlow, S. (2019). Protests, media coverage, and a hierarchy of social struggle. *The International Journal of Press/Politics*, 24(4), 508–30.

Mastro, D. E., Blecha, E., & Atwell Seate, A. (2011). Characterizations of criminal athletes: A systematic examination of sports news depictions of race and crime. *Journal of Broadcasting & Electronic Media*, 55(4), 526–42.

Moody, M., Subervi, F., & Oshagan, H. (2013). Ethnic/racial minorities' participation in AEJMC: How much and what type of progress? *Journalism & Mass Communication Educator*, 68(3), 269–81.

Mourão, R. R., Kilgo, D. K., & Sylvie, G. (2018). Framing Ferguson: The interplay of advocacy and journalistic frames in local and national coverage of Michael Brown. *Journalism*, 22(2), 320–40.

National Advisory Commission on Civil Disorders (1968). *Kerner Report*. U.S. Government Printing Office.

News Leaders Association (2019). 2019 diversity survey. *News Leaders Association*. https://www.newsleaders.org/2019-diversity-survey-results.

Noble, S. U. (2018). *Algorithms of oppression: How search engines reinforce racism*. New York University Press.

Poindexter, P. M., Smith, L., & Heider, D. (2003). Race and ethnicity in local television news: Framing, story assignments, and source selections. *Journal of Broadcasting & Electronic Media*, 47(4), 524–36.

Poindexter, P. M., & Stroman, C. A. (1981). Blacks and television: A review of the research literature. *Journal of Broadcasting*, 25(2), 103–22.

Reid-Brinkley, S. R. (2012). Ghetto kids gone good: Race, representation, and authority in the scripting of inner-city youths in the Urban Debate League. *Argumentation and Advocacy*, 49(2), 77–99.

Richardson, A. V. (2020). *Bearing witness while Black: African Americans, smartphones, and the new protest #journalism*. Oxford University Press.

Roberts, C. (1975). The presentation of Blacks in television network news. *Journalism Quarterly*, 52(1), 50–55.

Royal, C. (2017). Your journalism program is obsolete. *Nieman Lab.* https://www.niemanlab.org/2017/12/your-journalism-curriculum-is-obsolete/.

Sui, M., & Paul, N. (2017). Latino portrayals in local news media: Underrepresentation, negative stereotypes, and institutional predictors of coverage. *Journal of Intercultural Communication Research, 46*(3), 273–94.

Sweetser, K. (2020, July 30). Resources for adding diversity to your mass comm classrooms. *Glen M. Broom Center for Professional Development in Public Relations.* https://jms.sdsu.edu/broom_center/making_news_entry/resources-for-adding-diversity-to-your-mass-comm-classrooms.

Toll, C. (2015). Are minorities getting a fair shot at journalism jobs? *Nieman Reports.* https://niemanreports.org/articles/are-minorities-getting-a-fair-shot-at-journalism-jobs/.

Tuck, E., & Yang, K. W. (2012). Decolonization is not a metaphor. *Decolonization: Indigeneity, Education and Society, 1*(1), 1–40.

Yancy, G. (2008). Colonial gazing: The production of the body as "other." *Western Journal of Black Studies, 32*(1), 1–15.

PERSPECTIVE: CREATING SPACES OF COLLECTIVE UNLEARNING

Angie Chuang, University of Colorado

In my seventh year on the journalism faculty at American University, I was asked to develop a mandatory first-year experience course on race. I immediately wanted to run in the other direction. Until then, I had seen myself as a postprofessional scholar on the periphery of institutionalized academia, a second-career academic whose preparation for this life consisted of a master's degree and a thirteen-year reporting career in daily newspapers. Prior to academia, I had been a reporter focused on race and immigration issues, most comfortable in the unsupervised individualism of field reporting. I had not been a joiner at American University, staying in my own discipline-specific lane of journalism and race, in which I thought I was most qualified to make a difference as one of a handful of Black, Indigenous, People of Color (BIPOC) faculty teaching race-focused courses. Let the "real academics" take on the seemingly impossible, and likely thankless, task of creating a controversial course under the scrutiny of upper administrators, student services staff, university trustees, and the news media.

Long story short, I am writing this piece because I said yes, in spite of my misgivings and a bad case of impostor syndrome. It was late 2014, months after a summer and fall of unrest in cities like Ferguson, Missouri, and on college campuses—including my own—had compelled me to question everything about teaching, journalism, race, and the intersections of the three. As Danielle Brown Kilgo has elucidated in her chapter, when these inflection points arrive, we cannot continue doing what we had before. Signing on to an institutional, administration-driven effort would hardly seem radical to many, but for me it was. I was acknowledging that I had to infiltrate the system I had avoided—in effect, the machine of predominantly White higher education—to undergo the transformation *I* required.

My university had acknowledged that something needed to change. Empowered by my newly tenured status, I could help make the course impactful versus watered down and perfunctory. At the time, a growing number of colleges had zeroed in on a crisis in first-year student retention rates that disproportionately affected BIPOC students (Libassi, 2018). As this troubling trend came into focus in the early 2000s, widely offered or mandatory first-year experience courses had become common. According to a report produced by the U.S. Department of Education (2016), 52 percent of four-year institutions required all entering students to take first-year experience courses. Most of these courses included "cultural diversity" among a range of common topics, including campus resources and student development.

Administrators at American University had envisioned a yearlong experience, with a first semester on general college transition and, more remarkably, a second semester focused on race and social identity. It was that latter semester that I was tapped to develop and pilot. The two-course sequence, catchily titled "The American University Experience," or AUx1 and AUx2, would be taught in small seminar-style sections. "Race was an important jumping off point for the AUx2 course content, given what was happening in the country and on our campus at the time it was launched," said sociologist Andrea Malkin Brenner, the former director of the two-semester sequence and my collaborator in curriculum design. Brenner is now a private consultant, author, and first-year college transitions educator. "The course created a unique platform for students to have discussions across differences, not only about race and social identity, but also about gender, sexual expression, social class, religion, disability, and political identity" (personal communication, December 15, 2020).

The vast openness of this call for a prepackaged course on race, which would eventually be taught by a range of instructors to about two thousand students a year, unnerved me. Until then, so much of my own course design had been dependent on *me*. I had chosen discipline-specific materials that either had influenced me as a former reporter on one of the country's first regional daily newspaper race and ethnicity issues beats, at *The Oregonian*, or by journalists or journalism scholars I knew personally. That approach would not work for AUx2.

I found a wellspring of support and ideas as I ventured outside of my journalism and communication silo and sought out my colleagues and experts in critical race and gender studies, sociology, history, literature, psychology, and more. Because of conversations with them, I built a curriculum that, instead of focusing on separate units about each racial identity group, hinged on intersectional "moments," both historic and contemporary. These learning units included the impact of "Manifest Destiny" on both Native displacement/genocide and African slavery; the collaborations and tensions between the Abolitionist movement and early White feminists; the "Model Minority" myth's role in leveraging Asian Americans against Black and Brown communities; and the 2016 Pulse Nightclub mass shooting as a tragic but transformative catalyst among the LGBTQ, Latinx, and Muslim American communities for confronting violence and hate.

During the pilot semester's "Manifest Destiny" week, we discussed a video from the acclaimed animated educational television series *Schoolhouse Rock* called "Elbow Room." Aired in 1976, the lighthearted cartoon depicts early American colonists crowded in the Northeast corner of a U.S. map, in need of some "elbow room." Then an animated Thomas Jefferson merrily dispatches Lewis and Clark westward into the blank map. A stereotypically rendered Sacagawea appears in their boat, the only real acknowledgment that Native Americans existed, and the colorless map only comes to life as the settlers traverse "the most elbow room we've ever had." The song alludes to "fights to win land rights" (Ahrens, 1976), concluding:

> But the West was meant to be;
> It was our Manifest Destiny!

My students in 2016 had reactions ranging from discomfort to disbelief that "Elbow Room" was an actual educational video. Yet most had learned a similar version of the "Manifest Destiny" story of westward expansion as late as high school. We discussed conventional Western historical narratives of Columbus "discovering" the Americas, the first Thanksgiving, and global colonialism. "I didn't realize that learning about race in America meant I had to *unlearn* elementary, middle, and high-school U.S. history," one of the first-year students said.

Religious studies scholar Natalie Avalos (2018), a Chicana of Apache descent and now my colleague at the University of Colorado Boulder, argued that decolonizing the curriculum is not only about offering alternative perspectives but also about challenging and unmasking the reason false dominant narratives were constructed in the first place. "A decolonial approach makes the mechanisms of colonial power visible," she wrote (para. 1). Over the course of that pilot semester, I came to see that, in spite of my painstakingly built learning units and carefully chosen academic readings, the best catalysts for student discussions and reflections were most often a moment of incidental or spontaneous *unlearning*.

"Elbow Room," intended as a short breather between more traditionally academic material, came to set a tone for the course that, as one student quipped, "Everything I learned about race before college was wrong." This statement was intended as exaggeration, but many students were indeed surprised to learn, for example, that race has no genetic basis; that Martin Luther King Jr. was a complex strategist, not a speechifying saint; and that neither racism nor privilege should be viewed as individual but rather as systemic. Decolonizing the classroom requires this constant vigilance about the power structures of familiar ways of thinking, even if they appear at face value to be progressive. It requires the patience and willingness to, as Brown Kilgo puts it, normalize difference and allow students to challenge and work through unlearning in their own ways and with each other.

I passed the first-year experience course on to others after that pilot year, when an unexpected offer of employment took me to the University of Colorado Boulder in 2017. At American, AUx2 has transformed into other incarnations since then, reflecting changing times and staffing, and has encountered bumps in the execution of a worthy effort. Student media have reported that BIPOC students and instructors have felt isolated or alienated in class or among program staff, respectively. Nevertheless, I am grateful to have been a part of its early stages.

I joined CU Boulder's Journalism Department a changed teacher and person. I expanded the range of my courses by including fuller examinations of gender, sexuality, and socioeconomic class in conjunction with race in media. Intersectional approaches not only feel more aligned to the reality of social identity today but also are inclusive of a student body that is less racially diverse and more socioeconomically diverse than the one on my previous campus.

Nowadays my courses are far less about my past experiences and disciplinary comfort zones and much more about creating experiences of collective *unlearning*, of challenging conditioned beliefs and narratives—including my own. I am working to decolonize my own pedagogy, both in the content I present and also in my own awareness of my responses as a BIPOC woman and a nontraditional scholar in an academic setting. I am finding my place at the table as a "real academic" and, more importantly, accepting my responsibility as a teacher and agent of radical change.

References

Ahrens, L. (1976). Elbow room [Song recorded by S. Manchester]. https://www.schoolhouserock.tv/Elbow.html.

Avalos, N. (2018). Decolonial approaches to the study of religion: Teaching Native American and Indigenous religious traditions. *Religious Studies News*. https://rsn.aarweb.org/spotlight-on/teaching/anti-racism/decolonial-approaches.

Libassi, C. (2018). The neglected college race gap: Racial disparities among college completers. Center for American Progress. https://www.americanprogress.org/issues/education-postsecondary/reports/2018/05/23/451186/neglected-college-race-gap-racial-disparities-among-college-completers/.

U.S. Department of Education. (2016). *First year experience courses*. Institute of Education Sciences. https://ies.ed.gov/ncee/wwc/Docs/Intervention Reports/wwc_firstyear_102116.pdf.

2

Incorporating a Critique of Coloniality

Ilia Rodríguez, University of New Mexico

The turbulent summer of 2020 provided vivid, painful, and embodied reminders of the deep and outspread roots of institutionalized racism: the multiple police killings of African Americans; the inequities in healthcare that caused disproportionately high numbers of deaths among African Americans, Latinx, and Native Americans during the COVID-19 pandemic; and the Trump administration's threats to interfere with the U.S. Census process and suppress voting in minoritized communities. For many of us teaching journalism and media courses with a focus on race and cultural diversity, these crises, as well as the antiracism protests they spurred, gave a greater sense of urgency to our commitment to unpack systemic racism through critical thinking and dialogical practices.

My approach to these practices has been influenced by the critical communication pedagogy's view that teaching methods should include reflection on ways in which identity, embodied knowledge, and power are negotiated in the classroom (Cooks, 2003; hooks, 1994; Fassett & Rudick, 2016; Simpson, 2010; Simpson et al., 2011). My positionalities as a mixed race heterosexual woman, born and raised in colonial Puerto Rico and diasporic wanderer in the United States, bilingual, former journalist, and critical scholar certainly mark my teaching performance. Equally important, the interactions with my students at the University of New Mexico, a Hispanic-serving and Carnegie Research 1 institution in a minority-majority state, create unique opportunities for rich intercultural interactions in a colonized, border space. Hence, I strive to bring into my pedagogy conceptual tools that enable understanding and transformation of racial stratification and domination.

In this chapter I discuss, in particular, the incorporation of theorizing on coloniality, decoloniality, and critical race methodology into the teaching of journalism and media studies. These conceptual lenses allow for the analysis of the deeper epistemic foundations that have sustained hierarchization, racism, and liberal ideologies of diversity in modern society. These epistemic foundations also underlie normative practices and dominant narratives in academia as well as in media-related industries and professions. In this sense, the critique of coloniality and the commitment to decolonization of knowledge through reflection, media production, and activism are two sides of the same exercise. In the first part of the chapter, I synthesize theoretical insights from coloniality studies that I have found relevant for my teaching about media and diversity. In the second part, I suggest strategies for adding a coloniality/decolonial approach in lectures, discussions, class activities, assignments, and bibliographic resources. I also present references to research in media studies that offer examples of critical analysis.

COLONIALITY, DECOLONIALITY, AND CRITICAL RACE THEORY METHODS: SOME KEY INSIGHTS

Coloniality/decoloniality is a fragmented, global field of studies that includes the works of South Asian, African, Arabic, First Nations, Native American, and Muslim intellectuals. My discussion here is informed primarily by the contributions of Puerto Rican, Chicana/o, African American, Latin American, and Caribbean intellectuals to this interdisciplinary field. Coloniality has been defined as the Eurocentered structuring of knowledge that has over the centuries shaped perceptions, conceptualizations, and practices of cultural diversity (Grosfoguel, 2005). From this perspective, colonialism refers to sociohistorical processes, while coloniality and decoloniality refer to "the logic, metaphysics, ontology, and matrix of power created by the massive processes of colonization and decolonization" (Maldonado-Torres, 2016, p. 10). Coloniality thus endures long after most regimes of direct European colonial rule around the world were abolished by national independence struggles in the twentieth century (Grosfoguel, 2011; Mignolo, 2009, 2017). Coloniality and modernity have been conceptualized as two sides of the same coin, as modernity—a narrative of Enlightened progress through which the world's history has come to be understood—is an epistemological frame that is constituted by and inseparable from colonialism and enslavement (Dussel et al., 2005; Mignolo, 2000, 2007; Quijano, 2007).

Three central foci in coloniality studies have been of particular relevance to this discussion. One approaches coloniality as the imposition of Western epistemic foundations—or the logics of what constitute valid and authoritative knowledge, truth, certainty, and cognition—on non-Western cultures and how they undermine the ways of knowing and being of subaltern, colonized cultures. Such power, it has been argued, operates through (a) the presumed superiority of constructs like objectivity, rationality, universality, neutrality, and pragmatism; (b) the Western scientific paradigm and methods of quantification and standardization as sources of Truth and efficiency; (c) notions of linear time and progressive narrative of history; and (d) the logics of binary oppositions and hierarchical categorization as ways to understand society and nature (Pitts, 2017; Mignolo, 2009). A second point of critique concerns the invisibility of power in coloniality. Castro-Gómez (2010) referred to the "hubris of the point zero" in Eurocentric philosophies as a point of view that presumes to be beyond a particular point of view. It is a perspective that pretends to hold no point of view and hides behind assumptions of abstract universalism. In doing so, it obscures the particular racial, gender, sexual, and class positionalities of the knowing, enunciating subject. Mignolo described the point zero as the view that the Western knowing subject is positioned in a disembodied, "detached and neutral point of observation" while it "maps the world and its problems, and classifies people and projects" (2009, p. 1). A third focus of analysis traces the persistence of Western domination as a matrix of power sustained by White supremacy and the stratification of essentialized, social differences within the formations of patriarchy, modernity, and capitalism (Grosfoguel, 2005; Lugones, 2003; Quijano, 2000).

Therefore a main goal of decolonization of knowledge is to unpack how particular forms of representation and institutional practices that are presented as universal, neutral, rational, objective, pragmatic, natural, unlocated, or disembodied are historically grounded forms of coloniality rooted in ideologies of White supremacy, patriarchy, and the superiority of European and European American epistemologies and cultural formations (Castro-Gómez & Grosfoguel, 2007). Chicana/o, Black, and Asian American scholars have underscored that production of knowledge is situated in particular locations in the social structure of power, and nobody escapes class, sexual, gender, spiritual, linguistic, geographical, and racial intersectional positionings (Anzaldúa, 1987, 1990; Collins, 1990; Moraga & Anzaldúa, 1983; Nakayama & Krizek, 1995). Along these lines, Mignolo asked us to consider "[for whom] and when, why, and where knowledge is generated" (2009, p. 2). A decolonial critique thus questions what positionalities are invisible in discourses that assume a rhetoric of universality and emancipatory potential, such as democracy, individual and human rights, cultural diversity, modernization, and liberal pluralism, among others. For decolonial critics, the goal is not to eradicate

Western epistemology but to expose it as one form of situated knowledge and power grounded in particular racial, gender, and class investments that have unequal material and spiritual effects on peoples. The decolonial act opens space for pluriversal knowledges that give voice to people of color's ways of knowing, talking, feeling, and being that have been ignored, delegitimized, and even prohibited by coloniality as, for example, ancestral and locally grounded understandings, border thinking, the affective, and embodied knowledge. Thus, multivocality and horizontal dialogue (Maldonado-Torres, 2016), complex communication (Lugones, 2006), or even nondialogical communication (Veronelli, 2016) have been proposed as practices for decolonization.

I complement decolonial perspectives with discussion of Critical Race Theory (CRT) as a particular form of decolonizing knowledge. CRT centers race and intersectional identities in the analysis of U.S. racial stratification through institutional and social practices and their material effects on people of color (Decuir-Gunby et al., 2018; Delgado & Stefancic, 2001; Johnson & Neville, 2018; Martinez, 2018; Matsuda et al., 1993; Salinas et al., 2016; Zuberi & Bonilla-Silva, 2008). These institutions and practices include media industries and mediated discourses. CRT methodology calls attention to the need to unpack master narratives (or majoritarian stories) and counter-stories (Delgado, 1989; Solórzano & Yosso, 2001, 2002). Majoritarian stories center whiteness, male, middle and/or upper class, and heterosexual perspectives by constructing these social locations as natural, invisible, or normative. Counter-stories, on the other hand, tell about the experiences of people of color that are often distorted or ignored in master narratives; counter-stories can shatter complacency, challenge dominant discourses, and empower marginalized voices (Solórzano & Yosso, 2002).

THE HISTORICITY OF JOURNALISM AND MODERNITY/COLONIALITY

The lens of coloniality underscores the historicity of journalism to expose how its history, principles, conventional practices, and professional standards are not abstract, universal values but ideals rooted in the particular historical experience of U.S./European modernity/coloniality and the Western episteme. In U.S. media history courses, such reflection can be encouraged in two main ways. First, through an approach to journalism as a "paradigmatic profession of modernity" that since the 1980s has experienced a transition from "high modernity" to "liquid modernity" (Bogaerts & Carpentier, 2013; Deuze, 2005, 2007; Hallin, 1992, 2006; Koljonen, 2013). In class readings and discussion, the focus is on how the defining traits and professional practices of modern commercial journalism—since the late nineteenth century and particularly since the 1950s—have enacted core foundations of the Western episteme while concealing whiteness and other situated knowledge on issues of race, gender, and class. This critique can extend to the present as, for instance, the epistemologies of big data production and the new regimes of knowledge it produces are being questioned as a new version of coloniality in which diverse worldviews come into tension and particular voices and racial groups tend to be muted (Couldry & Mejías, 2019; Goldberg, 2019; Milan & Gutiérrez, 2015; O'Neil, 2016; Treré, 2018).

In a decolonial move, I also problematize how conventional categorizations of commercial journalism as holding the standards of professionalism, objectivity, general interest, and credibility have historically reduced media controlled by people of color to biased, subjective reporting that serves the functions of advocacy and cultural cohesion for particular groups (Rodríguez, 2006). An applied exercise—by itself or added to a more general assignment—is the comparison of news coverage of a selected historical event involving racial or other types of cultural conflict in one mainstream commercial and one minority-owned news outlet. Students may be asked to write essays (or engage in small group work) to explore how preferred angles, language, style, format, and sourcing relate to the (in)visibility of power, narratives and counter-stories of colonial/decolonial positions, and particular ways of understanding cultural difference.

Another teaching strategy in media history courses is to highlight blind spots in conventional historiographies of journalism and media developments despite growing inclusivity of historically underrepresented groups in recent decades. A first step is the discussion of the persistence of progressive or Whig narratives of media history—a linear narrative of continuous progress and improvement fueled by liberal values of freedom of speech, technological innovation, and greater inclusivity of women, racial minorities, and other historically underrepresented groups. Such narratives tend to eclipse discussion of coloniality, even in contexts where coloniality is central.

A classic example examined in class is the Spanish-American War—whose very labeling excluded the centrality of Cubans in the conflict. Media history textbooks give significant attention to news coverage of this war in 1898 as an example of jingoistic, rally-round-the-flag behavior in support of U.S. intervention against Spanish colonial rule in Cuba. It is also framed as an example of the sensationalism that characterized the excesses or extreme behavior of yellow journalism. However, most accounts overlook how the coverage illustrated the colonizing role of the press within the project of U.S. imperialism at the turn of the nineteenth century. Significantly, mainstream coverage of the war became a form of discursive practice that supported U.S. colonial rule and, reproducing discourses on racial stratification and otherness, justified U.S. occupation and colonial administration of the peoples of Puerto Rico, Cuba, Guam, and the Philippines in the aftermath of U.S. intervention. In class activities, I draw on my analysis of coverage of the U.S. military invasion of Puerto Rico and share examples of stories from U.S. newspapers (Rodríguez, 1998). In small group discussion or individual short essays, students examine how U.S. coverage reproduced racial stratification and muted local voices to reify White supremacy.

Discussion of the historicity of journalism in relation to modernity/coloniality can apply also to newswriting courses. It can complement introductory material about journalistic standards and values to problematize how assumptions of objectivity and universality, and notions of professionalism, present challenges to reporters covering racial issues when detachment/objectivity is placed over trust and community (Glasser et al., 2009; Robinson & Culver, 2019). In class exercises (small group discussion or oral presentations), students may select a story about a particular event involving cultural diversity and analyze (a) how standards may relate to invisibility of whiteness and issues of trust in communities covered; (b) how reporters' positionalities reproduce or challenge male, middle and/or upper class gaze, or heterosexual normativity; (c) how exclusion or inclusion of locally and culturally grounded knowledge, sources, and modes of communication affect quality of reporting; and (d) how students' own positionalities might lead to different approaches to reporting.

An application of critical race methodology in advanced newswriting courses involves the politicization of the notion of "story" as a discrete or self-contained account. Through discussion of the concepts of majoritarian story, counter-story, and discourse students are encouraged to consider how any account of a particular event or issue is linked to larger social discourses and ideological struggles. The goals are to foster higher levels of conceptual thinking and practice ideological analysis. As an applied exercise, the instructor may assign stories on issues pertaining to cultural diversity and ask students to work in small groups to identify implicit or explicit master narratives and counter-narratives that give meaning to the event and link it to preexisting issues and larger discourses (for example, the American Dream, color-blindness, U.S. liberal exceptionalism, or feminism).

LIBERAL MULTICULTURALISM AND THE AMERICAN DREAM IN MEDIA DISCOURSE

Liberal multiculturalism is one among other competing visions of cultural diversity that circulate in the culture (Belcher, 2016; Hesse, 1999; Squires, 2014). In my research on media discourse on diversity, it emerged as a salient ideology on how to manage cultural difference within the nation (Rodríguez, 2009). It recognized conflictive differences, inequality, racism, and social injustice in U.S. society and even looked at racial and social barriers to equality as systemic and structural. Yet it was one that implicitly supported the conciliation of differences through assimilation of whiteness and European American values among racial and ethnic minorities, immigrants, and other marginalized sectors. Within this ideology, the American Dream has functioned as a master narrative of assimilation.

More specifically, liberal multiculturalism centers individual pursuit of rights and assumes that equal opportunity and meritocracy are core features of the U.S. liberal democracy. Although historically and ideologically linked to the imaginary of White, European American national identity, it prescribes a set of values as universal values that, when assimilated by non-White subjects, makes possible the management of conflictive diversity (Rodríguez, 2009). Operating primarily through the narrative of the American Dream, it purports that successful integration into national culture is achievable through individual effort, hard work, free choice, and ability to control one's own future (Gooden & Myers, 2019; Hochschild, 1996, 2016; Schudson, 2004). It also privileges English language proficiency, formal educational achievement in U.S. schools, legal citizenship, and upward mobility as ways to successfully integrate cultural others within the national polity.

The American Dream is a majoritarian story that has reduced the experiences and voices of racialized peoples into a predictable narrative that celebrates the adoption of Eurocentered values as a condition for public participation in national culture and political life. It suggests a model of integration that, as Goldberg (1994) argued, sanctioned individual expressions of cultural difference—such as native languages, identification with symbols of national or ethnic origins, ancestry, etc.—in private life and consumer culture while imposing that the public sphere be ruled monoculturally by a set of European American values assumed to incarnate the national character.

By reproducing whiteness, liberal multiculturalism and the American Dream often disregard the representation of social relations among minoritized groups, unless they signal converging interests with White, mainstream society. And in instances when such relations are represented in media, research suggested that the discourse tended to focus on antagonism among minorities (Rodríguez, 2007; Squires & Jackson, 2010; Shah & Thornton, 2003). In this sense, popular media have produced a colonizing rhetoric of classification, stratification, and division. This pattern was evident even in the reporting of stories that were not about conflict among groups. For instance, my research on mainstream coverage of U.S. Census statistics on Latino population growth showed how mainstream media pitted African Americans and Latinx communities against each other as if competing in a race to be the largest ethnic minoritized group (Rodríguez, 2007).

A decolonial critique that decenters whiteness can trace the ideological effects of liberal multiculturalism and the American Dream master narrative by exploring how they (a) reify whiteness and coloniality and erase people of color's culturally grounded understandings, collective experiences, aspirations, and actions regarding individual, community, and national needs and goals; (b) ignore differentiated meanings of the American Dream and other purported national values for different communities; (c) conceal how the individualist pursuits of minoritized, immigrant, and working-class subjects to assimilate such values keep middle- and upper-class European Americans in positions of comfort and privilege; (d) often reduce the differentiated or oppositional ideologies of people of color to individual failure to achieve the dream; and (e) overlook how communities of color interact in positive and horizontal relations of solidarity with one another. As a class exercise, students may draw on a set of assigned readings on the American Dream narrative (for example, from Hochschild, 1996, 2016; Holtzman & Sharpe, 2014) to develop original essays or research that engage the five points of criticism listed here by applying text analysis to media texts featuring racial, ethnic, or immigrant groups.

Plurality of Identities, Citizenships, and Cultural Memberships within the United States

The decolonial act questions the reduction of national identity and culture to geographical origins, legality, or fixed cultural values and boundaries set by the European American lived experience. It seeks to highlight how colonization has forced people of color to participate simultaneously in various cultural formations—Indigenous, Western, ancestral, mestizo, modern, postmodern, traditional, national, diasporic, transnational, ethnic, etc.—as well as hierarchical structures of citizenship. For example, Chicana/o, Latinx, and Caribbean scholars have advanced notions of liminality, mestizaje, creolization, nepantla, diasporic, border thinking, transnational, and in-between cultures to theorize the cultural identities of colonized peoples (Glissant, 1989; Mignolo, 2000; Moraga & Anzaldúa, 1983; Saldívar, 2006). For instance, Anzaldúa's (1987) work, based on the Chicana experience of coloniality on the U.S.-Mexico border, underscores that varying modes of consciousness produce differing forms of cognition, creativity, and feeling.

The case of Puerto Rico is another telling example (Grosfoguel, 2003; Santiago-Valles, 1994). A U.S. unincorporated territory since 1898, where residents were first granted U.S. citizenship in 1917, Puerto Rico forces a recognition that U.S. colonialism and coloniality operate simultaneously until today. For instance, in her research about Puerto Ricans' sense of identity as U.S. citizens, Valle (2019) noted that participants defined U.S. citizenship as a formal status and a set of rights but expressed that their legal, citizen status does not grant them membership into U.S. national culture. The author argued that Puerto Ricans' experiences of U.S. citizenship are influenced by the marking of "Puerto Rico (as a place) and Puerto Ricans (as a people) as different and inferior" (Valle, 2019, p. 25). This positionality exposes U.S. citizenship as a stratified structure in which "Puerto Ricans have a colonial/racialized citizenship constituted by an unequal citizen status, differentiated citizen rights, and exclusion from the American national imaginary" (Valle, 2019, p. 26). The Puerto Rican case opens a door for discussion of the differentiated experiences of other people of color living in U.S. territories with nonsovereign status who are rarely visible in the U.S. national imaginary: Virgin Islands, Guam, American Samoa, and Northern Mariana Islands. A decolonial critique can thus expose the hybrid, transcultural, subordinate, and counter-hegemonic experiences of people of color living under U.S. government control.

The decolonial critique also enables critical reflection on mediated narratives on migration. It shifts conventional views of migration as a one-way flow (south to north) of individuals seeking economic opportunity and political freedom in the United States and other Western nations to a conceptualization of migration as (a) circular patterns of interaction shaped historically by colonial relations of domination; (b) dynamic cultural circuits that have resulted from slavery, economic exploitation, and U.S. imperialist/geopolitical interests as well as people's solidarity; and (c) collective movements featuring adaptation, cultural resistance, and transnational identifications.

From this perspective, I approached coverage of immigration policy between 2006 and 2014 in newspapers produced for U.S.-born African Americans as well as for Haitian, Jamaican, and African immigrant communities in the United States (Rodríguez, 2015). The analysis showed that these newspapers offered alternative perspectives to mainstream coverage by stressing the racist politics of immigration laws, advocating for the plight of Black immigrants from around the world, and giving voice to their personal narratives of migration. Furthermore, the newspapers created positions of identification for members of the African diaspora through construction of shared cultural markers, such as racial pride upon overcoming discrimination; the struggles of Black peoples to achieve an elusive American Dream in the United States; collective memory via references to slavery, contemporary economic exploitation that forces Black laborers to migrate for jobs, modern human trafficking, the middle passage, and European colonialism; and images of nostalgic and symbolic returns to Africa.

In this sense, the Black press has contributed to what Gilroy (1993) described as the historical legacy and cultural circuit of the Black Atlantic. Gilroy conceptualized the Black Atlantic as a cultural and political formation created by African diasporic peoples who have suffered from the Atlantic slave trade and its enduring historical consequences in Europe, the Americas, and the Caribbean. Gilroy's work called attention to the historical development of a modern, Western Black culture that is not specifically African, American, Caribbean, or British but a hybrid formation and cultural exchange with shared themes and experiences that transcend ethnicity and nationality. He considered this formation a counter-culture that has been constitutive of and constituted by European modernity and its "dubious political legacies" of coloniality (Gilroy, 1993, p. 47).

In conclusion, the theorizing and teaching strategies discussed here advance critical understanding of key concepts, themes, and practices that are integral parts of the journalism and media studies curricula. The critique of coloniality also encourages decolonial practices in media production among prospective social communicators at a critical time when the antiracist activism of our brave, younger generations opens new paths for social justice and institutional change.

REFERENCES

Anzaldúa, G . (1987). *Borderlands/La frontera: The new mestiza*. Spinsters/Aunt Lute.
Anzaldúa, G. (1990). En rapport, in opposition: Cobrando cuentas a las nuestras. In G. Anzaldúa (Ed.), *Making face, making soul—Haciendo caras: Creative and critical perspectives by feminists of color* (pp. 142–48). Aunt Lute Foundation Books.
Belcher, C. (2016). There is no such thing as a post-racial prison: Neoliberal multiculturalism and the White savior complex on Orange Is the New Black. *Television & New Media*, 17(6), 491–503.
Bogaerts, J., & Carpentier, N. (2013). The postmodern challenge to journalism: Strategies for constructing a trustworthy identity. In C. Peters & M. Broersma (Eds.), *Rethinking Journalism* (pp. 72–84). Routledge.
Castro-Gómez, S. (2010). *La hybris del punto cero: Ciencia, raza, e ilustración en la nueva Granada (1750–1816)*. Editorial Pontificia Universidad Javeriana.

Castro-Gómez, S., & Grosfoguel, R. (2007). *El giro decolonial: Reflexiones para una diversidad espistémia más allá del capitalismo global*. Siglo del Hombre Editores.

Collins, P. (1990). *Black feminist thought: Knowledge, consciousness, and the politics of empowerment*. Unwin Hyman.

Cooks, L. (2003). Pedagogy, performance, and positionality: Teaching about whiteness in interracial communication. *Communication Education, 52*(3–4), 245–57.

Couldry, N., & Mejías, U. A. (2019). Data colonialism: Rethinking big data's relation to the contemporary subject. *Television & New Media, 20*(4), 336–49.

Decuir-Gunby, J. T., Chapman, T. K., & Schutz, P. A. (Eds.). (2018). *Understanding critical race research methods and methodologies: Lessons from the field*. Routledge.

Delgado, R. (1989). Storytelling for oppositionists and others: A plea for narrative. *Michigan Law Review, 87*(8), 1411–41.

Delgado, R., & Stefancic, J. (2001). *Critical race theory: An introduction*. New York University Press.

Deuze, M. (2005). What is journalism? Professional identity and ideology of journalists reconsidered. *Journalism, 6*(4), 442–64.

Deuze, M. (2007). *Media work*. Polity Press.

Dussel, E., Krauel, J., & Tuma, V. C. (2000). Europe, modernity, and eurocentrism. *Nepantla: Views from South, 1*(3), 465–78.

Fassett, D. L., & Rudick, C. K. (2016). Critical communication pedagogy. In P. Witt (Ed.), *Communication and learning* (pp. 573–98). DeGruyter Mouton.

Fassett, D. L., & Warren, J. T. (Eds.) (2010). *The Sage handbook of communication and instruction* (pp. 361–84). Sage.

Gilroy, P. (1993). *Black Atlantic: Modernity and double consciousness*. Harvard University Press.

Glasser, T. L., Awad, I., & Kim, J. W. (2009). The claims of multiculturalism and journalism's promise of diversity. *Journal of Communication, 59*(1), 57–78.

Glissant, E. (1989). *Caribbean discourse: Selected essays*. University Press of Virginia.

Goldberg, D. T. (1994). *Multiculturalism: A critical reader*. Blackwell Publishers.

Goldberg, D. T. (2019). Coding time. *Critical Times, 2*(3), 353–69.

Gooden, S. T., & Myers, S. L. (2018). The Kerner Commission report fifty years later: Revisiting the American Dream. *RSF: The Russell Sage Foundation Journal of the Social Sciences, 4*(6), 1–17.

Grosfoguel, R. (2003). *Colonial subjects. Puerto Ricans in a global perspective*. University of California Press.

Grosfoguel, R. (2005). The implications of subaltern epistemologies for global capitalism: Transmodernity, border thinking, and global coloniality. In R. Applebaum & W. I. Robinson (Eds.), *Critical globalization studies* (pp. 283–92). Routledge.

Grosfoguel, R. (2011). Decolonizing post-colonial studies and paradigms of political-economy: Transmodernity, decolonial thinking, and global coloniality. *Transmodernity: Journal of Peripheral Cultural Production of the Luso-Hispanic World, 1*(1). http://escholarship.org/uc/item/21k6t3fq.

Hallin, D. C. (1992). The passing of the "high modernism" of American journalism. *Journal of Communication, 42*(3), 14–25.

Hallin, D. C. (2006). The passing of the "high modernism" of American journalism revisited. *Political Communication Report, 16*(1).

Hesse, B. (1999). It's your world: Discrepant M/multiculturalisms. In P. Cohen (Ed.), *New ethnicities, old racisms* (pp. 205–25). Zed.

Hochschild, J. L. (1996). *Facing up to the American dream: Race, class, and the soul of the nation.* Princeton University Press.

Hochschild, J. L. (2016). Chasing the American dream: Understanding what shapes our fortunes. *Political Science Quarterly, 131*(4), 856–58.

hooks, b. (1994). *Teaching to transgress: Education as the practice of freedom.* Routledge.

Holtzman, L., & Sharpe, L. (2014). *Media messages: What film, television, and popular music teach us about race, class, gender, and sexual orientation* (2nd ed.). Routledge.

Johnson, A., & Neville, M. L. (2018). Using counterstories to critique racism: Critical race theory, beloved, and the hate u give. In M. Macaluso & K. Macaluso (Eds.), *Teaching the canon in 21st century classrooms* (pp. 123–37). Brill | Sense.

Koljonen, K. (2013). The shift from high to liquid ideals: Making sense of journalism and its change through a multidimensional model. *Nordicom Review, 33*(1), 141–54.

Lugones, M. (2003). *Pilgrimages/Peregrinajes: Theorizing coalition against multiple oppressions.* Rowman & Littlefield.

Lugones, M. (2006). On complex communication. *Hypatia, 21*(3), 75–85.

Maldonado-Torres, N. (2007). On the coloniality of being: Contributions to the development of a concept. *Cultural Studies, 21*(2–3), 240–70.

Maldonado-Torres, N. (2016). *Outline of ten theses on coloniality and decoloniality.* Frantz Fanon Foundation. http://frantzfanonfoundation-fondationfrantzfanon.com.

Martinez, A. Y. (2018). The responsibility of privilege: A critical race counterstory conversation. *Peitho Journal, 21*(1), 212–33.

Matsuda, M. J., Lawrence, C. R., Delgado, R., & Crenshaw, K. (1993). *Words that wound: Critical race theory, assaultive speech, and the First Amendment.* Westview.

Mignolo, W. D. (2000). *Local histories/global designs: Coloniality, subaltern knowledges, and border thinking.* Princeton University Press.

Mignolo, W. D. (2007). Delinking: The rhetoric of modernity, the logic of coloniality, and the grammar of decoloniality. *Cultural Studies, 21*(2–3), 449–514.

Mignolo, W. D. (2009). Epistemic disobedience, independent thought, and decolonial freedom. *Theory, Culture & Society, 26*(7–8), 1–23.

Mignolo, W. D. (2017). Coloniality is far from over, and so must be decoloniality. *Afterall: A Journal of Art, Context and Enquiry, 4*(1), 38–45.

Milan, S., & Gutiérrez, M. (2015). Citizens' media meets big data: The emergence of data activism. *Mediaciones, 11*(14), 120–33.

Moraga, C., & Anzaldúa, G. (Eds.) (1983). *This bridge called my back: Writing by radical women of color* (2nd ed.). Kitchen Table/Women of Color.

Nakayama, T. K., & Krizek, R. L. (1995). Whiteness: A strategic rhetoric. *Quarterly Journal of Speech, 81*(3), 291–309.

O'Neil, C. (2016). *Weapons of math destruction: How big data increases inequality and threatens democracy.* Broadway Books.

Pitts, A. (2017). Decolonial praxis and epistemic injustice. In I. J. Kidd, J. Medina, & G. Pohlhaus (Eds.), *The Routledge handbook of epistemic injustice* (pp. 149–57). Routledge.

Quijano, A. (2000). Coloniality of power and eurocentrism in Latin America. *International Sociology, 15*(2), 215–32.

Quijano, A. (2007). Coloniality and modernity/rationality. *Cultural Studies, 21*(2), 168–78.

Robinson, S., & Culver, K. B. (2019). When White reporters cover race: News media, objectivity, and community (dis)trust. *Journalism: Theory, Practice & Criticism, 20*(3), 375–91.

Rodríguez, I. (1998). News reporting and colonial discourse: The representation of Puerto Ricans in the U.S. press during the Spanish-American War. *Howard Journal of Communications, 9*(4), 283–302.

Rodríguez, I. (2006). The Spanish-language and bilingual press of New Orleans in the crosscurrents of journalistic trends in the 19th and early 20th centuries. *Louisiana Communication Journal, 8*, 42–57.

Rodríguez, I. (2007). Telling stories of Latino population growth in the United States: Narratives of inter-ethnic conflict in mainstream, Hispanic, and African-American newspapers. *Journalism: Theory, Practice and Criticism, 8*(5), 573–90.

Rodríguez, I. (2009). "Diversity writing" and the liberal discourse on multiculturalism in U.S. mainstream newspapers. *Howard Journal of Communications, 20*(2), 167–88.

Rodríguez, I. (2015). The construction of black diasporic identities in news discourse on immigration in the U.S. black press. In V. Berry, A. Dayo, & A. Fleming-Rife (Eds.), *Black culture and experience: Contemporary issues* (pp. 235–55). Peter Lang.

Saldívar, R. (2006). *The borderlands of culture: Américo Paredes and the transnational imaginary*. Duke University Press.

Salinas, C. S., Fránquiz, M. E., & Rodríguez, N. N. (2016). Writing Latina/o historical narratives: Narratives at the intersection of critical historical inquiry and LatCrit. *The Urban Review, 48*(2), 264–84.

Santiago-Valles, K. A. (1994). *Subject people and colonial discourses: Economic transformation and social disorder in Puerto Rico, 1898–1947*. SUNY Press.

Schudson, M. (2004). American dreams. *American Literary History, 16*(3), 66–73.

Shah, H., & Thornton, M. C. (2003). *Newspaper coverage of interethnic conflict: Competing visions of America*. Sage.

Simpson, J. S. (2010). Critical race theory and critical communication pedagogy. In D. L. Fassett & J. T. Warren (Eds.), *The Sage handbook of communication and instruction* (pp. 360–67). Sage.

Simpson, J. S., James, C. E., & Mack, J. (2011). Multiculturalism, colonialism, and racialization: Conceptual starting points. *Review of Education, Pedagogy, and Cultural Studies, 33*(4), 285–305.

Solórzano, D. G., & Yosso, T. J. (2001). Critical race and LatCrit theory and method: Counter-storytelling. *International Journal of Qualitative Studies in Education, 14*(4), 471–95.

Solórzano, D. G., & Yosso, T. J. (2002). Critical race methodology: Counter storytelling as an analytical framework for education research. *Qualitative Inquiry*, *8*(1), 23–44.

Squires, C. R. (2014). *The post-racial mystique: Media and race in the twenty-first century*. New York University Press.

Squires, C. R., & Jackson, S. J. (2010). Reducing race: News themes in the 2008 primaries. *The International Journal of Press/Politics*, *15*(4), 375–400.

Treré, E. (2018). From digital activism to algorithmic resistance. In G. Meikle (Ed.), *The Routledge companion to media and activism* (pp. 367–75). Routledge.

Valle, A. J. (2019). Race and the empire-state: Puerto Ricans' unequal US citizenship. *Sociology of Race and Ethnicity*, *5*(1), 26–40.

Veronelli, G. (2016). A coalitional approach to theorizing decolonial communication. *Hypatia*, *31*(2), 404–20.

Zuberi, T., & Bonilla-Silva, E. (Eds.) (2008). *White logic, White methods: Racism and methodology*. Rowman & Littlefield.

PERSPECTIVE: TEACHING RACE WITHIN AN INTERSECTIONALITY FRAMEWORK

Nathian Shae Rodriguez, San Diego State University

Ilia Rodríguez's chapter highlighted the urgency in communication and journalism pedagogy to unravel institutionalized racism and open spaces in our classrooms for critical, intercultural dialogue among our students. I have argued elsewhere that classrooms in this discipline are not as inclusive of traditionally marginalized identities and more pedagogies with intersectional lenses are desperately needed (Rodríguez, 2020). To combat the racism and other isms plaguing our classrooms, Rodríguez (this volume) suggested employing coloniality, decoloniality, and Critical Race Theory as conceptual lenses to our pedagogical practices. I argue that we should go further and incorporate intersectional theories in our pedagogy that look at race in addition to other components of our students' identities. Quare theory (Johnson, 2001), joteria (Alvarez, 2014), multiplicity (Hames-Garcia, 2011), and theories of the flesh (Moraga & Anzaldúa, 2002), among others, all exist within an intersectional framework often employed in critical communication pedagogy approaches.

Intersectionality brings to light overlapping oppressions and ostracisms tied to marginalized identities that work in tandem to produce and maintain unified systems of injustices (Crenshaw, 1990). When applied to a critical communication pedagogy's goals of "(1) heightening awareness of hegemony, (2) identifying avenues for praxis, and (3) taking steps toward praxis—determining how to respond to instances of hegemony when they discern them" (Kahl, 2013, p. 2626), an intersectional framework can help empower marginalized students and help address the imbalance of power through pedagogical practices of inclusion, critique, and relevance (Fassett & Rudick, 2007). I echo Rodríguez's sense of urgency to address systems of oppression in higher education and offer an intersectional framework I call RAPID, an acronym that stands for Reflect; Amplify; Purposeful; Intersectional inclusive content; Decenter whiteness, privilege, and power. The RAPID framework situates the instructor as transformative to culture and power through developing a critical consciousness of power differentials, providing motivation and significance to experiences inside the communication classroom, and fostering dialogue through the

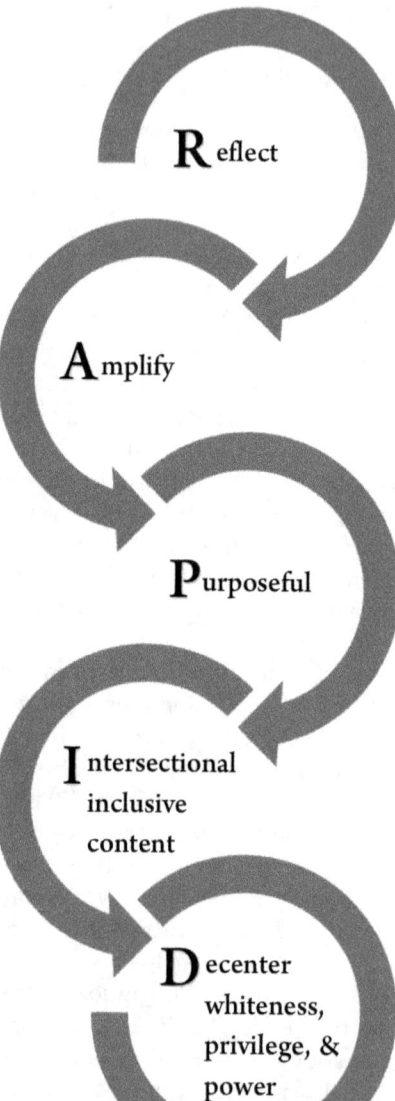

Figure 2.1. The RAPID Model. Nathian Shae Rodriguez, PhD

critique of power and hegemony in intersectional mediated content (Fassett & Rudick, 2007; Kahl, 2013; Rodríguez, 2020). Furthermore, the framework can be entered through any component, before or during a course, making it ideal for instructors to adopt.

First, instructors should **reflect** on their own positionality, where the individual stands in relation to others. Instructors should begin with the question, Who am I? This includes reflecting on your own intersectional identities of race, ethnicity, gender identity, sexuality, and others that may influence not only the ways you experience the world around you but also the way you come to think about it. Some follow-up questions include: What are you here to do? How can you help? What is needed of you? What is expected of you? This reflection will aid in identifying what your biases are and how you can mitigate them. An important question for those with more privileged identities to ask (and if you teach in higher education, you have academic privilege, among others, for sure) is: How can you use your privileges to help lift up traditionally marginalized identities in your classroom? Return to this component after you have completed all five of the components and reflect on what you have done. This is an iterative process, as is your pedagogy. One thing I have done personally is to utilize a living syllabus that responds in real time to the needs of your students. I define a living syllabus as recursive, modified as the course progresses in direct response to the temporal and spatial context of your course, including students and sociopolitical atmosphere. Such modifications might entail including marginalized voices and intersectional content outlined in the other components.

Amplify the voices of traditionally marginalized students. Listen! Then empower them to think critically and speak up. Advocate for them inside and outside of the classroom. Instructors should also amplify the voices of scholars from marginalized backgrounds by including readings from scholars of color and other intersectional backgrounds. You can also include diverse perspectives and voices by inviting scholars from marginalized identities to guest lecture or speak at institutional functions while advocating for and/or providing compensation. Most of us are also researchers; we can practice amplification in the academy by coauthoring pieces, providing mentorship, or offering help to scholars of marginalized identities.

The next component is to be **purposeful** in your intentions and interventions. Ask yourself: Are your actions hollow rebranding or do you really want to instigate change? Do not just say it, do it.

Be sincere and genuine or simply do not do it. Be contextual and consider time and space. What are your students experiencing in the sociopolitical atmosphere that you can purposefully address through your pedagogy? This can also mean taking a closer look at the conditions within your institution. What does administration "look" and "feel" like for your students, as well as your colleagues of color and other traditionally marginalized identities?

Intersectional inclusive content is a necessary component of RAPID. In addition to ensuring your class readings are inclusive of diverse voices and marginalized identities, be sure the mediated examples are also intersectionally inclusive and reflect the diversity of your students. Ask yourself: Do my students see themselves in my examples and assignments? Including intersectional content can be as simple as choosing commercials, songs, videos, or other mediated texts with diverse voices and identities. If your students are not particularly diverse, ask yourself how can you include intersectional content to have them engage with identities outside their own? Encourage your students to provide and create examples. Using online meme makers, video and audio software, and graphic design sites like Canva.com can be great to build into your pedagogy. Being intersectionally inclusive fosters an environment of open dialogue in which students can not only exemplify but also challenge and critique.

The final component is to **decenter whiteness, privilege, and power** by removing "white" as the structural center and making multiculturalism the center—sometimes referred to as decolonizing. Therefore white values, interests, culture, and histories are not the baseline and driving force behind everything. Every racial category should have access, input, and opportunity. White becomes a category like every other race and ethnicity. Furthermore, every identity should have access, input, and opportunity, so remember intersectionality at all times. Make sure you are focused on equity and not equality; your students all have varying needs. Have you made your syllabi and content accessible for students with disabilities? Your syllabi can also include information about gender neutral bathrooms on campus or give your preferred pronouns.

Another area within this component is to advocate for scholars and colleagues of color and other marginalized identities. These colleagues not only serve as representation for the marginalized students on your campus, but they are also performing invisible labor (also called cultural taxation by some) by mentoring and serving particular groups of students. Speak out for them, especially those who are untenured or nontenure track. Make ally a verb and do! Stand in solidarity with your colleagues and make space for them inside and outside of your institution. In addition to coauthoring pieces with them, you may also consider consulting with them when creating cultural content.

I identify as a queer, first-generation professor of color and have been battle tested as both a student and professor, aiding in the construction of this framework through phenomenology—lived experiences. However, anyone, regardless of identity or privilege, can employ it across a variety of courses. I will demonstrate the process with a personal experience from my "Media and Identity" course. I created the syllabus by reflecting on my own positionality and what my identity meant to students who shared similar intersections of it. I wanted to be purposeful in engaging those identities, as well as making sure other students from marginalized identities that I did not identify with also saw themselves in the course. I wanted to amplify those identities by incorporating a wide range of intersectional inclusive movie clips, songs, and advertisements, as well as assigning readings from diverse academics. Although I also included readings and viewings from white identities, they were not the main readings but rather additive readings to the course. As the semester started I got to know my students a little better and realized many used sports metaphors and often cited athletes in their examples. So I went back and added more sport-centric content that highlighted identity and added more time for the class to deconstruct Colin Kaepernick and Megan Rapinoe. In another semester of the same course, I noticed one student wrote extensively about his coming out experience as an Asian American. So I added YouTube clips from LGBTQ-identifying comedians Joel Kim Booster and Margaret Cho. The student, a senior at the time, stayed after class and tearfully thanked me for including a representation of himself that he had not seen in all of his academic career. I reflect on that experience before I plan every course.

The RAPID framework is an intersectional approach based on the tenets of critical communication pedagogy and helps instructors address how to combat racism and other isms by incorporating reflexivity, intentionality, and intersectionality. The framework can be employed in conjunction with intersectional theories as an iterative pedagogy that both reflects on and practices methods that call in to question hierarchies of power and identity in the classroom

(Fassett & Rudick, 2007). You can employ RAPID while planning a course or, if you are in the middle of a semester, you can employ it to appraise your students and the sociopolitical climate to adjust your pedagogy in real time. RAPID's intersectional praxis directly addresses overlapping systems of oppression that traditionally marginalized students experience (Crenshaw, 1990) and, as Rodríguez stated in her chapter, disrupts normative exercises of dominant narratives in academia.

References

Alvarez, E. (2014). Jotería pedagogy, SWAPA, and Sandovalian approaches to liberation. *Aztlán: A Journal of Chicano Studies, 39*(1), 215–28.

Crenshaw, K. (1990). Mapping the margins: Intersectionality, identity politics, and violence against women of color. *Stanford Law Review, 43*(6), 1241–99.

Fassett, D. L., & Warren, J. T. (2007). *Critical communication pedagogy.* Sage.

Hames-Garcia, M. R. (2011). *Identity complex: Making the case for multiplicity.* University of Minnesota Press.

Johnson, E. P. (2001). "Quare" studies, or (almost) everything I know about queer studies I learned from my grandmother. *Text and Performance Quarterly, 21*(1), 1–25.

Kahl Jr., D. H. (2013). Critical communication pedagogy and assessment: Reconciling two seemingly incongruous ideas. *International Journal of Communication, 7,* 2610–30.

Moraga, C., & Anzaldúa, G. (2002). *This bridge called my back: Writings by radical women of color.* Third Woman Press.

Rodriguez, N. S. (2020). An intersectional LGBTQ+ pop culture approach to critical pedagogy. In C. Carter Olson & T. Everbach (Eds.), *Testing tolerance: Addressing controversy in the journalism and mass communication classroom* (pp. 147–57). Rowman & Littlefield.

3

Committing to Excellence in Diversity and Accreditation

Mia Moody-Ramirez, Baylor University

A commitment to diversity, equity, and inclusion is a necessity in today's society—one that journalism and communication programs must take seriously. Students must be prepared to work with diverse populations to succeed as leaders in a diverse workforce and society—both domestically and internationally. Diversity is often defined as "any dimension that can be used to differentiate groups and people from one another . . . it's about empowering people by respecting and appreciating what makes them different, in terms of age, gender, ethnicity, religion, disability, sexual orientation, education, and national origin" (Global Diversity Practice, n.d., para. 1). Inclusion is defined as "a state of being valued, respected and supported . . . focusing on the needs of every individual and ensuring the right conditions are in place for each person to achieve his or her full potential" (HUD, n.d., para. 2).

Standard 3 of the Accrediting Council on Education in Journalism and Mass Communications (ACEJMC) offers guidelines to help faculty, administrators, and staff provide a diverse learning environment for students. While Standard 3 is possibly the most elusive benchmark for academic units to conquer, it remains vital for programs that want to remain competitive.

Regional academic accreditation agencies (for example, Middle States Commission on Higher Education, New England Commission of Higher Education, Southern Association of Colleges and Schools Commission on Colleges) originated to assess how schools were using student learning metrics to evaluate and improve their programs. Organizers established the structure for evaluating and accrediting journalism and mass communications programs in 1945, when the accrediting body was founded. It was originally called the American Council on Education in Journalism and then renamed the Accrediting Council on Education in Journalism and Mass Communications in 1980.

The accrediting body for journalism and communication programs crafted a standard focused on diversity in 1984 to help educators recognize the importance of diversity regarding faculty and students, as well as the awareness of inclusiveness. According to ACEJMC's website, commitment to diversity and inclusiveness is necessary: "To inform and enlighten, the professions of journalism and mass communications, whose professionals should understand and reflect the diversity and complexity of people, perspectives and beliefs in a global society and in the multicultural communities they serve" (n.d., para. 4). The organization offers guidance and encourages programs to develop curricula and instruction that "educate faculty and prepare students with the multicultural knowledge, values and skills essential for professional practice" (para. 5). It also emphasizes the importance of diversity and inclusion in faculty, staff, and students.

This chapter examines key definitions and provides an overview of the ACEJMC accreditation process. Next it looks at the history of ACEJMC's Standard 3 and offers some best practices for educators preparing for the accreditation process. It concludes with a look at future directions for the standard. Implications are important as units continue to struggle to infuse diversity in curriculum, enrichment opportunities, and other measures, such as recruiting and retaining diverse faculty, students, and staff (Daufin, 2001).

HISTORY OF ACEJMC AND STANDARD 12/STANDARD 3

The ACEJMC accreditation process includes a self-study in which the academic unit assesses itself on the standards. A council-appointed site team then visits the unit and reviews program documents, visits classrooms, and interviews administrators, students, faculty, staff, and other relevant personnel. From this information, the team recommends whether a unit should be (a) fully accredited, (b) provisionally accredited, or (c) denied accreditation. Units that are provisionally accredited have one or two years to correct deficiencies. Units denied accreditation cannot be reviewed again for two years. This second review is considered a new accreditation instead of a reaccreditation. ACEJMC traditionally focused on a program's curriculum and resources, such as faculty and facilities, when making accrediting decisions (Henderson & Christ, 2014).

In 2003, the total number of ACEJMC accreditation standards was reduced from twelve to nine. Originally Standard 3 was known as Standard 12, which was developed in 1984 in response to a Minorities Task Force and Minorities and Communication proposal urging ACEJMC to "adopt more aggressive and accountable efforts by journalism educators to increase enrollment by minority students and to improve the representation of minority faculty" (Ross et al., 2007, p. 11). According to the article, the proposal also called for ACEJMC to require accredited programs to develop courses that reflected contributions of minorities to the journalism industry. Standard 12 was adopted and published in the 1985–1986 academic year accreditation booklets; however, journalism units were given from 1985 to 1990 to prepare for compliance. In 1992, ACEJMC expanded and revised the standard using more forceful language.

In 2004, ACEJMC voted to add sexual orientation to race, ethnicity, and gender in its revised diversity standards for schools seeking accreditation or reaccreditation. The new provision applied specifically to the curriculum portion of the standards. Three years later, Ross et al. (2007) credited the standard for increasing non-White and female faculty and students in accredited journalism units. The study also concluded Standard 12 progress was evident in some schools, but not in others.

> Gains were greater for female faculty relative to those for non-White faculty. However, the general pattern is one of diversity increase. When compared with national and census data, the under-representation of both female and non-White faculty surfaces. Still, our data suggest that the units in our sample did respond to Standard 12 and "demonstrated a commitment to increasing diversity in their faculties." Indeed, our data indicate that since 1989 journalism and mass communication faculties have become more diversified in that the numbers and percentages of both women and non-Whites have increased. (Ross et al., 2007, p. 22)

In 2009, the competencies were updated when the new "diversity" competencies encouraged units to "demonstrate an understanding of gender, race, ethnicity, sexual orientation and, as appropriate, other forms of diversity in domestic society in relation to mass communications" and "demonstrate an understanding of the diversity of peoples and cultures and of the significance and impact of mass communications in a global society" (ACEJMC, n.d., para. 12). Before this modification, units were asked to encourage programs to "demonstrate an understanding of the diversity of groups in a global society in relationship to communications" (Henderson & Christ, 2014, p. 232).

The most recent trends in accreditation include streamlining it to make it less cumbersome for programs that desire to go through the accreditation process, which includes a self-study and site visit. Journalism educators around the world are closely following the developments of ACEJMC because the organization has been used as a model for accreditation bodies in other countries. Additionally, eight institutions outside the United States are accredited by ACEJMC.

IMPLICATIONS FOR TEACHING

Units contemplating the accreditation process must decide how to best navigate the assessment process. They must incorporate diversity into the program—and decide if the standard should be addressed by sprinkling content throughout course content or by offering it as a required standalone course. The strongest departments will do both by offering an approach that addresses diversity and inclusion across multiple classes and offers a capstone or standalone course that emphasizes the topic.

Accreditation is usually focused on the unit level; however, faculty members must do their part by focusing on classroom processes and interactions. Faculty members may use ACEJMC guidelines to become better instructors in the classroom. To emphasize the importance of domestic and global diversity, they must stay abreast of the trends essential for professional development. Faculty may contribute to diversity and inclusion efforts by infusing them into their course curriculum. For instance, syllabi may include diversity-related exercises, textbooks, and speakers. The goal should not be to keep the unit in compliance but to succeed beyond that marker. Also relevant in the accreditation process is the Scholarship of Teaching of Learning (SoTL), which involves faculty (sometimes in partnership with their students) undertaking systematic inquiry about student learning. It is informed by prior scholarship on teaching and learning. SoTL invites professionals to examine their own classroom practice, record their successes and failures, and ultimately share their experiences so that others may reflect on their findings and build upon teaching and learning processes.

The general goal is to foster programs that value diverse perspectives. Efforts to sprinkle such content across courses might include incorporating speakers from diverse backgrounds, monitoring diversity in course syllabi, and sponsoring programming and encouraging students to attend cultural events that help broaden their knowledge base of different cultures. One way to do this is to closely monitor course development. Faculty must include diversity elements in their syllabi—either in their teaching philosophy—or as a department diversity statement. Extending these practices to the accreditation process is advantageous for students, faculty, and staff. For example, using a survey helps units assess each faculty member's incorporation of domestic and/or global diversity content into courses. Survey findings help faculty assess how well they are addressing the topic. Questions might include: To what extent do the syllabi reflect learning outcomes related to diversity, equity, and inclusion, both domestically and internationally? To what extent has diversity been infused into all aspects of the curriculum? Do all majors under review get exposed to learning about how diversity and inclusion affect (a) their research and reporting; (b) message creation (multimedia, social, writing, etc.); (c) channels (print, online, on-air, paid, earned, shared, and owned from an audience perspective); (d) effect (audience impact); and (e) the management of communication teams (communications workforce)? How have diversity and inclusion learning outcomes been assessed and how have these results been looped back into curricular and cocurricular changes or enhancements? In addition, course syllabi should include learning outcomes that support multicultural outcomes (Fleming-Rife, 2013).

Another way to encourage diversity and inclusion is to assess how faculty are infusing diversity into course content. A starting point for assessing faculty efforts might be syllabi. Faculty must assess how diversity is defined and highlighted in each course syllabus. Faculty may also gauge their inclusion of diversity by conducting a keyword search of key terms (that is, culture, diversity, bias, framing, stereotyping, feminism, global, gender, racism, sexism, ageism, disabilities, Black, Hispanics, representation).

The overall visibility of diversity in the unit is also important. For instance, departments may choose to have a bulletin board and reading room to highlight diverse events and other contents. Members of the diversity committee may be responsible for maintaining both of them. A list of speakers must be maintained to include diverse speakers who share information on diversity research, panel discussions, etc.

Diverse student organizations—both professional and social—are imperative to student growth and development. Students must have access to programs that help them spread their wings and take on leadership roles that they might not undertake in other organizations. Professional organizations, such the National Association of Black Journalists, give student chapters the opportunity to sponsor activities such as job trainings and networking gatherings.

Faculty evaluations are also important. Units may consider including a question on evaluations regarding diversity and inclusion. They might also assess each course's overall goals and objectives. The purpose of this evaluation is to help the unit and faculty member understand each instructor's plans to incorporate diversity and inclusion efforts into course content.

Another way to approach accreditation from a teaching perspective is to look for exemplary work that might come from faculty members. Internal diversity awards may incentivize the importance of diversity and inclusion in curriculum by highlighting departments that are doing a good job. Awards might include Outstanding Diversity Faculty and Outstanding Diversity Alumni. Additionally, AEJMC sponsors the Equity and Diversity Award each year. It is one of the highest honors in diversity and inclusion for journalism and communication programs in the United States. It recognizes academic programs that are working toward and have attained measurable success in increasing equity and diversity. Programs must display progress and innovation in racial, gender, and ethnic equity and diversity over the previous three-year period. In 2020, Syracuse University won the award. The school hosts regular, informal forums that encourage students of color to discuss their experiences and make connections—with each other and with Newhouse School of Public Communications faculty, staff, and administrators (Loughlin, 2020).

Units are encouraged to develop standalone courses that focus specifically on diversity, equity, and inclusion. Course titles might include "Race, Gender, and Class in the Media"; "The History of Minorities in the Media"; and "The History of Women in the Media," and students should be able to design their own research studies around race, gender, class, sexual orientation, ability, and other identities (Fleming-Rife, 2013).

THE FUTURE OF DIVERSITY AND ACCREDITATION

The council has recently adopted revised ACEJMC standards, a process that takes place every ten years. The new standards will take effect in the 2022–2023 academic year. Because of the COVID-19 pandemic, the 2020–2021 accrediting cycle was postponed a year. All units on the traditional six-year visit schedule will instead be reviewed for work done in the previous seven years for one cycle.

Instead of nine, there will be just eight standards. Under Standard 2, Curriculum and Instruction, the ACEJMC Professional Values and Competencies have been reduced from twelve to ten and updated to reflect current industry and higher education expectations. Under the new Standard 4, faculty members are obligated to prepare students with the knowledge, values, and skills essential for professional practice as they relate to diversity and inclusion. Units must continue to update course content and goals to advance curricula development.

The updated diversity standard brings us closer to where departments need to be as a discipline. The updated standard helps programs assess key performance indicators (KPIs) within the diversity plan. Programs must look at the unit's evidence of progress in achieving those KPIs. Programs that are lacking or not making progress must outline a plan for adjustments and new techniques that will be employed to achieve the unit's goals.

In ACEJMC's updated diversity standard, plans will be evaluated based on how they tie directly to the student value and competency related to diversity. In other words, how do students benefit from the plan? Frequent updates are emphasized; units must discuss the diversity plan annually to discern improvements. Closing the loop is still important. If the unit has updated its plan within the past twelve months, it must assess its progress on previous plans and how the plan versions differ. Units must also evaluate the evidence they have for implementing and evaluating progress on the plan annually. They should incorporate learning outcomes into syllabi that link clearly to the ACEJMC diversity value. Questions might include: What should students be able to think or know, feel, and do as related to diversity, equity, and inclusion?

To reach these goals, professional development is keenly important. For instance, units must encourage faculty to complete professional development activities to enhance their ability to teach diversity and inclusion within their courses. The Accrediting Council has available several resources to assist schools with the accreditation process. Documents can be found under the resources tab at http://www.acejmc.org/resources.

ACEJMC Standard 2: Curriculum and Instruction
The unit provides a curriculum and instruction, whether on site or online, that enables students to learn the knowledge, competencies, and values that the council defines for preparing students to work in a diverse domestic and global society.

PROFESSIONAL VALUES AND COMPETENCIES

The Accrediting Council on Education in Journalism and Mass Communications requires that graduates of accredited programs be aware of certain core values and competencies and be able to

- apply the principles and laws of freedom of speech and press, in a global context, and for the country in which the institution that invites ACEJMC is located;
- demonstrate an understanding of the multicultural history and role of professionals and institutions in shaping communications;

- demonstrate culturally proficient communication that empowers those traditionally disenfranchised in society, especially as grounded in race, ethnicity, gender, and sexual orientation and ability, domestically and globally, across communication and media contexts;
- present images and information effectively and creatively, using appropriate tools and technologies;
- write correctly and clearly in forms and styles appropriate for the communications professions, audience, and purposes they serve;
- demonstrate an understanding of professional ethical principles and work ethically in pursuit of truth, accuracy, fairness, and diversity;
- apply critical thinking skills in conducting research and evaluating information by methods appropriate to the communications professions in which they work;
- effectively and correctly apply basic numerical and statistical concepts;
- critically evaluate their own work and that of others for accuracy and fairness, clarity, appropriate style, and grammatical correctness; and
- apply tools and technologies appropriate for the communications professions in which they work.

> **ACEJMC Standard 3: Diversity and Inclusiveness (Until 2022–2023)**
> The unit has an inclusive program that values domestic and global diversity and serves and reflects society.

INDICATORS

a. The unit has a written diversity plan for achieving an inclusive curriculum, a diverse faculty and student population, and a supportive climate for working and learning and for assessing progress toward achievement of the plan. The diversity plan should focus on domestic minority groups and, where applicable, international groups. The written plan must include the unit's definition of diversity and identify the underrepresented groups.

b. The unit's curriculum fosters understanding of issues and perspectives that are inclusive in terms of domestic concerns about gender, race, ethnicity, and sexual orientation. The unit's curriculum includes instruction in issues and perspectives relating to mass communications across diverse cultures in a global society.

c. The unit demonstrates effective efforts to recruit women and domestic minority faculty and professional staff and, where feasible, recruits international faculty and professional staff.
d. The unit demonstrates effective efforts to help recruit and retain a student population reflecting the diversity of the population eligible to enroll in institutions of higher education in the region or population it serves, with special attention to recruiting underrepresented groups.
e. The unit has a climate that is free of harassment and all forms of discrimination, in keeping with the acceptable cultural practices of the population it serves, accommodates the needs of those with disabilities, and values the contributions of all forms of diversity.

Accreditation site visit teams will apply this standard in compliance with applicable federal and state laws and regulations, as well as the laws of the countries in which non-U.S. institutions are located.

EVIDENCE

- A unit-specific written plan, including progress toward goals
- Syllabi and other course materials
- Coursework in international cultures and in international communication
- Records and statistics on faculty and staff hiring and on promotion and tenure decisions
- Records and statistics on student recruitment, retention, and graduation
- Records on part-time and visiting faculty and speakers

The written plan must include the unit's definition of diversity and identify the underrepresented groups.

ACEJMC Standard 4: Diversity and Inclusiveness
The unit demonstrates it has a diverse and inclusive program that embodies domestic and global diversity and that empowers those traditionally disenfranchised in society, especially as grounded in race, ethnicity, gender, ability, and sexual orientation.

INDICATORS

a. The unit has a written diversity plan that has been implemented and discussed annually for achieving an inclusive curriculum; a diverse, culturally proficient faculty, staff, and student population; and a supportive climate for working and learning and for assessing progress toward achievement of the plan. The diversity plan should focus on domestic minority groups and, when applicable, international groups. The written plan must include the unit's definition of diversity, identify underrepresented groups, and articulate key performance indicators upon which the unit intends to focus and improve.

b. The unit's curriculum creates culturally proficient communicators capable of learning with, working on, and advancing the value of diverse teams. The unit's curriculum includes instruction on issues of perspectives relating to mass communications across diverse cultures in a global society.

c. The unit demonstrates effective efforts to enhance all faculty members' understanding of diversity, equity, inclusion, and ability to develop culturally proficient communicators capable of learning with, working on, and advancing the value of diverse teams. The unit also demonstrates intentional efforts to recruit and retain faculty and professional staff who are from demographics that are historically, domestically marginalized.

d. In alignment with the institution's mission, the unit demonstrates effective efforts to help recruit, retain, and graduate a student population reflecting the diversity of the population the institution aims to serve.

e. The unit demonstrates that it has an inclusive climate, free of harassment and all forms of discrimination, in keeping with the acceptable cultural practices of the population it serve, accommodates the needs of those with disabilities, and values the contributions of all forms of diversity.

Accreditation site visit teams will apply this standard in compliance with applicable federal and state laws and regulations, as well as the laws of the countries in which non-U.S. institutions are located.

EVIDENCE

- A written diversity plan, posted to the unit's website, that includes key performance indicators (KPIs).
- The unit provides evidence of progress on achieving KPIs. Where there has not been progress, the unit describes adjustments and new techniques it is using to achieve it.
- A description of how the plan ties directly to the professional values and competencies related to diversity.
- Course syllabi reflect learning outcomes related to diversity, equity, and inclusion, both domestically and internationally.
- A grid in the self-study report that outlines where cultural communications proficiency is taught in the curriculum.
- Assessment reports that outline culture communication proficiency.
- For U.S. units, create three tables to describe demographics of faculty with categories used by their institutions for collecting and reporting data to reflect the six years under review. (Citizenship is not necessary to present.)
- Data on enrollment, retention, and graduation rates of underrepresented groups within the population; data on faculty/staff hiring; and data on promotion and tenure decisions.
- For units within institutions with the mission to serve specific genders, races, religions, or ethnicities, an explanation of how they retain and graduate underrepresented groups and enable their students to be prepared to work on diverse teams not represented at their university.
- Faculty vitae.
- Reports showing the impact of faculty professional development aimed at enhancing the ability to teach courses that develop culturally proficient communicators able to work on and advocate for diverse teams.
- Evidence of climate studies or other indicator of the unit's level of inclusion.

REFERENCES

ACEJMC (n.d.). *Principles of accreditation*. Retrieved February 8, 2021. https://www.acejmc.org/policies-process/principles/.

Biswas, M., Izard, R., & Roshan, S. (2017). What is taught about diversity and how is it taught? Update of diversity teaching at U.S. journal of mass communication programs. *Teaching Journalism and Mass Communication, 7*(1), 1–13.

Blom, R., Bowe, B. J., & Davenport, L. (2020). International expansion of the accrediting council on education in journalism and mass communications

(ACEJMC) curricular evaluation program. *The International Communication Gazette, 82*(8), 749–63.

Crichlow, V. J. (2017). The solitary criminologist: Constructing a narrative of Black identity and alienation in the academy. *Race and Justice, 7*(2), 179–95.

Daufin, E. K. (2001). Minority faculty job experience, expectations, and satisfaction. *Journalism & Mass Communication Educator, 56*(1), 18–30.

Fleming-Rife, A. (2013, December 20). Tips from the AEJMC teaching committee. *AEJMC.* https://www.aejmc.org/home/2013/10/diversity-into-curricula/.

Global Diversity Practice. (n.d.). *What is diversity and inclusion.* Retrieved December 19, 2020, from https://globaldiversitypractice.com/what-is-diversity-inclusion/.

Henderson, J., & Christ, W. (2014). Benchmarking ACEJMC competencies: What it means for assessment. *Journalism & Mass Communication Educator, 69*(3), 229–42.

HUD.gov (n.d). Diversity and inclusion definition. US Department of Housing and Urban Development. Retrieved December 19, 2020, from https://www.hud.gov/program_offices/administration/admabout/diversity_inclusion/definitions.

Loughlin, W. (2020, March 29). Newhouse School recognized with AEJMC Equity and Diversity Award. *Media, Law & Policy.* https://news.syr.edu/blog/2020/05/29/newhouse-school-recognized-with-aejmc-equity-and-diversity-award/.

Ross, F. G. J., Stroman, C., Callahan, L. F., Dates, J., Egwu, C., & Whitmore, E. (2007). National study on diversity in journalism and mass communication education, phase II. *Journalism & Mass Communication Educator, 62*(1), 10–26.

PERSPECTIVE: TEACHING DIVERSITY AT HBCUS REQUIRES A DEEPER DIVE

Robbie R. Morganfield, North Carolina A&T State University

On the first day of a "Black Press in the United States" class I was assigned to teach at North Carolina A&T State University, I asked students to tell me why they enrolled in the elective course that was filled beyond its original capacity.

Student after student conveyed to me points that fortified my growing belief that teaching diversity and inclusion at historically Black colleges and universities (HBCUs) is a far bigger task than trying to check off a box to meet an accreditation standard.

After serving more than fifteen years as a certified diversity facilitator and professor in sometimes resistant majority-White environments, I am now in my fifth year of discovering that teaching this subject matter at HBCUs is filled with the possibility to profoundly impact students who hunger to know and better understand themselves through the lens of history and culture.

Thus, the irony emerges that largely Black student populations at HBCUs need the same kind of academically centered knowledge of minority groups—including their own—that the Accrediting Council for Education in Journalism and Mass Communications has posited largely White student populations at majority-White institutions need. The difference perhaps lies in the fact that many HBCU students also want it.

According to Kim Smith, "Our students suffer from African American culture illiteracy" (personal communication, December 30, 2020). Smith is an associate professor of journalism at North Carolina A&T, where he has been on faculty since 2008. He echoed a conclusion I reached during a four-year stint at historically Black Grambling State University, where I served as head of the Department of Mass Communication before becoming an endowed professor at A&T in the fall of 2020.

"Look at the dilemma," Smith added. "The reality is you could spend four years teaching African American cultural literacy and nothing else, but we have got to teach these students how to write and get a job. So, what do you do? The fact is, we do not have any problem teaching White culture because it is already there. We—our students and faculty—live it every day."

Smith's words capture the paradox of today's HBCU experience that is often clouded by assumptions students will not get enough exposure to people and ideas of other cultures. This essay seeks to invite my HBCU colleagues to deeper conversations about developing more comprehensive approaches to diversity education at a time when an academically informed cross-cultural IQ could make our graduates more valuable resources in a workforce and world increasingly marred by clamor associated with differences.

Resurrecting Communication and Culture

At Grambling, mass communication majors could take "African Culture" as an elective outside of the department, but the few sections offered each semester typically filled up before many other students could secure a spot. That was part of the reason why I initiated conversations with departmental faculty that resulted in resurrecting a "Communication and Culture" course and designating it as a core requirement to ensure students would receive formalized instruction related to diversity and inclusion. The next challenge was getting both Black and non-Black professors up to speed to teach the course effectively. With limited time and resources, we defaulted to the use of an intercultural communication textbook I commended to the instructors based on my previous teaching experience. This could allow the unit to begin addressing two additional challenges that I also saw as opportunities. First, I wanted to challenge students and faculty to raise their level of consciousness about the depth of African American history and culture. There were signs that some equated popular culture with African American culture rather than seeing that as only one part of the culture. Second, I wanted students and faculty to have an academically centered understanding of themselves and others rather than relying solely on experiential factors.

Teachable Moments

I soon saw how much the class was needed after being invited to draw on my theological education and experience to lead one section of the course in dialogue about religion and worldviews.

After assuming responsibility for another section of the course during the final six weeks of the semester, I saw for the first time in my teaching at Grambling a single White student in a class of Black faces. Some of my Black students shared perspectives that reeked of ethnocentrism. "Black culture is superior," one student asserted. Another chimed in with agreement as my lone White student shrank into her seat. That became one of many teachable moments as I led students in a discussion about ethnocentric rhetoric, reminding them of instances when Black people have been subjected to the indignity of it.

It did not take me long to discover that a Black man teaching diversity at an HBCU looked and felt different than it did at a majority-White institution. I did not have to pump my brakes when broaching race-related subjects as I often felt I needed to do in largely White environments. I also never had a student storm out of the room in anger as I witnessed on one of my previous teaching stops, but that did not mean there were never times when Black students would resist with all that is in them the proposition that I placed before them on matters related to race and culture. Those moments often accentuated the somewhat unique experience of teaching about diversity at an HBCU and forced me to think in creative ways.

Higher Education of the N-Word

After noticing students across campus openly using "the n-word" to refer to one another, I began initiating debates in my classes about it. In my graduate-level "Opinion Writing" course, the topic elicited intense discussion as some students defended the usage of the word and others opposed it. The response was even more dramatic in an undergraduate reporting class I taught, with some students insisting, "It is our word. We can use it. Others cannot." I repeated throughout the discussions that my intent was to get students to think rather than tell them what to think. I personally found the use of the word to be abhorrent, but I told my students I wanted each side to make a case and allow the strongest argument to win.

I decided to organize a campus forum and invited some of my students to help me plan the event as part of a lecture series I organized each year. I would invite an outside speaker and set up a panel that would include students, faculty, and administrators. I also invited a student to serve as a moderator for the discussion and partnered with other classes to have student crews to record the event, so it could be broadcast on student media platforms. The "Opinion Writing" students were assigned to function as an editorial board and produce a piece for the campus paper. I did not tell them what position to take, but I did tell them to justify the position. The campus radio station began announcing the event and planned prior to the event to interview the guest speaker, who was the director of the African American Cultural Center at North Carolina State University. Grambling's president and several subject matter experts from within the university agreed to be on the panel, including the heads of our political science and sociology departments.

The event, dubbed "The Higher Education of the N-Word," was held in a small campus auditorium that quickly filled up. I kicked it off by showing a video clip from a situation comedy in which a group of mostly Black friends had gathered; when a rap song came on the radio, they all began dancing and singing along. But things turned intense when a White acquaintance in the room sang a portion of the song that included "the n-word." It was a light-hearted treatment of the issue that laid the foundation for serious conversation and contemplation during the roughly ninety-minute program.

The guest speaker, faculty members, and university president all made points that challenged students to think about the implications of the word and whether its usage was advisable. Afterward, students with a range of opinions on the matter said they had been greatly enlightened by the discussion. For weeks, students and faculty members would stop me in the hallway thanking me for the event and asking when the next round would be held. I was proud of the fact that the event highlighted a much bigger debate that has been unfolding in society about the use of the n-word and allowed my class to create a platform for exploring it from an informed perspective.

Writing this essay has crystallized a reality that I hope my HBCU colleagues will not miss: the experiential—being Black, White, or some other designation—cannot become a substitute for the intellectually centered preparation that both students and faculty need. Let us dig deeper together from the inside, out.

II
POSITIONALITY IN THE CLASSROOM

4

When the Lecturer Is a Minority

Alfred J. Cotton III, University of Cincinnati

As you have read in the previous chapters, teaching about race necessitates an awareness of the challenges in all facets of journalism and mass communication pedagogy. From managing student-professor relationships, to confronting the inherent whiteness and biases of much of the journalism and mass communication scholarship, to negotiating relationships with colleagues with differing approaches to and levels of passion for the value in including race in the journalism and mass communication curriculum, we have to take a holistic approach to navigating these struggles.

For many of us, teaching race as a person of color in a predominately white group adds another layer of complications with which our white colleagues are often unable or unwilling to empathize. We are often tasked with the responsibility or burden of teaching the race classes (Peuchaud, 2018). When we do choose to teach race, our perspective and social positioning within the academy, the discipline, and our own departments is often either not taken seriously or perceived as a bias (Hendrix, 1997, 2002). We are often not only engaging in the difficult intellectual labor of teaching race but also engaging in the labor of advocating to our colleagues why what we do is so important. Sometimes it involves advocating for the inclusion of racialized and intersectional pedagogy not only in race classes but also in the basic course and across the curriculum. Almost always, teaching race involves challenging the myths and stereotypes that accompany both the curriculum of teaching race in journalism as well as those racial myths within the profession. We are far too often carrying the weight of representation on our shoulders, particularly when teaching at predominantly white institutions (PWIs) and especially when we are the only one or one of a few who look like us within our departments. *Teaching Race* is, at its core, a book aimed at providing useful advice for instructors of race in journalism and mass communication. For this chapter, the focus is on the phenomenon of teaching race when the instructor is from a historically underrepresented racial group. For much of the chapter, I will be writing specifically from my perspective as a Black male at a PWI. The recommendations in this chapter encompass many aspects of that phenomenon, inside the classroom and out. To have a better understanding of the origins of my advice, I will begin briefly outlining my background and how it informs the approach to teaching race I am advocating here. I will also provide a brief discussion of scholarship on being a person of color in the academy. Finally, I will conclude with advice and recommendations for faculty of color who teach race at a PWI.

MY BACKGROUND

I am a Black male tenure-track assistant professor in the journalism department of an urban research university in the Midwest. I attended PWIs for both my undergraduate and graduate education. My path through my doctoral program may seem familiar to many faculty reading this. When I began, there were only two Black faculty members (one African, one African American) teaching in the graduate program, only one of whom would still be there by the time I earned my degree. My dissertation committee consisted of white faculty members (save the outside reviewer). Two of the other three Black graduate students in the program when I got there did not complete their degrees. I dealt with both microaggressions and blatant racist behavior from my classmates and the dismissal of research topics from white professors. I also took more time to finish my dissertation than most in my cohort.

A year after defending my dissertation, a discourse analysis of news narratives of police killings of Black men, I applied for a position at my current institution where I am currently the only Black faculty member in a small journalism department. The position called for a scholar with a background in teaching courses related to race as well as someone with a track record of scholarship on race. Specifically, the job advertisement was to teach a course on race and reporting as well as the "Principles of American Journalism" intro course and to serve as the advisor to our campus chapter of the National Association of Black Journalists, in addition to the typical research requirements. My experiences in my present and previous faculty roles have been consistent with those experiences outlined in the literature on what faculty of color go through at PWIs.

SCHOLARSHIP ON BEING A MINORITY EDUCATOR

Faculty of color have been (Bowie, 1995) and continue to be underrepresented (Turner, 2003) demographically across the academy, as well as within journalism and mass communication (Chakravartty et al., 2018). Faculty of color have been found to trail behind their white counterparts in opportunity for advancement and access to resources (Allen et al., 2000). They have reported lower job satisfaction, increased service obligations, and higher levels of job-related stress (Laden & Hagedorn, 2000; Turner et al., 1997). The literature has pointed to a climate for faculty of color that restricts free expression (Allison, 2008) while simultaneously placing unfair burdens on us so that our racial identities become our occupational identities (Stanley, 2006). There also exists a phenomenon where faculty of color often feel "presumed incompetent" by their white colleagues (Hopson, 2000; Muhs et al., 2012). Recognizing the intersectionality of identity in these occupational phenomena means understanding the reality that these statements ring true doubly for women of color (Bowie, 1995; Muhs et al., 2012; Spitzack & Carter, 1987; Thomas & Hollenshead, 2001).

For years, scholars have suggested structural and procedural changes that would not only improve job satisfaction for faculty of color at PWIs but also improve the institutions themselves (Tillman, 2001). As Jones said, "I suggest that Brothers of the academy adopt a model of scholarship development that will continue to support our research interests while continuing to add to the array of research that is conducted" (2000, p. 326). Similarly, my advice in this chapter is holistic in highlighting how my work as a scholar of news narratives can intersect with my students' journalistic work.

MINORITY EDUCATORS IN THE CLASSROOM

A more pointed arena of the literature on the experience of faculty of color on campus is research on the relationships with faculty of color and white students. Faculty of color at PWIs often encounter resistance from white students in the classroom (Stanley, 2006; Stanley et al., 2003) including insubordination, challenging grades, and questioning the instructor's personal narratives. Bower (2002) stated that white students might be more likely to have doubts about the expertise of underrepresented faculty. Bernal and Villalpando (2002) noted evidence of white students who "feel marginalized" taking courses on race and culture exacting revenge through negative course evaluations. Hendrix (1997) found in their study that white students held their Black instructors to a "more stringent" standard than their white counterparts when judging their perceived subject matter expertise. These myths and stereotypes about the inferiority of faculty of color persist among both the white student body and among our white colleagues, perpetuating many of the markers of job dissatisfaction discussed earlier. What follows in my pedagogical advice may provide some opportunities for faculty hoping to bridge those gaps.

MY ADVICE

A consistent teaching philosophy is crucial for teaching success. A teaching philosophy can generally be understood to be a set of guiding principles and practices an educator engages in to facilitate student learning (Fung, 2005; Goodman, 1988; McEwan, 2011). Lesson plans can succeed or fail based on the whims of your students on a given day. Syllabi can prove to be ineffective halfway through a semester. A teaching philosophy, however, can endure regardless of a particular situation or group of students. Therefore whether you are teaching a class on race or incorporating race into a class where diversity was not previously a focus, consistency in the execution of a trusted set of principles will be crucial. As Sawers et al. said, "An instructor's teaching philosophy tends to be constant across physical domains" (2016, p. 28). Their study found a statistically significant relationship between teaching philosophy and student engagement while using active learning strategies in an active learning classroom.

Teaching philosophies are varied and often individualized. My philosophy centers on reflexivity and community-focused journalism. Whether you decide to take the exact approach I pitch in this chapter or adapt it to fit your particular needs and extant philosophy, what you should take from this is how valuable reflexivity is both for you as an instructor of color and for your students as racially aware future journalists.

MY COURSES

I currently teach a rotation of courses on race and reporting, public affairs reporting, and our basic course. The race class, "Advanced Reporting: Race and Reporting," is an upper division undergraduate course aimed at both enhancing students' abilities to reconceptualize race in their journalism practices as well as evaluate their understanding of how messages from journalism and mass communication texts work to define race in the larger societal conversation.

In "Public Affairs Reporting," I provide students with the knowledge of government operations, structure, and proceedings at the local, state, and federal levels. The major assignments in that course involve reporters covering various beats (for example, government, crime and public safety, fire and emergencies, and business). One of the main points of emphasis in that class is how public affairs journalism is essentially community-minded and community-focused journalism. Being a successful public affairs reporter requires understanding the community on which you are reporting (Merritt & McCombs, 2003). In order to accomplish that, a journalist must have a dedication to being a part of that community and avoiding the potential for professionalism standards of detachment and objectivity to widen the gap between journalists and the communities they cover. Important here is that even though this class is not a "race class," students must come to understand how respecting the diverse makeup of these communities leads to more accurate and fair reporting. With all of these classes, my teaching philosophy remains the same.

MY PHILOSOPHY OF TEACHING JOURNALISM

I believe the best instructors do more than transmit knowledge and information to students. A great instructor fosters a desire for learning and exploration in their students as well as gives them the tools to make use of that information well after the end of the term. My teaching philosophy is not strictly constructivist or traditional but rather exists somewhere between the two on a "continuum" (Sawers et al., 2016). Among the important concepts within my teaching philosophy are reflexivity and an emphasis on community-centered (often local) journalism practices. Additionally, I reinforce the lessons from Jones (2000) mentioned earlier by applying a holistic and collaborative approach by infusing lessons from my own scholarship into how I teach my students to do journalism.

Reflexivity

Too often, industry standards of objectivity leave journalists detached from the source or subject of their reporting. Regardless of the connectedness of the journalist, the results of the investigations and interviews are affected by the researcher's presence inside or outside of the community. This is what necessitates reflexive introspection (Davies, 2008). Ahva said journalistic reflexivity is about a "capacity for self-awareness" (2013, p. 791) and McDevitt and Ferrucci added, "Reflexivity in normative theory is viewed as accountability through transparency, and thus meaningful reflexivity must manifest in what the press expresses openly to its readers" (2018, p. 11). If we want to teach our student journalists to be accountable, we must maintain they apply reflexivity to all their work.

Community Focus

The second major concept I found most helpful in my approach to teaching race was community-centered journalism. Community-centered journalism education shifts the traditional industry-centered approach to journalism education from training our students to become professionals working in an industry to training them to become members of a community advocating for their fellow community members' needs. If we accept that one of the central aims of journalism is to give people the information they need to be free and self-governing citizens within a democracy (Kovach & Rosenstiel, 2014), how better to understand what those citizens need than to be a part of their community?

Community-centered journalism pedagogy works to improve the effectiveness of teaching race in the journalism and mass communication curriculum by forcing students to see what type of people live in their community. When public service reporting is tied directly to a clear image of who that public is, everyone in the process benefits. Of the benefits of community-centered journalism, Mensing said, "Requiring students to collaborate in an ongoing manner with interested members of a community would deepen their understanding of how communities work and of what people need and want from journalism" (2010, p. 518).

Another beneficial tool for community-centered journalists is the counter-story. If "objective" journalism is simply white male journalism disguised as democracy, journalism instructors must work diligently to challenge those hegemonic constructs so that our students can create journalism that tells a whole and better truth. One way of doing that is to put our students in positions to tell stories that run counter to those hegemonic, white-centered stories. Counter-storytelling "[builds] community between both whites and non-whites by relying on principles of narrative theory in order to effectively tell stories that reduce alienation and build bridges across racial divides" (Alemán, 2017, p. 76).

Robinson made her goals obvious teaching a course titled "Journalism for Racial Justice: Amplifying Voices in Local Communities," which she said "trained advanced journalism students to practice better reportorial techniques by showing them how to make connections with 'regular, non-official people,' rethink traditional norms of journalism, and perform as civic actors themselves" (2017, p. 304).

As scholars of journalism, we understand the power of journalism in the social construction of reality (Adoni & Mane, 1984) for its audiences. As such, we must recognize the power we are instilling in our students to construct their audiences' realities. Teaching race to journalism students naturally involves teaching them to define race for members of a community. When our students understand that power and the inherent responsibility that comes with that power, and have a strong ethical foundation upon which to exercise that power, everyone in the journalistic process benefits.

STRATEGIES, COURSE DESIGN, AND LESSON PLANS

Van Dijk (2011) argued that the news media internationally, both in practices and content, perpetuates racist norms. He argued this occurs across all areas of the journalistic process including hiring, news values, beats, source selection, story selection, topical coverage, perspective, foregrounding and formatting, quotations, writing style, and rhetoric. A critical approach to teaching race involves making students aware of how the industry is already perpetuating both implicit and explicit racist structures, whether those are stereotypes and racial myths (Johnson et al., 2009; Sui & Paul, 2017) or a lack of empathetic coverage of communities of color (Kaufhold, 2019). It also involves compelling students to become aware of how their own behaviors, and even what they have learned from your colleagues, have conditioned them not to challenge those structures. This is why reflexivity is so beneficial to teaching race to journalism and mass communication students.

Only with a reflexive approach, both from the instructor and from the students practicing journalism, can we identify our own racial fault lines. A framework of the Maynard Institute, "fault lines" are conceptual or ideological fissures in understanding that, when crossed, can cause turbulence in our collective understanding of those important concepts and ideologies (Miller & Hsu, 2008). Being reflexive in our journalistic decision making involves understanding our own implicit and explicit biases. In my reporting classes, using the guidance from Christian's (2012) *Overcoming Bias: Journalist's Guide to Culture & Context*, I repeatedly challenge my students to ask the following questions of themselves:

- What preconceptions do you bring to different situations?
- What do you notice?
- What don't you notice?
- How do you categorize people and events?
- How does your upbringing affect your inability to interact with people unlike you?
- Is your mind able to tolerate some ambiguity in a situation, or do you need things to be concrete and quickly defined?

Rethinking their own habitual thinking before beginning any journalistic inquiry allows student journalists to navigate better the mental processes that bias their thinking. Students can benefit greatly from looking inward in order to report better on the world outside themselves.

This tactic can be particularly useful for faculty of color, especially if you are instructing your students to think inwardly while also participating in that reflexive introspection yourself. Students (particularly white students) will be less likely to see this activity as a threat if you are also engaging. I want to emphasize strongly how crucial it is when dealing with race and other identity constructs in the classroom to participate in these activities *with* your students. You can alleviate some fear and trepidation students may face when confronting race by showing them how comfortable you are confronting topics that make others uncomfortable.

Another activity I typically engage in with my students that helps white and non-white students alike understand race, as well as other social constructs, is the diversity wheel activity. Developed by Loden and Rosener (1991), the activity involves having students think of their identity as majority or minority in a number of areas, such as financial status, appearance, gender identity, political belief, race, religion, and income. When students understand they embody many differing identities from in-group and out-group perspectives, they can better see where they are in relation to others who are racially different.

CONCLUSION

I have outlined here for underrepresented faculty teaching at PWIs a set of practices centered on collaboration, reflexivity, and being community focused. Being in the minority in the classroom presents many systemic challenges to pedagogical success but also positions that instructor to engage with their students in ways white instructors at PWIs cannot. Those challenges are mitigated by employing a consistent and holistic teaching philosophy that portrays the lecturer as a teacher, advisor, and researcher by openly addressing both the lecturers' and the students' racial identities and positionings through reflexive practice and by finding a way to do community-focused work that forces students to confront their preconceptions about people who may be different from them.

REFERENCES

Adoni, H., & Mane, S. (1984). Media and the social construction of reality toward an integration of theory and research. *Communication Research, 11*(3), 323–40.

Ahva, L. (2013). Public journalism and professional reflexivity. *Journalism, 14*(6), 790–806.

Alemán, S. M. (2017). A critical race counterstory: Chicana/o subjectivities vs. journalism objectivity. *Taboo: The Journal of Culture and Education, 16*(1), 73–91.

Allen, W. R., Epps, E. G., Guillory, E. A., Suh, S. A., & Bonous-Hammarth, M. (2000). The Black academic: Faculty status among African Americans in U.S. higher education. *The Journal of Negro Education, 69*(1/2), 112–27.

Allison, D. C. (2008). Free to be me? Black professors, white institutions. *Journal of Black Studies, 38*(4), 641–62.

Bernal, D. D., & Villalpando, O. (2002). An apartheid of knowledge in academia: The struggle over the "legitimate" knowledge of faculty of color. *Equity & Excellence in Education, 35*(2), 169–80.

Bower, B. L. (2002). Campus life for faculty of color: Still strangers after all these years? *New Directions for Community Colleges, 118,* 79–88.

Bowie, M. M. (1995). African American female faculty at large research universities: Their need for information. *Innovative Higher Education, 19*(4), 269–76.

Chakravartty, P., Kuo, R., Grubbs, V., & McIlwain, C. (2018). #CommunicationSoWhite. *Journal of Communication, 68*(2), 254–66.

Christian, S. E. (2012). *Overcoming Bias: Journalist's Guide to Culture & Context.* Routledge.

Davies, C. A. (2008). *Reflexive ethnography: A guide to researching selves and others* (2nd ed.). Psychology Press.

Fung, M. Y. (2005). A philosophy of teaching practicum: Construction of a personal theory of teaching and learning. *Teacher Development, 9*(1), 43–57.

Goodman, J. (1988). Constructing a practical philosophy of teaching: A study of preservice teachers' professional perspectives. *Teaching and Teacher Education, 4*(2), 121–37.

Hendrix, K. G. (1997). Student perceptions of verbal and nonverbal cues leading to images of Black and white professor credibility. *Howard Journal of Communications, 8*(3), 251–73.

Hendrix, K. G. (2002). Did being Black introduce bias into your study?: Attempting to mute the race-related research of Black scholars. *Howard Journal of Communications, 13*(2), 153–71.

Hopson, R. K. (2000). Toward the language and scholarship of freedom and resistance: Coming to terms with being a young, Black male academic in America. In L. Jones (Ed.), *Brothers of the academy: Up and coming Black scholars earning our way in higher education* (pp. 71–82). Stylus.

Johnson, J. D., Olivo, N., Gibson, N., Reed, W., & Ashburn-Nardo, L. (2009). Priming media stereotypes reduces support for social welfare policies: The mediating role of empathy. *Personality and Social Psychology Bulletin, 35*(4), 463–76.

Jones, L. (2000). Conclusion: The community of scholars' model: African American scholarship in higher education. In L. Jones (Ed.), *Brothers of the academy: Up and coming Black scholars earning our way in higher education* (pp. 325–30). Stylus.

Kaufhold, K. (2019). Mediating empathy: The role of news consumption in mitigating attitudes about race and immigration. *Newspaper Research Journal, 40*(2), 222–38.

Kovach, B., & Rosenstiel, T. (2014). *The elements of journalism: What newspeople should know and the public should expect* (3rd ed.). Three Rivers Press.

Laden, B. V., & Hagedorn, L. S. (2000). Job satisfaction among faculty of color in academe: Individual survivors or institutional transformers? *New Directions for Institutional Research, 2000*(105), 57–66.

Loden, M., & Rosener, J. B. (1991). *Workforce America! Managing employee diversity as a vital resource*. McGraw-Hill.

McDevitt, M., & Ferrucci, P. (2018). Populism, journalism, and the limits of reflexivity: The case of Donald J. Trump. *Journalism Studies, 19*(4), 512–26.

McEwan, H. (2011). Narrative reflection in the philosophy of teaching: Genealogies and portraits. *Journal of Philosophy of Education, 45*(1), 125–40.

Mensing, D. (2010). Rethinking [again] the future of journalism education. *Journalism Studies, 11*, 511–23.

Merritt, D. B., & McCombs, M. E. (2003). *The two W's of journalism: The why and what of public affairs reporting*. Routledge.

Miller, L., & Hsu, E. (2008). Fault lines: The Maynard Institute's diversity framework. In R. Izard (Ed.), *Diversity that works: Report and recommendations of a conference on succesful programs in higher education diversity* (pp. 118–23). Manship School of Mass Communication.

Muhs, G. G. Y., Niemann, Y. F., González, C. G., & Harris, A. P. (2012). *Presumed incompetent: The intersections of race and class for women in academia*. University Press of Colorado.

Peuchaud, S. R. (2018). Objectivity, advocacy, and critical pedagogy in the race, gender, and media classroom: Individual, interpersonal, and structural tensions and recommendations. *Journalism*. Advance online publication.

Robinson, S. (2017). Teaching journalism for better community: A Deweyan approach. *Journalism & Mass Communication Quarterly, 94*(1), 303–17.

Sawers, K. M., Wicks, D., Mvududu, N., Seeley, L., & Copeland, R. (2016). What drives student engagement: Is it learning space, instructor behavior or teaching philosophy? *Journal of Learning Spaces, 5*(2), 26–38.

Spitzack, C., & Carter, K. (1987). Women in communication studies: A typology for revision. *Quarterly Journal of Speech, 73*(4), 401–23.

Stanley, C. A. (2006). Coloring the academic landscape: Faculty of color breaking the silence in predominantly white colleges and universities. *American Educational Research Journal, 43*(4), 701–36.

Stanley, C. A., Porter, M., Simpson, N., & Ouellett, M. (2003). A case study of the teaching experiences of African American faculty at two predominantly white research universities. *Journal on Excellence in College Teaching, 14*(1), 151–78.

Sui, M., & Paul, N. (2017). Latino portrayals in local news media: Underrepresentation, negative stereotypes, and institutional predictors of coverage. *Journal of Intercultural Communication Research, 46*(3), 273–94.

Thomas, G. D., & Hollenshead, C. (2001). Resisting from the margins: The coping strategies of black women and other women of color faculty members at a research university. *The Journal of Negro Education, 70*(3), 166–75.

Tillman, L. C. (2001). Mentoring African American faculty in predominantly white institutions. *Research in Higher Education, 42*(3), 295–325.

Turner, C. S. (2003). Incorporation and marginalization in the academy: From border toward center for faculty of color? *Journal of Black Studies, 34*(1), 112–25.

Turner, C. S. V., Myers, S. L., & Creswell, J. (1997). *Bittersweet success: Faculty of color in academe*. Presented at the Annual Meeting of the Association for the Study of Higher Education, Albuquerque, New Mexico.

Van Dijk, T. A. (2011). Teaching ethnic diversity in journalism school. *GRITIM Working Paper Series, 7*. https://repositori.upf.edu/bitstream/handle/10230/11648/GRITIM(7).pdf.

PERSPECTIVE: WHEN THE LECTURER IS BIRACIAL OR MULTIRACIAL

Elliott Lewis, Syracuse University

The class began, as my classes often do, with a question. "How many of you have ever been stopped by the police because of your race?" I ask the students. It is my way of launching a discussion about diversity issues in news coverage. No hands go up.

"Seriously?" I say. "None of you?"

I am not terribly surprised. Of the thirteen students seated in my radio news course this particular semester, none are Black.

At Syracuse University, the predominantly White institution where I teach broadcast journalism and communication law, less than 7 percent of undergraduates identify as African American. As of the fall of 2020, 55 percent identified as White, 10 percent as Hispanic, 7 percent as Asian, and 4 percent as multiracial. But those university-wide numbers are rarely reflected in my classroom. In my first three years as a faculty member in the Newhouse School of Public Communications, I cannot recall having more than three students of color in any single undergraduate course that I have taught. It is worth noting my graduate-level classes have been considerably more racially diverse.

Nonetheless, I often face a class with few students who have experienced the sort of racial encounters with law enforcement that cause many communities of color to view police with at least suspicion if not outright hostility. Few of my students understand the repercussions of journalists mishandling issues of race in news coverage. Like many men of color, I have indeed been stopped by the police on account of race. The situation never escalated to the point of violence. Still, the details of how it happened is a story I share with my students for several reasons.

First—and there is no other way to say this—some students think I am White. Sharing my story provides an opportunity for me to clarify that and introduce them to the nuances of racial identity. As I often put it, I consider myself "more Black than White but more biracial than anything else." Second, it exposes the dangers of using generic racial descriptions in crime stories. It is a pitfall too many newsrooms still fall into today, and I hope my students will learn to avoid it when they enter the profession. Third, it serves as a starting point for a broader ethical conversation about journalistic principles of fairness, objectivity, separating the personal from the professional, and whether there are times when one's own experience may be used to enhance news coverage.

"The Suspect Is a Black Male..."

It happened when I was sixteen years old. My mother, an olive-complexioned woman of Black and White ancestry, had recently remarried to a brown-skinned Black man. He and I were heading home after picking up a pizza when we noticed the flashing red and blue lights behind us. We pulled over, and the officer, who was White, approached the driver's side window.

"Hi, there," he said. "Out getting some pizza, ay?" noticing the Domino's Pizza box I had on my lap. "Can I see your license and registration?" he asked my stepfather.

"Sure," he said. "What's this all about?"

"I'll come back and explain it in a minute," the officer answered.

He returned to his patrol car and began talking on the police radio. Meanwhile, another officer, also White, pulled up in a second patrol car behind him. Both of them then came back to our vehicle, one on either side of the car.

"The reason we stopped you is that we had a report of a robbery involving two Black males," the first officer said, now realizing he had stopped the wrong people.

"One of them had a goatee," the second officer said. Neither my stepfather nor I did. "Of course, you could have shaved that off," he added.

"We're sorry for the inconvenience," the first officer said. "Enjoy your pizza."

And with that, they sent us on our way. The officers were courteous throughout, and their handling of the matter could have been a case study in how to avoid making a tense situation worse. But we were still rattled by the encounter—that we had been stopped on the grounds we supposedly matched the description of the suspects.

"Bullshit, we matched the description," I tell my students when I recount the story. It is one of the rare moments when I deliberately swear in class. "The cops pulled us over because we matched the suspects' race. If the suspects had been two White males, do you think they would have pulled over every car with two White guys sitting in it?" I ask rhetorically. And therein lies the danger in using generic racial descriptions in news stories. Such descriptions are rarely helpful in narrowing down a criminal suspect. Instead they provide fodder for majority communities to feel justified in viewing anyone of the specified minority group with suspicion. Absent further identifying details, vague descriptions that include race do more harm than good.

Racial Dynamics in the Newsroom

More than ten years after I was mistaken for a robbery suspect, I sat in a television newsroom watching my station's 11 p.m. newscast as we aired a crime story that included a suspect description—a "Black male" with few other identifying characteristics.

"Why did we run that description?" I asked my assistant news director, who was White.

"That was the information police provided, and we pass along whatever information they have, whatever will help the cops," he said nonchalantly.

Help the cops do what? I wanted to say. Stop and harass Black people? My news manager's explanation directly contradicted the guidance offered by the *Associated Press Stylebook*, both then and now. The 2020 edition advises journalists to think carefully before identifying someone by race. "Where suspects or missing persons are being sought," the descriptions should be "detailed and not solely racial" (The Associated Press, 2020, p. 250) the *Stylebook* advises. "Any racial reference should be removed when the individual sought is apprehended or found" (p. 250).

"That description was not helpful," I told the assistant news director.

"Well," he conceded, "I guess I've never been stopped by the police on account of my race."

"Well, I have," I told him.

Those descriptions carry real-world implications for people of color—something that I knew from firsthand experience, but my assistant news director had little appreciation for. It is just one example of how a more diverse, more inclusive newsroom can lead to better editorial decision making.

Check Your Opinions—Not Your Life Experience—At the Newsroom Door

As this example illustrates, my life experience as a biracial American is not something I should attempt to "turn off" when I enter the newsroom. But it should not cloud my view of my professional responsibilities either. The kinds of stories we are training most of our students to write require them to check their opinions at the newsroom door. Covering a "pro-choice" rally? Your opinion on abortion rights has no place in the story. Assigned to witness an execution? Your feelings on the death penalty do not belong in the piece. Too often, I find myself having to remind students, "You are writing a news story, not an essay sprinkled with quotes."

That said, many life experiences are worth drawing upon to help a newsroom improve its coverage. A journalist who grew up on a farm may have a different perspective on international trade policy and its impact on agriculture than a big-city reporter who relates more to Wall Street than to rural America. A newsroom staffed with young, single people may not prioritize education stories in the same way journalists with school-aged children would. In other words, we should plan on checking our opinions at the newsroom door but not our life experience. Instead we should try to leverage diverse experiences to build a better news product.

Professor-Generated Content

In an academic setting, campus media outlets can provide a laboratory for exploring the diversity that is all around us. When *Comedy Central*'s Trevor Noah visited Syracuse University in 2019, I used the biracial comedian's appearance as the topical hook for an eight-minute segment on multiracial identity that I produced for WAER, Syracuse University's NPR station. My sources each had a different view on what being biracial meant to them. One was Jason Gruber, a student who had been in my class the previous semester. I asked him what race he initially thought I was.

"When I heard your name, Elliott Lewis, I was like, 'This professor is going to be White; this is going to be another White professor.' When I saw you, I was like, hmmm, I don't know. It's kind of throwing me off a little bit," Gruber said. "Then once you introduced yourself as biracial, I was like, oh, it makes sense. Yeah . . . we see each other."

Stories like this can be repurposed in the classroom to teach any number of lessons. This particular piece is an example of first-person reporting, an approach that I would argue should be used sparingly but does have a place in our media landscape. The style seemed appropriate for my long-form feature story, a different genre from fast-paced, deadline-driven, daily journalism. The piece also highlights some broadcast reporting fundamentals: the use of natural sound, the sensitivity needed when covering often marginalized groups, and the diversity of perspectives found within communities of color.

Leveraging our life experiences to produce more well-rounded content can be accomplished without devolving into opinion-driven journalism or compromising other traditional values of our craft. As Dorothy Tucker (2020), president of the National Association of Black Journalists, said in an interview on NPR's *All Things Considered*, "You bring to the table who you are. But as a journalist, you are fair, and you are accurate, and you are balanced. And that is the job that we have, and that is the job that we do."

References

The Associated Press. (2020). *The Associated Press Stylebook* (55th Ed.). Basic Books.

Bolt, C., & Lewis, E. (2019, January 24). *Local stories show realities of biracial identity for people and families*. WAER. https://www.waer.org/post/local-stories-show-realities-biracial-identity-people-and-families.

Office of Institutional Research (2020). *Student enrollment by career and ethnicity*. https://institutionalresearch.syr.edu/wp-content/uploads/2020/09/02-Syracuse-University-Student-Enrollment-by-Career-and-Ethnicity-Fall-2020-Census.pdf.

Tucker, D. (2020, July 20). Black journalists weigh in on a newsroom reckoning [Interview]. *All Things Considered; NPR*. https://www.npr.org/2020/07/02/886845421/black-journalists-weigh-in-on-a-newsroom-reckoning.

5

When the Faculty Is a Majority

Brian J. Bowe, Western Washington University/
The American University in Cairo

People in the academy have a variety of experiences with racism. Faculty and students of color experience vivid and inescapable confrontations with bigotry. White faculty, on the other hand, are afforded the privilege of being oblivious to racism's very existence if they so choose. That is because structural racism's underlying logic makes it easy for those in the majority to not notice the trauma that it inflicts. Peeling back those blinders is necessary, if uncomfortable, work. But as a colleague recently said to me, the work of dismantling white supremacy in journalism education—and within journalism itself—is *every* white professor's responsibility.

This chapter examines the need for majority (generally speaking, white) faculty to share in the labor of teaching about race in journalism and mass communication programs. Research has suggested that the responsibility for teaching diversity in journalism programs has disproportionately been left to faculty of color and treated as an add-on rather than being integrated into all parts of the curriculum (Baldasty et al., 2003; Biswas et al., 2017). Given that imbalance, the work of building racially just journalism education needs to be shouldered more equitably.

However, if faculty represent a key part of the solution, there is evidence that some may lack the necessary cultural tools to do the work. For example, a recent study found that journalism faculty in one large program rated *themselves* as highly culturally competent but were critical of the competence of their faculty peers (Erba et al., 2020). In this same study, 10 percent of respondents reported being at the receiving end of hostility, and most of this involved insensitive comments from faculty—suggesting that instructors may overestimate their own cultural competency.

When race-related issues are taught in journalism and mass communication programs, they are often lumped together with gender, class, nationality, and ethnicity under a broad umbrella of "diversity" (Baldasty et al., 2003). A survey of journalism programs found that more than four-fifths of programs offered a standalone diversity class but only a little more than a quarter of the classes reported were required for students (Biswas et al., 2017). This means that such classes may be most often taken by those who are predisposed to be interested in them rather than reaching the people who most need them.

Even when white faculty hold strong personal beliefs about the importance of diversity, equity, inclusion, and social justice, the very structure of higher education caters to their ease. As Baladsty et al. noted, "Whites should recognize that when we have dealt with race, we have often done so in a way that is comfortable for us" (2003, p. 9). But this sense of comfort allows the logic of white supremacy to run in the background, similar to the way an operating system governs the basic functions of a computer outside of the user's direct attention. Of course, for those who do not benefit from the privileges whiteness affords, this operating system is more than buggy—it is dangerously dysfunctional and dehumanizing.

In particular, white men like me have a long history of avoiding these necessary conversations, more often representing the problem rather than contributing to the solution. This chapter acknowledges that many of us faculty have work to do. It starts with a discussion of the importance of decentering whiteness in journalism and journalism pedagogy and then moves to a discussion of some ineffective strategies that are sometimes used by white faculty. Then it discusses the benefits of using a Scholarship of Teaching and Learning (SoTL) approach. Finally, an example of one exercise in practice is discussed.

DECENTERING WHITENESS IN JOURNALISM EDUCATION

There has been much conversation in recent years about the urgent need to decenter whiteness in higher education generally, and in journalism and mass communication specifically. As "an ideological system that prizes white skin and confers privilege" (Alemán, 2014, p. 73), whiteness is deeply embedded across the academy, in ways both obvious and subtle. Frequently, discussions about decentering whiteness occur at the curricular level, focused on reviewing syllabi to be mindful of whose voices are amplified and whose are absent in the coursework. This is particularly important work in journalism classes because many of the field's longstanding professional norms mask their roots in white supremacy (Alemán, 2014).

Journalism and mass communication industries carry important civic responsibilities, and reforming the ways future professional communicators are educated can have an outsized effect on public discourse. Mass communication workers direct attention and give audiences cues about what is important in public life, helping them form beliefs and attitudes about people and issues outside of their direct experiences. In the words of Kovach and Rosenstiel, journalists "identify a community's goals, heroes, and villains" (2014, p. 12)—with people of color habitually placed on the negative end of that construction. Traditional media practices have contributed mightily to the demonizing, stereotyping, and otherizing of people of color. News media often have presented mediated presentations of marginalized groups that "superimpose a pro-white preference over an anti-minority bias" (Fleras, 2016, p. 23).

More than a half-century has passed since the Kerner Commission concluded that "the media report and write from the standpoint of a white man's world" (National Advisory Commission on Civil Disorders, 1967, p. 368), yet little has changed. The systemic whiteness of news media is so pervasive that first the Kerner Commission, and later Fleras (2016), proposed thinking of mainstream journalism as the "white press" or "white ethnic media."

The perspective Kerner was critiquing remains an ossified part of journalism pedagogy, with uncritical reliance on conventional news values such as timeliness, conflict, and prominence, which may present an impediment to fairly and inclusively reporting on communities of color (Alemán, 2014; Robinson & Culver, 2019). Adherence to the concept of objectivity—particularly "an objectivity that falsely equates diverging sides of an issue or privileges elite sources" (Robinson & Culver, 2019, p. 376)—is another problematic concept that is embedded in journalism teaching (Brown Kilgo, this volume). One corrective to this idea is the emerging paradigm that Nielsen (2020) named the "Interactive Race Beat." Reporters working in this paradigm have viewed this traditional notion of objectivity "as dangerous and outdated," in part because it centered "whiteness, particularly elite, male whiteness, as a norm" that has treated the existence of racism as an open question (p. 199).

REFORM FROM THE NEWSROOM TO THE CLASSROOM

Journalism education is implicated in the deficiencies of journalism practice. Left unexamined, some traditional pedagogical approaches in journalism and mass communication perpetuate whiteness and promote "a worldview that excludes the perspective of racially disenfranchised communities—even when students of color are enrolled in the classroom," observed Alemán (2014, p. 86). Such values of news production have tended to flatten the lived experiences of people of color and other marginalized groups, and they have persisted from the classroom to the professional field (Robinson & Culver, 2019).

However, race-conscious reform in higher education has an important human aspect as well as a curricular one. The curriculum is delivered by real, flesh-and-blood human beings who possess individual identities that cannot be left at the classroom door. Good faculty bring much of themselves into their teaching, but white faculty have experienced some particular barriers to incorporating antiracist pedagogy. These barriers have included a lack of institutional commitment, pressures related to tenure and promotion, and "an internalized struggle with being perceived as nonexperts in anti-racism and equity discourse" (Phillips et al., 2019, p. 9). These are barriers that white faculty must overcome to join in the process of subverting the embedded logic of white supremacy and building a more inclusive higher education.

There have also been maladroit approaches that white faculty sometimes employed in dealing with race. One ineffective strategy has been to simply ignore it altogether, falling back on naïve and harmful notions of so-called color-blindness, which in reality has functioned as a slippery kind of covert racism (Bonilla-Silva, 2017). This silence has taken a variety of forms. Faculty may have designed their syllabi so that topics related to race were unlikely to come up. They might not quickly have spoken up to correct problematic student comments. Perhaps they did not pay attention to which students were speaking up and which students were not. Overall, this approach has been emblematic of an inability to deal with race in real time.

The motivations for adopting this approach have been several. White professors may be ambivalent about the seriousness of racism in the academy or the profession, they may be afraid of the consequences of getting something wrong, and they may believe that they lack the appropriate tools to discuss race. However, all of these motivations are inappropriate because they are ultimately centered on an instinct for self-protection rather than a focus on helping students (Sue, 2016).

Faculty silence on race primarily has had detrimental effects on students of color—retraumatizing and otherizing them and allowing microaggressions to fester. This hesitancy to engage has resulted in a "conspiracy of silence about race that allows those in power to live in comfort, naiveté, and innocence, while people of color continue to live quiet lives of desperation, attempting to speak, but having their voices unheard or silenced" (Sue, 2016, p. xv). However, the inability to frankly engage in dialogue on topics of race and racism also has had negative effects on white people, hampering their empathy and compassion for others and increasing feelings of self-denigration and self-deception (Sue, 2016). As such, silence has been harmful for students of all identities, as well as for faculty members.

A corrective for this strategy is for faculty to understand their duty to confront their anxieties about engaging with race in their teaching. As Ijeoma Oluo argued, "If we continue to treat racism like it is a giant monster that is chasing us, we will be forever running. But running won't help when it's in our workplace, our government, our homes, and ourselves" (2018, p. 7). We might add, especially in our classrooms.

At the other end of the spectrum from the silent types are those white faculty who weaponize social justice terminology in ways that are more self-serving than genuine (Gray, 2018). This phenomenon—also described as "performative wokeness"—has been defined as "a disingenuous demonstration of an acute awareness of social issues that affect marginalized populations" (Watson, 2020, p. 241). The performatively woke may use the proper critical terminology—and chastise colleagues who do not—but they have failed to reckon with the pervasive anti-blackness that permeates their institutions in decisive actions as well as words (Gray, 2018; Watson, 2020). In the public relations realm, this idea has been related to a strategy of "woke-washing," which describes statements of allyship that elide a sustained commitment to social justice (Sobande, 2019).

This performative approach has played out in faculty meetings and committee assignments, in tear-filled stories about a moment of racial awakening or detailed narratives acknowledging one's own privilege. At its core, it is wrong headed because it centers the white experience of racism. Such performance often masks weakness, allowing the white faculty to reap the benefits of greater credibility of appearing to be on the correct side of diversity work without any sort of action or personal sacrifice (Kalina, 2020; Phillips et al., 2019). Furthermore, because they center whiteness, performative approaches often focus on remedial work for white students rather than building adequate space for students of color to thrive.

Counteracting performative allyship is, of course, genuine allyship based on authenticity. True support for antiracist work is based in a continuous, reflexive, and proactive interrogation of whiteness and intersectionality, coupled with leveraging privilege to promote solidarity and support for people of color (Erskine & Bilimoria, 2019).

In other words, it requires action.

STARTING FROM WHERE YOU ARE

No matter who is doing the teaching, when teaching race, instructors cannot walk away from their own identities and lived experiences. Decentering whiteness does not mean annihilating the individual but rather reforming systems. Previous research has suggested that authentically engaging racial identity in teaching requires "a positive, supportive classroom that employs a collaborative learning style" that has helped students reformulate their understanding of race (Brunson, 2000, p. 3). Some successful strategies for effective classroom dialogue about race include bringing one's own racial or cultural identity into the conversation, acknowledging one's personal biases and imperfections, becoming comfortable about discussing race and racism, and creating space to cocreate knowledge with students (Phillips et al., 2019; Sue, 2016).

Overall, teachers should foreground authenticity. Rather than pretending race does not exist or that they have it all figured out, they should bring their true selves to the table and use their own journey to model an open-minded spirit of inquiry. However, white faculty must take special care when drawing from their own experiences in their teaching. While being transparent about their own process can be instructive, they should be mindful about whether they are speaking more to white students (that is, "I know because I have been there") at the cost of providing space for students whose identities the instructor does not share. It is important for faculty to pay attention to whether all students are able to see themselves in their teaching.

It is one thing to foreground authenticity, but, as noted earlier, this may be difficult to do for faculty who lack appropriate cultural competency. This is where tapping into the community of teaching scholars is crucial: we learn much more together than we learn separately. However, it is important that the white faculty take responsibility for their own learning rather than leaning on the people of color in their institutions to educate them—which is another source of uncompensated labor for faculty of color. The SoTL provides one effective way of sharing, iterating, and improving teaching practice, particularly in the development of student-centered, antiracist pedagogy. In the SoTL perspective, educators reflexively use their own teaching as a research agenda, sharing the results of their work publicly (Boyer, 1990; McKinney, 2007, 2013).

The SoTL process taps into the shared wisdom of practitioners (Nelson, 2001) by helping educators move back and forth between individual reflection on teaching and the broader body of knowledge. SoTL is, as Hutchings suggested, "both 'meta' and deeply engaged" (2003, p. 58). SoTL projects can simultaneously revitalize faculty and improve learning outcomes (McKinney, 2013). This is because SoTL carries "a bias toward innovation, and often toward more active roles for students that engage them more meaningfully in the content, ways of knowing, and forms of practice that characterize a field" (Hutchings et al., 2011, p. 11). Furthermore, disseminating the results of SoTL research publicly is a responsibility because it helps build a body of knowledge that others may draw upon in an effort to improve teaching generally (Bishop-Clark & Dietz-Uhler, 2012).

The next section details a project that developed out of a SoTL platform. The activity described here is based on an exercise called the Collaborative Lit Review Matrix, which was developed by Jasmina Najjar of the American University of Beirut and published online as part of a series of community-building resources produced in partnership between OneHE and Equity Unbound. This collaborative project offers an online repository of open-access teaching tools created by a diverse group of international scholars (Najjar, n.d.). With its focus on practice-driven and evidence-based pedagogy, these openly licensed community-building resources are a vibrant example of SoTL in practice.

UNPACKING A MEDIA BIAS ASSIGNMENT

In the fall of 2020, I was teaching a senior seminar capstone course at Western Washington University. Not only was the COVID-19 pandemic raging, but students were also preoccupied with the protest movements that were sparked by the police killings of George Floyd and others. These protests that were particularly active and controversial in the Pacific Northwest, even factoring into the presidential campaign. As the debates among students and their families continued, these budding journalists were keenly interested in the presence of bias in and fairness of the coverage.

Because several students specifically called out "media bias" as a topic of interest, I created this group assignment based on Najjar's literature review matrix. The assignment was designed to unpack the scholarly understanding of what bias means in order to help students think through the coverage they encountered and, ultimately, in their own work. The matrix activity was adapted for a journalism capstone course for senior-level undergraduate students. This course focuses on mass communication theory and culminates in large-scale student research projects. In terms of learning outcomes, the matrix gave the opportunity to practice writing literature reviews, which are a part of the final projects.

To begin with, the students were provided with a curated collection of scholarly articles that approached media bias from a variety of perspectives, including current works and some that went back decades. Each student was assigned one article, and the class was broken into groups of six, meaning each group was responsible for six scholarly works. Each group was provided with a blank matrix that asked to provide the article's citation, how the article *defined* bias, and how the article *measured* bias. Once each group had filled out its matrix, the group was then asked to collaborate on one paragraph about the definition of bias and one paragraph about the measurement of bias.

In the next step, all of the group paragraphs were collected and distributed to the entire class. A couple of themes emerged. Some groups pointed out that bias can be present in the news content people consume. This can mean unequal or preferential coverage for one side in a debate or uneven sourcing within stories. This also includes portraying one side of an issue more positively or negatively than the other side. Of particular interest, bias can mean depicting members of minority groups differently. Other groups talked about bias in terms of audience perceptions. Sometimes media consumers perceive preferential coverage for one side based on audience members' own political opinion. Bias sometimes occurs when people avoid news media that they believe is biased toward the other party or by selecting news media that are biased toward their own.

After reviewing all of the class submissions, an online discussion was launched asking students to reflect on whether the definitions of bias that they encountered captured what *they* think of when they think about media bias or whether there was something missing. Student comments included critiques of the concept of "objectivity" and the types of sources that have traditionally been preferred by journalists, and the question of the personal biases of journalists was raised. The institutional nature of news organizations was another concern, with students wondering whether coverage was sometimes skewed for economic considerations. Some of the responses also reflected on the line between inappropriate bias and skewing a story by providing a false balance.

Organically, these students were raising the issue in their discussions that have been critiqued as elements of journalism that serve to otherize members of marginalized groups (see Nielsen, 2020; Robinson & Culver, 2019). In the process, they began to interrogate their own practices. All students were invited to connect the learning material to their own experiences. There was still opportunity for the professor to draw connections that the students had not seen or offer correctives to naïve or erroneous thinking. However, the intellectual horizons of the class were broadened, and the students were able to identify the things that were important to them in ways that influenced the trajectory of the teaching. They were also able to begin to develop the vocabulary to effectively critique media coverage.

Ultimately, the literature review that the students came up with together was better than what they would have done separately, in part because they were able to leverage more voices in the process. This is a description of the first time using this assignment. In the future, I plan to develop a full-scale SoTL project with other key concepts to test its efficacy in more detail. But as a pilot, it was successful in helping students engage the debate over media bias in a more thoughtful way.

CONCLUDING THOUGHTS

As journalism professors (many of us current or former practicing journalists), many of us carry the baggage of outdated and unjust assumptions. As Alemán noted, "As it stands now, journalism pedagogy precludes future journalism practitioners from unlearning White privileged assumptions and perceptions of race, racism, and diversity" (2014, p. 86). White faculty must join in this unlearning process.

By leveraging a SoTL approach in this unlearning process, we can collectively assist in the development of a signature pedagogy for journalism and mass communication studies centered on diversity, inclusion, equity, and justice. Signature pedagogies are discipline-specific teaching techniques that help students "practice the intellectual moves and values of experts in the field" (Chick et al., 2009, p. 3). Creating a space for student-centered, justice-oriented, discipline-specific pedagogies to develop in a systematic way throughout journalism education is an important outcome if we hope to reform our teaching—and the profession.

REFERENCES

Alemán, S. M. (2014). Locating whiteness in journalism pedagogy. *Critical Studies in Media Communication, 31*(1), 72–88.

Baldasty, G., Bramlett-Solomon, S., Deuze, M., Liebler, C., & Sanchez, J. (2003). Has the dream stalled? *Journalism and Mass Communication Educator, 58*(1), 7–24.

Bishop-Clark, C., & Dietz-Uhler, B. (2012). *Engaging in the scholarship of teaching and learning: A guide to the process, and how to develop a project from start to finish* (1st ed.). Stylus Publishing.

Biswas, M., Izard, R., & Roshan, S. (2017). What is taught about diversity and how is it taught? A 2015 update of diversity teaching at U.S. journalism and mass communication programs. *Teaching Journalism & Mass Communication, 7*(1), 1–13.

Bonilla-Silva, E. (2017). *Racism without racists: Color-blind racism and the persistence of racial inequality in America* (5th ed.). Rowman & Littlefield.

Boyer, E. L. (1990). *Scholarship reconsidered: Priorities of the professoriate*. Carnegie Foundation for the Advancement of Teaching.

Brunson, D. A. (2000). Talking about race by talking about whiteness. *Communication Teacher, 14*(2), 1–4.

Chick, N. L., Haynie, A., & Gurung, R. A. R. (2009). From generic to signature pedagogies: Teaching disciplinary understandings. In R. A. R. Gurung, N. L. Chick, & A. Haynie (Eds.), *Exploring signature pedagogies: Approaches to teaching disciplinary habits of mind* (1st ed.). Stylus.

Erba, J., Geana, M. V., Aromona, O. O., & Johnson, J. A. (2020). Perceptions of cultural competence among students, staff, and faculty in a school of journalism and mass communications. *Journalism & Mass Communication Educator, 75*(1), 98–115.

Erskine, S. E., & Bilimoria, D. (2019). White allyship of Afro-Diasporic women in the workplace: A transformative strategy for organizational change. *Journal of Leadership & Organizational Studies, 26*(3), 319–38.

Fleras, A. (2016). Theorizing minority misrepresentations: Reframing mainstream newsmedia as *if* white ethnic media. In G. Ruhrmann, Y. Shooman, & P. Widmann (Eds.), *Media and minorities: Questions on representation from an international perspective* (pp. 21–28). Vandenhoeck & Ruprecht.

Gray, J. M. (2018, October 1). Performing wokeness. *Harvard Crimson*. https://www.thecrimson.com/column/better-left-unsaid/article/2018/10/1/gray-performing-wokeness/.

Hutchings, P. (2003). The scholarship of teaching and learning in communication: A few words from the Carnegie Academy. *Communication Education, 52*(1), 57–59.

Hutchings, P., Huber, M. T., & Ciccone, A. (2011). *The scholarship of teaching and learning reconsidered: Institutional integration and impact*. Jossey-Bass.

Kalina, P. (2020). Performative allyship. *Technium Social Sciences Journal, 11*, 478–81.

Kovach, B., & Rosenstiel, T. (2014). *The elements of journalism: What newspeople should know and the public should expect* (3rd ed.). Three Rivers Press.

McKinney, K. (2007). *Enhancing learning through the scholarship of teaching and learning: The challenges and joys of juggling*. Anker Pub. Co.

McKinney, K. (2013). Introduction to SOTL in and across the disciplines. In K. McKinney & N. L. Chick (Eds.), *The scholarship of teaching and learning in and across disciplines* (pp. 1–11). Indiana University Press.

Najjar, J. (n.d.). *Collaborative literature review matrix*. OneHE. https://onehe.org/eu-activity/collaborative-literature-review-matrix/.

National Advisory Commission on Civil Disorders. (1967). *The Kerner Report*. Princeton University Press.

Nelson, C. (2001). Why should you publish your best teaching ideas? *The National Teaching & Learning Forum, 10*(2), 10–11.

Nielsen, C. (2020). *Reporting on race in a digital era*. Springer International Publishing.

Oluo, I. (2018). *So you want to talk about race*. Seal Press.

Phillips, J. A., Risdon, N., Lamsma, M., Hambrick, A., & Jun, A. (2019). Barriers and strategies by white faculty who incorporate anti-racist pedagogy. *Race and Pedagogy Journal: Teaching and Learning for Justice*, 3(2). https://soundideas.pugetsound.edu/rpj/vol3/iss2/1/.

Robinson, S., & Culver, K. B. (2019). When white reporters cover race: News media, objectivity and community (dis)trust. *Journalism*, 20(3), 375–91.

Sobande, F. (2019). Woke-washing: "Intersectional" femvertising and branding "woke" bravery. *European Journal of Marketing*. Advance online publication. https://www.emerald.com/insight/content/doi/10.1108/EJM-02-2019-0134/full/html.

Sue, D. W. (2016). *Race talk and the conspiracy of silence: Understanding and facilitating difficult dialogues on race*. John Wiley & Sons.

Watson, T. N. (2020). A seat at the table: Examining the impact, ingenuity, and leadership practices of Black women and girls in PK-20 contexts. *Journal of Educational Administration and History*, 52(3), 241–43.

PERSPECTIVE: WHEN THE MAJORITY LECTURER IS IN THE MINORITY

Gregory Adamo, Morgan State University

The first time I taught a class centered on race, it was at a large traditionally White research university. Before showing a documentary about the early days of the Civil Rights Movement, I asked the class what they knew about the movement. An African American student quickly answered, "Martin Luther King and Rosa Parks." I asked what else. The same young man again replied, "Martin Luther King and Rosa Parks." This student had an idea on where I might be going, for we were about to watch "Awakenings," the first episode of Henry Hampton's groundbreaking documentary series *Eyes on the Prize*, a series that focused on the *stories* of that movement.

Two decades later, I continue to begin the semester by showing "Awakenings." I am now at a historically Black college and university (HBCU), where I have taught for more than fourteen years. I introduced "Women, Diversity, and Mass Media" as a course at Morgan State University ten years ago. It is a version of a class I first taught as an adjunct at Rutgers University and then introduced at Stockton University in New Jersey. With a class covering both race and gender, I am able to use theoretical approaches such as Gaye Tuchman's (2000) symbolic annihilation and Stuart Hall's work on contesting stereotypes (see Jhally, 1997). I find these foundational in exploring issues of identity. I must also note that having a class that attracts women and gender studies students helps with course enrollment as this is an elective, not a required class in Morgan State's School of Global Journalism and Communication.

Teaching about race is directly related to my research. My first book focused on African American television creators. It was based on interviews conducted in the late 1990s for my dissertation and then in the early and mid-2000s, which I turned into *African Americans in Television: Behind the Scenes* (Adamo, 2010). I have continued this work with book chapters exploring race and entertainment media. During the years that I administered the graduate program in telecommunications management at Morgan State, I worked to integrate issues of race into a number of my classes, seeing it as essential in preparing the students—almost all of whom were African American—with an in-depth understanding of issues of race and media. When I reached out to former students about their thoughts of having a White professor teaching about race, a graduate alum pointed to my personal background: "Him having a Black ex-wife and bi-racial children gives him a different perspective and interactions with Black people than the average White professor."

My goal with *Eyes on the Prize* is not so much to teach journalism and media students the civil rights history they may not have been taught in public schools. Instead it is to focus on the stories that Henry Hampton tells—stories that journalists failed to tell at the time of the movement and, for the most part, continue to ignore today. That is, the *stories* of those unsung activists that were integral to the movement.

The entire *Eyes on the Prize* series explores many of these stories, but in the first half of "Awakenings," the focus is on people like Jo Ann Robinson. She was an activist who was on the board of the Montgomery Improvement Association, organizing the carpool system that helped African Americans get to and from work during the long bus boycott. The Rev. Dr. Martin Luther King Jr. once said of Robinson, "Apparently indefatigable, she, perhaps more than any other person, was active on every level of the protest" (Robinson, 2019, para. 7).

I had never heard of Robinson until watching Hampton's series when it was first broadcast on PBS in the late 1980s. I often joke with students about the "things I was never taught in New York City public schools." That idea is central to not only the discussion of *Eyes on the Prize* but also to my approach throughout the semester. Many students report that the same holds true today as the American school system and American media prioritize the "great man" approach and limit the stories told about much of our history. I find that most students entering the class are going through the same journey that I did five decades ago and, in fact, continue to go through today as I explore the work of current journalists and media creators.

Bowe's statement that "it is important for faculty to pay attention to whether all students are able to see themselves in [your] teaching" helps explain why I believe the approach I use in teaching about race at an HBCU has worked (this volume, p. 80). Yes, there is information that I impart that the students may not know, but central to my teaching about race and ethnicity is that there are issues and history that I do not know and I take joy in learning about.

The central tenet of how I teach about race is: What do we know, what do we not know, and, most importantly, why? These are the questions I encourage students to ask themselves throughout the semester and hopefully long after. I admit to the students that I ask myself those questions all the time. I agree with Bowe's caution about White faculty treating their life experiences as the norm, but I have found for the most part that the "norm" for Black students entering my "Women, Diversity, and Mass Media" class is they do not know many of the histories and stories that we explore in the course. This does not seem to be simply due to their not learning this in K–12. It may be due, in part, to the kind of undergraduates we have at Morgan State. In their work on a new approach to developing communication skills in urban-educated millennials—which used their experiences at Morgan State as a model—Verdelle et al. found that our students "have a dimmed or diminished connection to their interests and passions" (2018, p. 204). This being my experience, I encourage students' passions by having them explore media images of African Americans.

Beginning the semester with *Eyes on the Prize* allows me to emphasize the importance of minority group creators. I discuss the fact that Henry Hampton was African American—that his identity was central to Hampton's goal of telling the story from a Black perspective. Hampton saw that the story of the movement had "always been done by Whites who depicted Black folks as poor, downtrodden, and brutalized primitives" and that his version would show that "it was the strength of Blacks that made the Civil Rights Movement happen, with support from some Whites" (McKinley, 1998, para. 10). This theme is one that I carry throughout the semester, tying it to the work that the students may someday create as journalists or media producers. Bowe rightfully reminded us that fifty years ago the Kerner Commission criticized the news media for the practice of creating work from the standpoint of a White man's world. Hampton's *Eyes on the Prize* is an example of what is possible when the lens belongs to a Black creator. Journalism and media students at HBCUs need to be reminded of this concept in discussions of recent work such as Ava DuVernay's documentary *13th* and Misha Green's HBO miniseries *Lovecraft Country*, work that I find them excited about.

Early in the semester, I connect the epistemological approach of "what do we know" to entertainment media by showing *Smoke Signals*, the first widely distributed film written, directed, and produced by Native Americans. Students enjoy this film, and it allows us to ask ourselves what we know or do not know about First

Nations people. What I learned growing up was through the media: movies, television, and news created by White people. Like me, from Staten Island, New York, my students—the majority of who have grown up here in Baltimore or the Baltimore-DC corridor—have had minimal, if not no, interaction with Native Americans in their lives. I assign students to listen to the episode "100 S Broadway Part 1" from the award-winning podcast series *Out of the Blocks*. The podcast is produced here in Baltimore by a White man and a Black man. This particular episode profiles members of North Carolina's Lumbee tribe who immigrated to Baltimore after World War II. They came for factory and construction jobs.

Subsequently, the Baltimore American Indian Center "has been a cultural hub for the transplanted Lumbee people and other Native Americans in the city" (Henkin, n.d., para. 1). The discussion and assignment then centers on what we do not know about American Indians, and I am able to apply symbolic annihilation theory (Tuchman, 2000). I introduce this topic by looking at media depictions and our knowledge of Native Americans, or lack thereof. So our semester-long journey includes applying this idea to various racial, ethnic, and sexual identities. I am also able to tie this back to the creators of these depictions by discussing the *Out of the Blocks* episodes from the Pine Ridge Reservation. Produced with Arlo Iron Cloud of KILI Radio, Voice of the Lakota Nation, this work is an example of refutation of one of the practices of White media: "parachuting" into a community, interviewing some of the members, and then leaving with media content created through a White lens.

We must remember to listen to how our students see this work, how it can sometimes be tough to consume as a minority group—something that, as a White person, I will never really know. One student, a returning African American woman, told me, "I believe that as long as the professor is culturally competent, sensitive to the topic of race, but also open to dialogue about race without biases, it's all good." Some students may be resistant, like when a former undergraduate recalled:

> When I initially found out my professor was a White male, I thought "What the hell can he teach me about race in the media? I live [every day] as a Black woman, he can't teach me nothing new." I eventually warmed up to the idea and gave it a chance.

We must remind ourselves of Bowe's call to foreground authenticity, bringing our true selves to the table, and own our journey to "model an open-minded spirit of inquiry" (p. 80).

References

Adamo, G. (2010). *African Americans in television: Behind the scenes*. Peter Lang.

Henkin, A. K. M. (n.d.). *100 S Broadway, part 1*. https://www.wypr.org/post/100-s-broadway-part-1.

Jhally, S. (Director). (1997). *Stuart Hall: Representation & the media* [Motion picture on DVD]. Media Education Foundation.

McKinley, J. (1998, November 24). Henry Hampton dies at 58; Produced "Eyes on the Prize." https://www.nytimes.com/1998/11/24/movies/henry-hampton-dies-at-58-produced-eyes-on-the-prize.html.

Robinson, J. A. (2019, August 2). A heroine of the Montgomery Bus Boycott. *National Museum of African American History & Culture*. https://nmaahc.si.edu/blog-post/jo-ann-robinson-heroine-montgomery-bus-boycott.

Tuchman G. (2000). The symbolic annihilation of women by the mass media. In L. Crothers & C. Lockhart (Eds.), *Culture and politics: A reader* (pp. 150–74). Palgrave Macmillan.

Verdelle, A. J., Dorsey-Elson, L., Kopano, B., Mekler, L. A., & Carveth, R. (2018). Beyond distraction: Using technology to support communication skills development for urban-educated millennials. In A. Atay & M. Ashlock (Eds.), *Millennial culture and communication pedagogies: Narratives from the classroom and higher education* (pp. 199–218). Lexington Books.

6

When the Lecturer Is International

Masudul K. Biswas, Loyola University Maryland

International faculty in U.S. universities play an important role by contributing to institutional diversity, as well as the global competitiveness of higher education institutions (Munene, 2014). International faculty bring global perspectives into their teaching and expand a student's horizon of learning (Webber & Yang, 2014). Simultaneously, international faculty confront a unique set of challenges, such as the perception about them being "less credible" educators while adjusting to a new workplace and academic culture outside their home countries (Alberts, 2008; Duru & Akinro, 2020; Herget, 2016). Against this backdrop, in addition to teaching other communication and journalism courses, international faculty members sometimes are assigned to teach race and diversity courses, either based on their own experiences in a foreign-born population or for their academic specialization or interest in diversity and the media. The challenges that foreign-born faculty members confront in U.S. universities can influence how they approach teaching a course. Therefore before getting into their approach to teaching culturally sensitive diversity and race topics in U.S. classrooms, this chapter, at the beginning, will identify international faculty experiences in U.S. universities and academic communities' perceptions about them.

Two terms—international faculty and foreign-born faculty—are used interchangeably in this chapter. The foreign-born population in the United States includes anyone who is "not a U.S. citizen by birth," including naturalized U.S. citizens (U.S. Census Bureau, 2020). International faculty who, over the time, become U.S. citizens are considered foreign-born U.S. citizens.

INTERNATIONAL FACULTY EXPERIENCE IN U.S. UNIVERSITIES

Foreign-born faculty confront more challenges and adjustment issues in the beginning years of their teaching careers compared to their U.S.-born counterparts (Alberts, 2008). Past research identified these unique challenges that foreign-born faculty encounter while teaching at U.S. universities: prejudices and biases, accents, and adjustments to academic systems and student expectations (Duru & Akinro, 2020; Lee & Janda, 2006; Omiteru et al., 2018; Herget, 2016).

A major prejudice that international faculty confront is that they are considered less credible and they are not as knowledgeable as their U.S.-born counterparts (Duru & Akinro, 2020; Kim et al., 2011; Manrique & Manrique, 1999). Because of how they talk and their accents, they are considered "outsiders" (Duru & Akinro, 2020; Munene, 2014). Some students sometimes undermine foreign-born faculty members' abilities and credibility in teaching certain courses, such as writing and cultural studies (Lee & Janda, 2006; Omiteru et al., 2018). Munene (2014) was critical of U.S. academia's double standard that overlooks prevailing misperceptions of international faculty while appreciating their roles in institutions' global competitiveness.

Another common challenge that international faculty confront is with their accents or how they speak English. Teaching undergraduate students on nonurban, less diverse campuses could be more challenging for international faculty as students may not have much exposure to foreign accents (Alberts, 2008; Herget, 2016). International faculty often receive low scores in students' course evaluations mainly because of their accents. In some cases, as Herget (2016) argued, students blame an international faculty member's accent even though they are not doing their part in a class, such as asking the instructor questions for clarification and working on their assignments properly. Lee and Janda (2006) argued that foreign-born, as well as native-born, minority faculty have not been well accepted by some students on less diverse campuses where faculty and students are predominantly White.

INTERNATIONAL FACULTY PERSPECTIVES

This chapter also reflects on the teaching race and diversity experiences of thirteen foreign-born faculty. International faculty interviewed for this research completed their undergraduate education outside the United States but earned graduate degrees in the United States. A number of these faculty members became naturalized U.S. citizens. Faculty interviewed were working either as tenured or tenure-track faculty members in U.S. universities located in the South, Midwest, or Northeast. Of them, nine faculty taught in public universities and four faculty taught in private universities during the time of interviews, in October and November 2020. The interview pool consisted of seven male and six female faculty members, and four of these faculty members were teaching in programs accredited by the Accrediting Council on Education in Journalism and Mass Communication (ACEJMC). These foreign-born educators have been teaching at U.S. universities for various durations from two months up to twenty-five years. This purposefully selected group of interviewees are originally from countries in Africa, East Asia, Europe, Latin America, the Middle East, and South Asia. In accordance with the informed consent agreement, this chapter will not include interview participants' names and institutional affiliations.

TEACHING RACE AND DIVERSITY

Teaching a course on race and diversity in multicultural U.S. society can be a challenging task for a foreign-born faculty member because their lived experience in the United States is much shorter than that of native-born minority faculty members. Additionally, prevailing prejudices about foreign-born faculty being "less credible" do not put them in a favorable position in teaching sensitive topics of diversity and race. Despite these challenges, a number of foreign-born faculty members have shared some of their approaches to teaching diversity and race for the purpose of this chapter, and they also addressed some classroom and pedagogical challenges while teaching such courses.

Not all faculty members interviewed in this research taught a course on diversity or race. Some of them taught a course on global communication, such as international public relations, while the rest infused diversity content in all courses that they regularly taught. Therefore the rest of this section is organized in two subsections: (a) international faculty members' teaching approaches to diversity in three course settings in journalism and communication programs: U.S. diversity courses, global diversity courses, and infusing diversity content in other courses; and (b) how they go about addressing some of the classroom and pedagogical challenges they confront while teaching diversity.

Teaching U.S. Diversity Courses

There are two types of courses on teaching diversity in multicultural U.S. society. One type of course is a survey course on diversity, and another type of course is designed around a specific social group, such as Asian

Americans and the media. Faculty interviewed for this research taught both of these types of courses.

Faculty members who have taught a diversity course in a journalism and communication program found more ways to be creative with their teaching approaches with such courses than in some other rigidly structured journalism courses, such as media writing and news editing. For example, one faculty member has used a wide range of learning assessment methods, more than exams and quizzes, which included a "point to ponder" activity for each textbook chapter. For a discussion on inclusion, he designed an "inclusion-exclusion" activity in his classroom where he assigned a number of randomly selected students to join a number of student groups. The task of each group was to ignore the new members during group conversation. The idea behind this activity was to convey this message to the students: When you suffer, you remember it. This has been how marginalized students on campus or marginalized populations in our society have felt or remembered their experience of exclusion and discrimination.

A faculty member, originally from Argentina and teaching at a private university, described her teaching approach in an undergraduate, elective diversity course ("Latino and Latin American Media"). Half of this course was focused on the representation of Latinos in mainstream U.S. media and the roles of Spanish-language and bilingual media geared toward Latino communities in the United States. The rest of the course served the purpose of teaching global diversity by focusing on the political economy of the Latin American media system. In her seminar-style class, undergraduate students wrote papers and participated in guided discussion to reflect their understanding of course topics. One of the class discussions dwelled on how the *Associated Press Stylebook* is not correct about some of the terms associated with Latinx identity.

A Bangladesh-born faculty member teaching at another private university blended historical and sociological backgrounds of stereotypes associated with racial and ethnic minorities with discussion on contemporary representation of these identities in U.S. entertainment media, such as TV commercials, YouTube videos, TV shows, and Hollywood films. In his class, students were trained to take a sociological approach to analyzing representation of identities in media content and read a social history book on the sociology of group conflict and change in the context of diverse identities. In addition to writing multiple reflection papers and participating in numerous guided class discussion, students conducted a content analysis project with a focus on representation of race, ethnicity, gender, or class in TV commercials or television shows. Before assigning this project, the instructor taught students how to conduct a content analysis project. Based on the findings, students were expected to write a four- to five-page research paper along with their completed codebook for their content analysis. In writing this paper, students were expected to discuss their findings in the context of their learning of relevant historical and sociological backgrounds of stereotypes and other study findings on media representation.

Global Diversity

The strength of having foreign-born faculty members teach a global diversity course is their ability to share firsthand global media and communication experiences with the students, in addition to what students can learn from assigned readings, textbooks, and other course materials. A faculty member, who is originally from the Dominican Republic, extensively exposed students to public relations practices in other Latin American countries in her international public relations class in addition to the public relations industry in other regions. Unfortunately, the majority of textbooks highlighted case studies from only a select few, developed countries. Hence, her professional experience in the Dominican Republic allowed her to share some firsthand experience with public relations in a different culture. Another faculty member who had international journalism experiences in South America brought her global media perspective to teaching courses like "Journalism and Democracy" and "Latin American Media," which explored international media systems in respective political contexts.

Infusing Diversity

The majority of the faculty members interviewed for this research have not taught a course on diversity. Instead they incorporated diversity content in other courses they regularly have taught in public relations, advertising, and journalism. Some of them baked their global journalism and communication experiences into their lectures. For example, when teaching media ethics and news reporting courses, a faculty member brought his firsthand experience of news reporting in the Iranian media system and shared the differences in journalistic practices between societies. When she taught global marketing in an advertising class, a South Korea–born faculty member found it very easy to explain the difference between Eastern and Western cultures because she lived in both cultures. She shared examples from Korea and discovered that her students were familiar with Korean pop music, also known as K-pop. Students were not only able to relate to the faculty member's interest, but they also found such connections with the instructor interesting and engaging, leading them to do more research in international marketing and advertising classes on the role of popular K-pop bands, such as Bangtan Boys (BTS).

Student diversity on campus and in classrooms can motivate a foreign-born faculty member to internationalize course content and activities. One faculty member added a good number of examples from Latin American countries in her advertising courses because a majority of her students were Hispanic or Latinx. She argued that student diversity in her department made her a better professor because she constantly updates her course content to make the classes relevant to students. Having a lot of first- and second-generation immigrant students from Africa, Asia, Latin America, and the Middle East allowed another faculty member, who grew up in Germany, to be more creative with her teaching approach to a journalism class. She also made efforts so that course content and assignments were relevant and practical for the students. Because of her students' family connections in other countries, she has created an international story assignment in her journalism course. Another faculty member, who teaches at a metropolitan university in the Midwest, commented that when he included international aspects of public relations practices in his introductory public relations course, those discussions got the students excited and interested to dig deeper. The majority of his students have been second-generation immigrants.

Two faculty members shared how they infused diversity in a required course. One faculty member incorporated diversity and inclusion in his senior digital media capstone class through clients' projects. In various semesters, this instructor created partnerships with social innovation project teams, charities, and nonprofits serving underserved immigrants from Latin American and African countries, individuals with disabilities, and other marginalized groups, such as incarcerated women in a major Mid-Atlantic city. Students worked on web, multimedia, and graphic design projects for these clients with small budgets who desperately needed help with communication. At the end of the day, this faculty member found his joy in teaching this capstone course for two reasons: (a) these nonprofits and charities utilized student-created design and content for fundraising for programs geared toward promoting inclusion or ensuring equity for socially disadvantaged groups, and (b) students gathered valuable perspectives about underserved and marginalized groups that they might not have gained otherwise. Another faculty member incorporated discussion on diverse identities, including racial, ethnic, religious, and sexual identities, and diverse news sources in a writing course. For example, in her fall 2020 virtual class, she brought a guest speaker, who is a Native American student, in to talk about how media covered Native Americans right after CNN's use of an on-air graphic labeling "Something Else" for voters who were not White, Latinx, Black, or Asian. The speaker not only shared her personal feelings about such media coverage and labeling, but she also offered some tips on the use of terminologies associated with Native Americans. This faculty member assessed such diversity learning outcomes through course assignments. For example, in a news writing assignment, students were required to include every stakeholder's voice in a story (for example, sources cannot be all male). Likewise, if the issue affected multiracial groups, then students were required to interview a diverse group of people for the story.

DEALING WITH BIASES: ACADEMIC EXPERIENCE VERSUS LIVED EXPERIENCE

Foreign-born faculty members should adopt three strategies to deal with biases in their teaching and classroom discussion. One of them is to create a safe classroom environment for race- or identity-related discussions by telling the students that an instructor may not be an expert of all identities; both students and instructors can have their own biases, but everyone needs to have an open mind to accept and correct the mistakes they make. Faculty members should prepare very well for teaching a class on race and diversity to offer adequate historical and social backgrounds of serious topics such as prejudices, stereotypes, and racial disparities. Additionally, faculty members should avoid speaking in absolute terms and with generalizations.

Two faculty members, while teaching diversity, told their students that, as professors, they may have their own biases and that they are not experts of all cultural identities. One of them had been living in the United States for about twenty years and is an expert of Latinos and the media, while another faculty member had been teaching diversity courses for five years with academic training and research specialization in diversity and the media. Students were welcome in their classes to point out if faculty members made biased comments. They think being frank with students created a safe classroom environment for participating in discussions on race and diversity. One of them also accommodated different types of students in her pedagogical practice. If students felt too shy to say something on a diversity topic in the classroom, they were allowed to email her their questions or comments. While engaging in discussion on diversity, this faculty member told her students, "We all are going to make some mistakes," and encouraged them to correct those mistakes. She also encouraged her students to ask someone from the community that they were covering to get an answer on the appropriate use of ethnicity-specific terms.

A faculty member teaching at a majority-minority campus in the South told her students that she does not say something in terms of absolute, such as it is always true or "everyone in the community believes this way." Rather she has used hedging words, such as "sometimes" or "sometimes it may happen." By saying these, the instructor set expectations for students on how they should write and talk about race and media. Another faculty member in his diversity and the media course taught his students how to distinguish facts from opinion and how to avoid generalizations of research findings on media representation in writing.

Two faculty members said that they spent more time preparing for a course or topic on diversity than in preparation for other types of courses and topics simply to avoid any form of incomplete information or biases and to get ready for all sorts of questions. They incorporated research and additional background information into their lectures and presentations while sharing contemporary examples to explain the quality of cultural and racial representation. One faculty member mentioned she thought a lot on how she would articulate a response to a question on race and cultural differences.

Another faculty member, who taught cultural difference between Eastern and Western cultures in an advertising class, trained her students with an evidence-based approach, such as through the use of a wide range of reference materials, to avoid cultural bias in classroom discussions and assignments on cultural differences. She thought that her lecture on cultural differences based on statistics, research, and industry reports was a model for her students to replicate. No student had questioned her for being culturally biased.

Some of the faculty members took additional time in explaining historical and sociological context or designed fun but relevant activities before introducing a topic on media and social identity. As implied in the interviews, like their colleagues and any other professional, international faculty grew on their job, too. They got more creative with engaging class activities and efficient in dealing with challenging classroom situations around race-related discussions when they taught a diversity course over a period of time.

COUNTERING THE NOTION OF "LESS CREDIBLE"

By preparing well for teaching a topic on race and diversity and being very mindful about their own biases, a foreign-born faculty member also can address a misperception of being "less credible" compared to U.S.-born faculty members. A faculty member teaching at a less diverse campus brought in "a lot of context," which included additional historical background to the discussion of religion and media. Despite not being a Christian, he shared his knowledge on Christianity with the students.

For example, in his lecture, he told his students that it is very common in the United States to hear the use of Christians and Catholics separately. Both are forms of Christianity, and the Catholics were there for more than one thousand years before reformers like Martin Luther arrived. The foreign-born faculty member said, "I bring in [this type of] knowledge so that [students] understand this guy is not talking trash." He wants his students to recognize that he is a knowledgeable person, and he did not always need to refer to a textbook.

Another faculty member mentioned that teaching innovations, such as creating a new course and reviving an existing course, can get an international faculty member noticed in the department and helps in countering prejudices about their abilities.

DEALING WITH PREJUDICES

Another challenge a foreign-born faculty member confronts while teaching a course on diversity and the media is some students' deeply entrenched perceptions about certain identities.

For example, an instructor of diversity and the media, who was generally happy with his students' diversity learning outcomes, observed that some of his students were not willing to change their unfavorable opinions toward Muslims and interracial relationships. This faculty member attempted to counter prejudice about Muslims by showing an infotainment video on interfaith dialogue and by sharing his Muslim friends' experiences as a religious minority. To understand differences and similarities among religions, his students watched a humorous, as well as a very insightful, TED Talks video called *The Interfaith Amigos: Breaking the Taboos of Interfaith Dialogue*. In this video, three religious leaders—representing Muslims, Jews, and Christians—frankly talked about how faith can bring people together and how faith can also create division. Despite watching this video, some students sometimes did not change their perceptions about Muslims. In response, he shared about his own upbringing in a religiously diverse Indian society, which has the world's third largest Muslim population (120 million). Though he is not a Muslim, he has secondhand experience through many of his Muslim friends as religious minorities in precarious situations, such as the repercussions of the 9/11 terrorist attack, disputes around the Babri Masjid (a mosque in Ayodhya, India), and other terror attacks.

CONCLUSION

The foreign-born faculty perspectives included in this chapter were not generalizable to every foreign-born faculty member teaching at a U.S. journalism and communication program. However, their experiences of teaching race and diversity courses and how they mitigated some of the pedagogical and classroom challenges could offer teaching ideas to any faculty member. Moreover, foreign-born faculty members can help a journalism and communication program achieve an accreditation standard not only through their hire but also through their teaching of global diversity in their program's curriculum. One of the accreditation standards set by the ACEJMC (ACEJMC, n.d.) focuses on the values of domestic and global diversity. When international faculty members have academic specialization in diversity and the media, they can also contribute more to programs' attainment of diversity goals through curriculum by teaching both domestic and global diversity issues. Two foreign-born faculty members thought that having a foreign-born faculty member in classrooms can itself be an international experience for students because of their distinct accent and global experience.

Faculty experience has always been an integral part of teaching experience, especially for first-time full-time international faculty members who needed to make adjustments to new academic standards and practices, as well as undergraduate student expectations. Faculty interviewed for this chapter recognized that diversity on campus positively impacted their teaching experience in U.S. universities, although some of them seem to have more positive teaching experience in a more diverse campus than those at less diverse campuses. Campus location can indirectly impact some international faculty members' teaching innovations pertaining to diversity and inclusion. Faculty members teaching at a university in a majority-minority city or a diverse city find more ways to be creative with their infusion of diversity in traditional journalism and communication courses because they can forge partnerships with community organizations that serve people of color and underserved communities. It is likely that campuses in urban areas have a more diverse student body, including first- and second-generation of immigrant students, that a foreign-born faculty member can easily relate to, making it easier for them to develop the course content relevant to the students.

REFERENCES

ACEJMC. (n.d.). *Nine accrediting standards*. Accrediting Council on Education in Journalism and Mass Communication. Retrieved December 7, 2020. http://www.acejmc.org/policies-process/nine-standards/.

Alberts, H. C. (2008). The challenges and opportunities of foreign-born instructors in the classroom. *Journal of Geography in Higher Education, 32*(2), 189–203.

Duru, A. V., & Akinro, N. (2020). Navigating academia away from home: Exploring the challenges of African-born academics. In Uche T. Onyebadi (Ed.), *Multidisciplinary issues surrounding African diasporas* (pp. 80–102). IGI Global.

Herget, A. (2016, August 18). *Foreign-born faculty face challenges*. HigherEdJobs. https://www.higheredjobs.com/articles/articleDisplay.cfm?ID=1012.

Kim, D., Twombly, S., & Wolf-Wendel, L. (2012). International faculty in American universities: Experiences of academic life, productivity, and career mobility. *New Directions for Institutional Research, 2012*(155), 27–46.

Kim, D., Wolf-Wendel, L., & Twombly, S. (2011). International faculty: Experiences of academic life and productivity in U.S. universities. *The Journal of Higher Education, 82*(6), 720–47.

Lee, G-L., & Janda, L. (2006). Successful multicultural campus: Free from prejudice toward minority professors. *Multicultural Education, 14*(1), 27–30.

Manrique, C. G., & Manrique, G. G. (1999). *The multicultural or immigrant faculty in American society*. The Edwin Mellen Press.

Munene, I. I. (2014). Outsiders within: Isolation of international faculty in an American university. *Research in Post-Compulsory Education, 19*(4), 450–67.

Omiteru, E., Martinez, J., Tsemunhu, R., & Asola, E. F. (2018). Higher education experiences of international faculty in the U.S. Deep South. *Journal of Multicultural Affairs, 3*(2), 1–18.

U.S. Census Bureau. (2020). *About foreign born*. U.S. Census Bureau. Retrieved November 4, 2020. https://www.census.gov/topics/population/foreign-born/about.html.

Webber, K. L., & Yang, L. (2014). The increased role of foreign-born academic staff in US higher education. *Journal of Higher Education Policy and Management, 36*(1), 43–61.

PERSPECTIVE: WHEN THE LECTURER IS FROM A DIFFERENT CULTURE

Mariam F. Alkazemi, Virginia Commonwealth University

Recently, I read a social media post by an international faculty member using the hashtag #LoveNotTourism. As I looked into the hashtag, I found resources for international couples facing legal obstacles to reuniting during the coronavirus pandemic. I began to wonder about the challenges facing international faculty when moving to and throughout the United States. I remembered a sign I came across as I explored Richmond, the home of Virginia Commonwealth University, and learned about the racial inequities in our past and present. The sign commemorated *Loving v. Virginia*, a U.S. Supreme Court case that legalized interracial marriage in the United States. Faculty members must remember that the remnants of historical conflicts need to be studied because of their propensity to resurface. Towns and cities that house universities across the world are not immune to conflict, and it is important for faculty members to become educated about the issues that affect their students and host communities. This is especially the case for educators who were raised in vastly different cultures and have the difficult task ahead of them to learn more about the intricacies of a nation's culture, as well as distinct local customs and traditions.

International Communication

International communication courses urge students to examine the political, legal, and social realities of the various countries in which communication is occurring. As journalism schools have grown around the world, journalism and mass communication educators must examine culture in relation to the profession. As a bicultural scholar-teacher, I have spent my professional and personal life between two vastly different cultures. I have taught at two Southeastern research institutions in the United States and a private university in Kuwait. I am sharing some of my teaching experiences in different types of classrooms, including ones where students were gender-segregated. My personal and professional experiences have allowed me to engage in research that furthers our understanding of how cultural conditions influence media consumption, media organizations, and media education.

Journalism and mass communication programs in a singular world region, like the Arab world, are not uniform. For instance, Al Nashmi et al. (2018) examined the curricula and faculty members in ten universities that offer a degree in journalism and mass communication in Arab states. They found differences among the programs in the employment of a different proportion of Arab and non-Arab faculty. In other words, some Arab universities hire more professors who may be less familiar with Arab culture than certain peer institutions.

As there is a large number of international educators in the Arab Gulf states, my colleagues examined the cultural aspects of the educational environment. Designed by an intercultural communication scholar, Fahed Al-Sumait, and a linguist, Marta Tryzna, the Intercultural Assessment Project involved an effort to measure intercultural communication competence (ICC) in Kuwait due to the high number of foreign-born educators in the region. Their work was inspired by Lily Arasaratnam's (2009) framework. I developed analyses and wrote reports for this project, some of which are shared in the next section.

Intercultural Communication Competence

The first step to assessing ICC is to understand the idea's conception. Arasaratnam (2009) cited Spitzberg and Cupach's (1984) research that ICC is a tool that allows individuals to be effective in achieving their goals and appropriate in different contexts. In building on decades of research, she developed measurements of ICC that relate to three components from previous literature: affect, cognition, and behavior. Affective ICC is the ability to feel empathy and emotionally connect to individuals from other cultures. Cognitive ICC is the ability to understand enough about another person from a different culture to interpret their behaviors correctly. Finally, behavioral ICC is the ability to seek intercultural encounters and adapt or change according to interaction with someone from a different culture. Arasaratnam and Doerfel measured the three components of ICC, called for "culturally unbiased measures" (2005, p. 142), and suggested rigorous testing in various cultural settings as a way forward.

My colleagues adapted some of these measures to examine how individuals' university education, as well as knowledge of languages, gender, and age, affected their ICC (Al-Sumait et al., in press). Affective ICC was significantly different between students with two or four years and those with one year of university experience. However, there were no differences with regard to behavioral or cognitive ICC components. In other words, students can feel empathy for individuals from a different culture without seeking those experiences and without understanding them enough to interpret their communication. In another study, we found that there were fewer than ten courses whose titles were related to intercultural communication in each Arab Gulf state, except for the United Arab Emirates (Tryzna et al., 2019). This showed a gap that universities can fill even where expatriates outnumber nationals, as in many of the Gulf States.

Knowledge of more than one language increased the affective and behavioral ICC scores among Kuwaiti respondents (Al-Sumait et al., in press). However, those who knew four or more languages had lower cognitive ICC scores. In other words, exposure and familiarity of different languages does not automatically translate to more ICC. Beyond the students' ICC skills, the diversity of the faculty helped me realize that not all of us were trained to think of education in similar ways. In trying to understand cultural references, norms, and stereotypes, I traveled to gain deeper exposure.

When I was in Kuwait, I often found myself attempting to play the role of a cultural translator—a role that was both pleasant and frustrating at times. In the United States, many institutions of higher education have offices to help further faculty's pedagogy offering workshops for faculty members. Some offices for diversity and inclusion may provide workshops to help explain issues of race, gender, and neurodiversity. At such workshops, international faculty members should seek cultural translators. If the faculty member is working at an institution where such resources are not available, they should seek other faculty members who had to overcome cultural differences themselves as well as faculty members with the kind of historical and institutional knowledge that comes from working at a university for a long time. International faculty members should ask explicitly about offensive words and behaviors in the culture, ranging from body language to explicit language to avoid. Further, these faculty members should be careful to think about discrepancies between behaviors portrayed in media content and in their own social environment, such as racial and gender-related slurs. By learning to identify cultural norms, one can focus on behaving and expressing oneself effectively and appropriately.

Scholarship of Teaching and Learning

While learning an entirely new language and culture is not feasible for academics who teach abroad, a review of literature can surely help improve the cognitive ICC component. Because of the limited knowledge about international universities (Gearhart & Cho, 2020), faculty teaching abroad should not hesitate to explore research from other fields, including area studies, political science, anthropology, and sociology, to inform their teaching within a culture different from one's upbringing. This self-study allows for the development of courses that integrate pedagogy and strategies for effective and appropriate intercultural communication. Further, the lesson plans and the research on which they are founded could lead to valuable scholarship of learning and learning projects (see Ni et al., 2015), which allows other faculty to learn from those experiences as well. In today's globalized world, academics should examine markers of their identities and the identities of their loved ones. Identifying differences in values is important because it allows for one to adjust to a new environment and develop self-awareness, which could strengthen our effectiveness in the classroom.

References

Al Nashmi, E., Alkazemi, M. F., & Wanta, W. (2018). Journalism and mass communication education in the Arab world: Towards a typology. *International Communication Gazette, 80*(5), 403–25.

Al-Sumait, F., Tryzna, M., Alkazemi, M. F., & Boone, E. L. (in press). Examining multicultural educational experiences and intercultural communication competence in Kuwait. *Journal of Intercultural Communication*.

Arasaratnam, L. A. (2009). The development of a new instrument of intercultural communication competence. *Journal of Intercultural Communication*, 20. http://www.immi.se.proxy.bsu.edu/intercultural/nr20/arasaratnam.htm.

Arasaratnam, L. A., & Doerfel, M. L. (2005). Intercultural communication competence: Identifying key components from multicultural perspectives. *International Journal of Intercultural Relations, 29*(2), 137–63.

Gearhart, S., & Cho, J. (2020). Mapping the history of *Journalism & Mass Communication Educator*: 30 years of publication (1990–2019). *Journalism & Mass Communication Educator, 75*(4), 375–91.

Ni, L., Wang, Q., & De la Flor, M. (2015). Intercultural communication competence and preferred public relations practices. *Journal of Communication Management, 19*(2), 167–83.

Spitzberg, B. H., & Cupach, W. R. (1984). *Interpersonal communication competence*. Sage.

Tryzna, M., Alkazemi, M. F., & Al-Sumait, F. (2019). Examining the intercultural outcomes of internationalized education in the Arabian Peninsula. In P. Turner, S. Bardhan, T. Holden, & E. Mutua (Eds.), *Internationalizing the Communication Curriculum in an Age of Globalization: Why, What, and How* (pp. 164–84). Routledge.

III
GUIDANCE AND MENTORSHIP

7

Teaching Diversity in Immersive Learning Courses

Gabriel B. Tait, Ball State University

It was 5:00 a.m. We were waiting for the last class member to arrive. The "Advanced Photojournalism" students at Arkansas State University had been preparing all semester for this special opportunity. Teaching at a primary White institution, each semester I immerse my students into a community outside their norm as a way to broaden their cultural understandings. When the final student arrived, they apologized: "I'm sorry, Dr. Tait. This is something we have worked on all semester, and I think I failed already."

I smiled.

We were preparing to make our two-and-a-half-hour trip from Jonesboro, Arkansas, to Oxford, Mississippi, to participate in the Lens Collective Multimedia storytelling workshop—an exclusive four-day workshop where students were invited into various communities to develop and produce multimedia stories about the people and places in the Mississippi Delta. We would extend our drive time by stopping in Memphis, Tennessee, to visit the Lorraine Motel and the National Civil Rights Museum (the place where Rev. Dr. Martin Luther King, Jr. was assassinated in 1968). We would also visit the Withers Collection Museum & Gallery on the famous Beale Street to check out the latest photographic additions to the civil rights collection of photographs by Ernest C. Withers before heading over to Gus's World Famous Fried Chicken for lunch.

My mission for this immersive experience was to help our students learn the history of the community, have them experience the sights and sounds of an urban context in which they might work, and assure that we, as an accredited program, were fulfilling the ACEJMC Professional

Values and Competencies. This particular immersive learning experience was aligned with three competencies to (a) demonstrate an understanding of gender, race, ethnicity, sexual orientation, and, as appropriate, other forms of diversity in domestic society in relation to mass communications; (b) demonstrate an understanding of the diversity of peoples and cultures and of the significance and impact of mass communications in a global society; and (c) understand concepts and apply theories in the use and presentation of images and information.

My students joined over thirty-five other invited students from seven universities across the country and worked in teams to tell stories from the Delta region that would focus on cultural preservation through digital storytelling. One of the key aspects of the workshop was that Delta participants invited the student teams into their community. For this immersive assignment, teams of three partnered with one of fifteen mentors (either professors or working professionals) to receive hands-on coaching as they developed their projects. While my students participated in the workshop, I served as a mentor in the program.

Even though one of my students was late for this trip, each student succeeded in the workshop and passed the class with flying colors. They each grew professionally and personally due to the immersive nature of their multimedia community engagement projects. Now, since this excursion, I have moved from Arkansas State University to Ball State University, but I still constantly employ immersive learning opportunities in my classroom to help my students develop professional skills while preparing them for the postcollege world. This chapter offers insights and opportunities for educators who are considering using the immersive learning framework in diverse communities to bridge the pedagogic gap between theory and experience, to improve interactions between students and their faculty members, and to develop meaning for community partnerships between the university and the constituents in the community.

IMMERSIVE LEARNING

When we talk about immersive learning, there can be some ambiguity to the concept. It is not ambiguous in terms of the purposes for the immersive learning experiences, but the term is contextual in how universities and their community partners define the outcomes for the necessary experience. Scholars have noted that immersive learning (De Freitas et al., 2010; Mustian et al., 2017; Thomas & Mucherah, 2016) can be viewed as a more focused version of service learning. Service learning and immersive learning are two pedagogical approaches that an educator should consider when planning to maximize the academic experience by integrating their students into the local (or regional) community. *Service learning* or *civic engagement* models of student learning (Einfeld & Collins, 2008; Keen & Hall, 2009) have been generally grounded in an experiential education model (Eyler & Giles, 1999) where universities and faculty instructors provide opportunities for students to serve a particular community. In essence, the community becomes the de facto classroom.

The students' engagement in the community becomes an avenue for the instructor to arrange a way for the students to gain a tertiary experience of what it is like to give back to the community. For scholars like Jacoby (1996), who was largely credited for the definition of "service learning," the key points of this approach have been that participants "give back" and "reflect" on their interactions of giving back.

Community partners, students, and faculty members come together to identify challenges and solutions to address these issues. This collaborative approach to problem solving and service brings about a unique set of possibilities and potential encounters (for example, project objective planning, documentation requirements, timeline and scheduling negotiations, etc.). As an explanation of how we approach the immersive learning experience for our students at Ball State University, our immersive statement reads:

> Immersive learning projects are high-impact learning experiences that involve **collaborative student-driven teams**, guided by **faculty mentors**. Students **earn credit** for working with community partners such as businesses, nonprofits, and government agencies to **address community challenges** through the **creation of a product** that has a lasting impact. (Ball State University, 2021b)

Within the immersive learning framework, institutions must be intentional about supporting their faculty (for example, faculty release time, grant and funding opportunities, assistance in proposal development and project planning, community connection initiatives, etc.) as they utilize innovative approaches to the learning (see Ball State University, 2021a). In a recent immersive learning proposal, a community partner and I wrote the following abstract:

> This immersive learning project provides an environment where students will work toward building an advanced understanding of diversity and contribute to an ongoing community revitalization project. As part of the project, students will partner with staff and members of the Ross Community Center (and by extension, the Thomas Park/Avondale community in Muncie) to develop visual ethnographies, documenting community issues, opportunities, and goals that contribute to community revitalization.

It should be noted that the shift toward immersive learning is not just between the institution and the faculty member, but it is also between the students and the faculty member and the faculty member, students, and the community partner. A triangular approach should presuppose that all sides are equal. The faculty member and the institution are one leg of the triangle, the students are another leg of the triangle, and the community partner often serves as the foundation because they willingly open their doors, provide access to their community members, and provide the facilities needed to accommodate programs that are generally not built into the mission of the organization. In the next section, I will share my background to help readers understand why I am a proponent for immersive learning experiences.

MY STORY

I am a product of the immersive learning framework. As a fifth-grade student at Manchester Elementary School in Pittsburgh, Pennsylvania, I traveled with my classmates to Washington, DC, to visit our nation's capital, talk with our elected leaders, and experience various museums. While I am sure immersive learning was not the label for Mr. Parks' teaching style, he believed in getting our class out of our traditional urban environment. Unfortunately, my immersive experiences following this fifth-grade experience have been few and far between.

As a communication and photojournalism student at Slippery Rock University, nearly thirty years ago, I was provided the opportunity to travel to Edinburgh, Scotland, for a student exchange program. I chose Edinburgh, Scotland, for several reasons—first, the media and communication program was one of the top in the United Kingdom, and second, Scotland is an English-speaking country and I did not have to learn another language. As I settled into my classes and learned the context of Scotland, I found myself trying to engage in experiences that would allow me to learn about that community and practice my craft. These cross-cultural experiences were not planned by my university or exchange program.

This student exchange was immersive in that I was an international student in a foreign country. There was a presupposition that, because I was an international student, learning and growing would be linked to me being in a culture that was different than my own. I took full advantage of being in another country, working as an unpaid freelance photojournalist at the Scotland *Evening News*. The *Evening News* was the largest evening newspaper in the community. I served as a freelance photojournalist and had a number of photographs published over the course of my five months in the country. I also traveled with a friend of mine to Egypt to work on a documentary on the continent of Africa. My immersive learning or student exchange scenario in Scotland provided me a much larger opportunity to see the world and gain practical experiences from within the educational environment.

In 2002, I was an embedded journalist with the *St. Louis Post-Dispatch* attached to the 4th Infantry Division in Iraq with a unit of combat engineers. My assignment with the *Post-Dispatch* was to document life up close and personal as the soldiers were in battle. I would sleep, eat, and travel where the soldiers did. For all intents and purposes, I was a member of the unit without a weapon (well, I did have a camera).

I gained a greater perspective of how my work impacts others, in addition to the practical skills that I learned while participating in the immersive experiences described earlier. I also learned how to work and communicate effectively with others who did not share my experiences, opinions, and perspectives about diversity, equity, and inclusion. These are some of the skills and practices I believe our students will gain as they participate in immersive learning projects. Based on my personal growth from these experiences, I argue that immersive learning is the instructor's intentional focus to provide a realistic, contextual learning experience for their students where they are learning and sharing their experiences for the greater good. My immersive learning experiences extended beyond my educational exchange program and shaped the way I approach teaching and community engagement.

WHY TEACH DIVERSITY AS AN IMMERSIVE LEARNING TENET?

In a message attributed to John Wesley, he is quoted saying the famous phrase, "I look upon all the world as my parish" (1739/1990, p. 67). While Wesley was speaking in the context of his faith, he looked at all of his interactions as opportunities to engage communities and learn more about who they were. I take a similar approach in my teaching style. I want my students to be intentional about crossing cultural, religious, ethnic, socioeconomic, philosophical, and/or racial boundaries to learn who people are. This, understanding and representing communities, is the essence of what we do as mass communication and journalism professionals. We are trying to learn about the people with whom we are seeking to communicate. While traditional pedagogical methods can be used to teach diversity and similar subjects, immersive learning techniques allow students to engage with the topic in ways that enhance not only their practical knowledge but also their critical thinking and storytelling skills. The more knowledge and understanding of diversity that students have, the better equipped they are to apply that knowledge in their various personal and professional contexts.

Waddell (2011) further illustrated the valuable impact that diversity centered immersive learning engagements have for the educator and students alike. She noted how changing "racial/ethnic populations in public schools" (p. 23) and institutions of higher education have demanded that our students are aware by engaging with increasingly diverse populations (Bowman & Brandenberger, 2012; Craft, 2018; Patton, 2005; Royce, 1982; Steinberg, 1993). This means that some form or tenet of diversity, albeit racial, ethnic, cultural, socio-economic, religious, gender and/or sexual orientation, may intersect with the student at some point in their academic life. Interacting with persons different than us builds a bridge (Zusman, 2016) that can reshape our worldviews and help us grow in the capacity to accept that the world is not monolithic.

Holsapple (2012) noted that college in general, and service learning opportunities specifically, are the first time most higher education students experience significant interactions with diverse neighbors in this "living laboratory with great potential for them to learn and grow" (p. 5). However, Holsapple cautioned that service learning programs are "largely absent from the larger discussion of improving students' exposure to interactional diversity" (p. 5). Other scholars (Bushouse, 2005; Keen & Hall, 2009; Zempter, 2018) asserted that service learning experiences need to be grounded in both curricular and cocurricular learning and differentiate the "community service only" component from student learning as an intended goal. These service learning projects help students experience the classes in a civic way where the objectives for the community and deeper understanding for themselves intersect.

Up until this point, I have talked about service learning and immersive learning as ways to understand theoretically (Doberneck et al., 2010) how to engage our communities. Now it is important to drill down to some of the meat and potatoes of the immersive learning experience. There are some clear thoughts that need to be considered when developing an immersive learning experience.

PLANNING AND EXECUTING AN IMMERSIVE LEARNING EXPERIENCE

During my tenure as a professor at two different institutions, my students have engaged in more than twenty immersive learning experiences. These experiences range from my students serving as student photojournalists for university events to traveling out of state to document communities and provide visual records of these environments. Each of these experiences has been built into my syllabi as community or cultural engagement events. For example, in one class our students traveled to Memphis, Tennessee, to engage in a diverse community. Here is a description from our syllabus:

> MEMPHIS PHOTOJOURNALISM ASSIGNMENT: This semester our class will take at least two photojournalism trips to Memphis. We work on a photojournalism project that explores how Memphians understand the I AM A MAN campaign following the 50-year MLK assassination. Students collect demographic data and will take portraits of persons who are wearing the I AM A MAN sign. These educational trips are mandatory and will take place on a Friday or Saturday. Class time will be adjusted.

When focusing on diversity, I utilize the following values and competency standards: (a) demonstrate an understanding of gender, race, ethnicity, sexual orientation, and, as appropriate, other forms of diversity in domestic society in relation to mass communications and (b) demonstrate an understanding of the diversity of peoples and cultures and of the significance and impact of mass communications in a global society (ACEJMC, n.d.). Here is an example of two goals and outcomes:

> **Goal:** To mentor students with visually reporting diverse interest of their community.
> **Outcome:** Students will create strong visual content that illustrates diverse and global society, which includes diversity of gender, race, ethnicity, sexual orientation, religion, culture, and national origin.
>
> **Goal:** To help students develop critical thinking skills in story development.
> **Outcome:** Students will develop a wide array of story ideas from news events and research of the community.

To guide the students throughout the semester toward the previously mentioned goals, students were required to participate in lectures, critiques, and discussions that examined their work and the work of their colleagues. Early semester lectures reviewed basic techniques in audio, lighting, and video as a refresher in photojournalism and visual storytelling. As the semester advanced, so did the expectations. Students were required to research their assignment locations, provide demographic background of their communities, and present their findings to the class during weekly feedback and critique sessions. During our student-led, in-class critiques, students would comment on other students' work. They would discuss if the stories' ideas aligned with the diversity standards outlined in the syllabus. After students completed their assignments, we would have an oval table discussion. We would have an informal content audit of all of the photographs produced. We would also examine the gender, race, ethnic, and socioeconomic background of the people in the complete take.

Our classes operated from the working premise that one of the best methods for learning about photographs comes from reviewing and discussing them. The ultimate goals of these sessions were to increase the students' cultural and diversity awareness and prepare them for their immersive learning experiences. Student assessment was measured through these critiques and one-on-one mentoring meetings with each student. These meetings affirmed Zygmunt-Fillwalk et al.'s (2010) argument in how the immersive learning opportunities within communities strengthen teachers' repertoires and provoke new ways of thinking about how different settings create possibilities and constraints for student growth. I would, however, be remiss if I did not mention there may be challenges when trying to weave diversity into one's immersive learning experiences.

RESISTANCE TO IMMERSIVE LEARNING EXPERIENCES

As a professor who has utilized the immersive learning approach in most of his classes, I have found that there is great resistance for students to get out of the proverbial bubble and engage the community on their terms. There are often reasons that are unknown to the instructor at the time. So it is important for the instructor to lay out their expectations at the beginning of the class. I tell my students in advance that we will have a number of immersive experiences. I provide for them the dates so they can plan their schedules accordingly. I also give them a day off during the normally scheduled class time. Such is the case in my "Diversity and Media" class at Ball State University when I have my students attend a religious organization (for example, an Islamic mosque, a Jewish synagogue, or a Christian African American church) for a site visit. These site visits are open for all students, and I provide for them the opportunity to self-select where and when they would like to attend. This requires that the instructor be organized on the front end. This is where a covenantal approach to the expectations of the class is beneficial between the students and faculty member. Faculty members need to assure that their students understand the cost-benefit (or value learning benefit) of engaging with the community that they will eventually, if not already, serve and work alongside. As professors of higher education, it is imperative that we understand that students have jobs, have fractured homes, and are just trying to get by, and our immersive learning experience should bridge potential gaps in the student learning process.

BENEFITS OF IMMERSIVE LEARNING

The immersive learning experience allows students to reflect on how they can apply their skills in real-world contexts and, in some cases, causes the students to pursue different courses of study or career paths. In addition, immersive learning experiences expose students to an array of contexts and challenges outside of the classroom. As the students navigate those contexts and challenges, they are able to apply the knowledge they have gained in the classroom while also gaining and/or refining essential communication, leadership, and critical thinking skills. For example, one of my former photojournalism students was accepted into an illustrious workshop. While she performed well during the workshop and was even offered a position, after experiencing the fast-paced exercise with newsroom-like deadlines for production, she decided that photojournalism was not the field she wanted to pursue. While this experience was not one that I had anticipated for the student, it did accomplish the goals outlined in the syllabus. The student did have a diverse experience. The student was able to critically think about her assignment and her life goals. And ultimately, the student decided that a different career path was for her. This is the essence of providing a diverse space for your students to grow into work through the particularities of their academic experiences. In my conclusion, I will offer a few tips for faculty members who may be considering using an immersive learning model to expand their students' learning.

CONCLUSION AND TAKEAWAYS

Colleagues often laugh at me when I tell them some of the ways that I am going to get the students out in the community. They tell me that I am ambitious and that I am demanding of the students. While both of these points are true, the end result is to provide an experience that "produces learning" (Barr & Tagg, 1995, p. 13). Not all immersive learning experiences have worked as planned. Some have been utter failures. If a faculty member is looking to build on the immersive learning framework, they will want to consider the following three steps: (a) develop an agreement between you and the community partner, (b) be selective in the students that you enroll in your immersive learning class, and (c) develop a communication team.

Develop an Agreement Between You and the Community Partner

I am currently working with a community partner who runs a nonprofit organization focused on helping a community with a diverse population and several resource gaps. Frequently we communicate by email. As we have discussed our partnership and related items via email, we have created a rolling document that allows us to memorialize our conversation. An agreement document assures that both the community partner and the faculty member understand all of the agreed-upon elements. This allows the faculty member and community partner to manage one another's expectations. It also establishes an appropriate framework in which the students can and will work.

Be Selective with the Students You Enroll

This point is probably one of the most critical of your planning process. If your class has the latitude to select your students, the faculty member will want to be intentional about who is on their team and what the goals of the class or immersive learning experience are meant to be. This reduces the level of reservation between the community partner and the student and the community partner and the faculty member. If this immersive learning experience is in a general or required class, it is important that the faculty member aligns their immersive experiences with other opportunities that all students can accept and participate in.

Develop a Communication Team

The final tip I would offer for a faculty member looking to increase their immersive learning experiences, and diversity engagement by extension, is to develop a communication team. Immersive learning experiences are about documenting the work that you have done so the student and the funding agent can see how their money is being used to address what you have said you were going to do. A student communication team is significant. In my experience as a professor in the Department of Journalism, we have all of the persons we need to be able to assemble a great communication team. You will want a person who can photograph or video record the interactions of the class with the community. You will want a person who can develop a public relations strategy. You will want a person who can work with the organization to develop a social media presence. In today's world, the communication team is probably as important as the students who will be participating in this immersive learning interaction. Documenting the work that you are doing also builds sustainability for future projects.

REFERENCES

ACEJMC. (n.d.). *Nine accrediting standards.* http://www.acejmc.org/policies-process/nine-standards/.

Ball State University. (2019). *Strategic plan—Destination 2040: Our flight path.* https://www.bsu.edu/about/strategic-plan.

Ball State University. (2021a). *For faculty.* Office of Immersive Learning. https://www.bsu.edu/about/administrativeoffices/immersive-learning/for-faculty.

Ball State University. (2021b). *Immersive learning.* Office of Immersive Learning. https://www.bsu.edu/about/administrativeoffices/immersive-learning.

Barr, R. B., & Tagg, J. (1995). From teaching to learning: A new paradigm for undergraduate education. *Change, 27*(6), 12–25.

Bowman, N. A., & Brandenberger, J. W. (2012). Experiencing the unexpected: Toward a model of college diversity experiences and attitude change. *The Review of Higher Education, 35*(2), 179–205.

Bushouse, B. K. (2005). Community nonprofit organizations and service-learning: Resource constraints to building partnerships with universities. *Michigan Journal of Community Service Learning, 12*(1), 32–40.

Craft, A. R. (2018). Creating connections, building community: The role of oral history collections in documenting and sharing campus diversity. *Serials Review, 44*(3), 232–37.

De Freitas, S., Rebolledo-Mendez, G., Liarokapis, F., Magoulas, G., & Poulovassilis, A. (2010). Learning as immersive experiences: Using the four-dimensional framework for designing and evaluating immersive learning experiences in a virtual world. *British Journal of Educational Technology, 41*(1), 69–85.

Doberneck, D. M., Glass, C. R., & Schweitzer, J. (2010). From rhetoric to reality: A typology of publicly engaged scholarship. *Journal of Higher Education Outreach and Engagement, 14*(4), 5–35.

Einfeld, A., & Collins, D. (2008). The relationships between service-learning, social justice, multicultural competence, and civic engagement. *Journal of College Student Development, 49*(2), 95–109.

Eyler, J., & Giles, D. E. (1999). *Where's the learning in service-learning?* Jossey-Bass.

Holsapple, M. A. (2012). Service-learning and student diversity outcomes: Existing evidence and directions for future research. *Michigan Journal of Community Service Learning, 18*(2), 5–18

Jacoby, B. (1996). Service-learning in today's higher education. In B. Jacoby (Ed.), *Service-learning in higher education: Concepts and practices* (pp. 3–25). Jossey-Bass.

Keen, C., & Hall, K. (2009). Engaging with difference matters: Longitudinal student outcomes of co-curricular service-learning programs. *The Journal of Higher Education, 80*(1), 59–79.

Mustian, A. L., Lee, R. E., Nelson, C., Gamboa-Turner, V., & Roule, L. (2017). Jumping into the deep end: Developing culturally responsive urban teachers through community-immersive partnerships. *The Educational Forum, 81*(4), 467–81.

Patton, M. Q. (2005). Diverse and creative uses of cases for teaching. *New Directions for Evaluation, 105,* 91–100.

Royce, A. (1982). *Ethnic identity: Strategies of diversity.* Indiana University Press.

Steinberg, S. (1993). The world inside the classroom: Using oral history to explore racial and ethnic diversity. *Social Studies, 84*(2), 71.

Thomas, K. E., & Mucherah, W. M. (2016). The contextual difference: Developing preservice teacher efficacy through immersive learning experiences. *Education and Urban Society, 48*(4), 364–83.

Waddell, J. (2011). Crossing borders without leaving town: The impact of cultural immersion on the perceptions of teacher education candidates. *Issues in Teacher Education, 20*(2), 23–36.

Wesley, J. (1739/1990). June 11, 1739. In W. R. Ward & R. P. Heitzenrater (Eds.), *The works of John Wesley Volume 19: Journal and diaries II (1738–43)* (pp. 65–68). Abingdon Press.

Zempter, C. (2018). Intercultural praxis in service-learning contexts. *Western Journal of Communication, 82*(5), 575–94.

Zusman, A. (2016). *Story bridges: A guide for conducting intergenerational oral history projects.* Routledge.

Zygmunt-Fillwalk, E., Malaby, M., & Clausen, J. (2010). The imperative of contextual cognizance: Preservice teachers and community engagement in the schools and communities project. *Teacher Education Quarterly, 37*(2), 53–67.

PERSPECTIVE: CULTURAL UNDERSTANDING OF DIVERSE COMMUNITIES

Aqsa Bashir, University of Florida

Given America is such a rich tapestry of cultures and races, it is interesting that the topic of race and cultural understanding has just gained momentous dialogue on a national level. Hofstede defined culture as "the collective programming of the mind distinguishing the members of one group or category of people from others" (Hofstede Insights, n.d., para. 1). Hence, the concepts of race and culture are as necessary to address in the academic classroom as are unbiased statements of diversity and inclusion in ecopolitical fields.

As an academician, how I got into teaching cultural communication was all by careful tactic. The first semester as a PhD student we were enrolled in the phenomenal Julie Dodd's teaching seminar. Dodd is now a retired professor from the University of Florida who is a legend in teaching mass communication and journalism. She has influenced countless upcoming instructors and guided graduate students on how to be empathic and kind teachers. During this seminar we had to design a course that we could potentially teach in the future. I had seen a thirst for cultural education among the American students I interacted with. They seemed keen on learning about the different cultures that international students like me came from, and so I designed my course around two things I knew best: culture and advertising. I pitched my "International Advertising" course in the spring of 2016 and I was teaching it a year later.

As an international instructor, I was interested in helping students understand cultural differences that existed around the world. While the globe was being Americanized through international business and media, it still held its distinct culture and values in different parts of the world. This cultural awareness has been essential for designing and pitching campaigns across borders. The students easily grasped the concept of cultural understanding that refers to gaining knowledge about a different culture.

The Internet offered a plethora of resources to facilitate their learning. One of my favorite go-to sources is Hofstede's Cultural Insights, which provides cultural knowledge on several countries based on six basic cultural dimensions. This model is used to describe a particular culture in comparison to another in reference to power distance, individualism, masculinity, uncertainty avoidance, long-term orientation, and indulgence (Hofstede Insights, n.d.). Additionally, official country websites can offer other key insights to the political, economic, and cultural environment.

The first day I walked into a class of twenty-five students I was not surprised: 90 percent of the students were White, about 7 percent were Hispanic, and 3 percent were Black. And just like Holt (2017), I was wondering, do we discuss standard ads that aired during the Super Bowl or shall we dabble right into representation of race and diversity in ads? The first few weeks we did the latter. We took our time talking about the cultural differences that existed in the United States and how brands were just now beginning to focus on these submarkets. This helped my students understand the concept of cultural sensitivity in the context of their own culture. Semester after semester, students questioned the effectiveness of showing a Latinx or Black person in a Coca-Cola commercial, because everyone drinks Coke, right? That was a very valid question and one that detoured our cultural lecture onto a consumer behavior track. (After two semesters, I had this lecture pulled up and ready to go on cue.) I always gave them a simple one-word answer: *research*.

Research has indicated that a sense of belonging leads to brand commitment and loyalty in any field (Bashir et al., 2018). It is a tried and tested method throughout the world that if consumers feel represented in the commercials, they will most likely try the product. And this needs to be translated and represented to different cultural markets in a nonderogatory, nonstereotypic way.

Learning has gone both ways in my classroom. Sometimes it is my students teaching me a thing or two about their cultures. I came from a monoracial culture where everyone was South Asian. We differentiated based on our cities, our religion, and the tone of skin color, but there was no "racial diversity" that needed to be addressed. So when the race talk started, I too was learning. Being a racial minority in the United States, teaching racial diversity added seriousness to the topic.

I strongly believe representation and celebration of race and diversity is necessary. Hence, throughout the course I constantly show students examples of ads and brands that historically prospered by exploiting racial and gender stereotypes (Davis, 2020). The most recent cases were Nivea's *Re-civilize Yourself* (Nudd, 2011), Sprite's *She's Seen More Ceilings than Michelangelo* (Mettler, 2016), and replacing Aunt Jemima's name on pancake mix and syrup with the name Pearl's Milling Company (Hsu, 2020; Vigdor, 2021). Back when the folks at Quaker Oats first started marketing their product in the early 1920s, the mascot Aunt Jemima was a mammy with a checkered headscarf, the classic *Gone With the Wind* representation of Black house help. In light of recent social justice protests, Quaker Oats, the parent brand of Aunt Jemima, joined others to rebrand images to be more culturally sensitive (Taylor, 2020). The debut of Pearl's Milling Company in 2021 followed similar rebranding efforts at other companies. Mars Inc. changed Uncle Ben's Rice to become Ben's Original, and those chocolate-covered vanilla ice cream bars formally known as Eskimo Pies are now Edy's Pies, which were named after founder Joseph Edy (Associated Press, 2020; Valinsky, 2020).

I tell my students that precampaign research will enable them to avoid blunders like the ones mentioned here, while postcampaign research will enable them to understand the effectiveness of the campaign. Examples like these cautioned the students that research does pay off.

Students often ask, Why not leave race out of the classroom because everyone is equal in here? Absolutely correct, but having left the celebration of race and diversity out of the classroom has led to our communication styles being insensitive and ignorant. And the last thing an advertiser wants to be in this social media age is perceived as ignorant of its target market. I emphasize the fact that advertising is a medium of cultural sensitivity because it is ubiquitous and easily accessible.

Teaching for me is just like advertising: I am trying to get the message across to an audience that either is forced to be there, is skeptical to be there, or really wants to be there on the first day of class. Whichever category my students are in, my aim is to make them love the course and be there willingly on the last day of class. Teaching diversity and race in communications will take time and effort. Though it has taken our media and business environment forty odd years to finally put out "diversity statements," I believe it is our better-late-than-never calling as educators to instill cultural and race appropriation into our students who will be influencing the management and leading the industry in the next few decades.

References

Associated Press (2020, September 23). Goodbye to "Uncle Ben": Rice brand to change its name to "Ben's Original." *The Los Angeles Times*. https://

www.latimes.com/business/story/2020-09-23/uncle-bens-rice-new-name-bens-original.

Bashir, A., Wen, J., Kim, E., & Morris, J. D. (2018). The role of consumer affect on visual social networking sites: How consumers build brand relationships. *Journal of Current Issues & Research in Advertising, 39*(2), 178–91.

Davis, J. F. (2020). Representation matters: An illustrated history of race and ethnicity in advertising. *Advertising & Society Quarterly, 21*(3). doi:10.1353/asr.2021.0002.

Holt, L. F. (2017). Bringing their tomorrow into today: Why it's essential to teach diversity in advertising education. *Journal of Advertising Education, 21*(2), 15–17.

Hofstede Insights (n.d.). *National culture.* https://hi.hofstede-insights.com/national-culture.

Hsu, T. (2020, July 17). Aunt Jemima brand to change name and image over "racial stereotype." *New York Times.* https://www.nytimes.com/2020/06/17/business/media/aunt-jemima-racial-stereotype.html.

Mettler, K. (2016, August 5). She's seen more ceilings than Michelangelo: Brutally refreshing Sprite ads called "brutally sexist." *The Washington Post.* https://www.washingtonpost.com/news/morning-mix/wp/2016/08/05/shes-seen-more-ceilings-than-michelangelo-brutally-refreshing-sprite-ads-called-sexist/.

Nudd, T. (2011, August 18). Nivea apologizes for wanting to "re-civilize" Black man. *AdWeek.* https://www.adweek.com/creativity/nivea-apologizes-wanting-re-civilize-black-man-134226/.

Taylor, K. (2020, June 17). Aunt Jemima will change its name and its mascot, with PepsiCo saying its origins are based on a racial stereotype. *Business Insider.* https://www.businessinsider.com/aunt-jemima-is-changing-its-name-mascot-over-racial-stereotype-2020-6.

Valinsky, J. (2020, October 7). Eskimo Pie is getting rid of its derogatory name. *CNN Business.* https://www.cnn.com/2020/10/06/business/eskimo-pie-name-change/index.html.

Vigdor, N. (2021, February 9). Aunt Jemima has a new name after 131 years: The Pearl Milling Company. *New York Times.* https://www.nytimes.com/2021/02/09/business/aunt-jemima-renamed-pearl-milling-company.html.

8

Diversity Issues in Campus Newsrooms and Agencies

Tamara Z. Buck,
Southeast Missouri State University

"I want to see all of the football pictures before they go to print," the digital editor told her colleagues as the editor-in-chief (EIC) and sports editor consulted over printed page proofs one morning. The digital editor, a Black woman, was the only student of color in the newsroom during the exchange.

"What's wrong with them?" the EIC asked. His question seemed warranted, as his colleague's job description did not involve working with the print issue at all. In fact, she was present that day only to upload story packages to the website and schedule social media posts.

"I'm tired of my friends talking trash because we don't know how to color correct and are making them look like dark blobs on the page," the digital editor said matter-of-factly. "They don't ever complain about how I make the pictures look online."

Without another word, the EIC handed her the page proofs and asked her how to improve the images. What followed was a ten-minute workshop on the proper editing of photos of Black people for publication on bright white newsprint, which has a tendency to absorb color and misrepresent dark skin tones. I smiled without moving from my desk on the sidelines as I watched this exchange, which included several White staffers looking over the Black editor's shoulder as she worked. In the past, this discussion would have been fraught with unease as a mostly White staff was confronted by a Black colleague who pointed out a diversity misstep.

This event happened some seven years after I assumed the role of faculty adviser to our predominantly White campus's student newspaper.

From day one, I have worked to monitor, mentor, and advise my students when required on all issues related to journalism, including the need to create a diverse and inclusive organizational culture that would produce the same in our content. We had addressed many diversity concerns over the years, but this time, my students did not need me, and that was because diversity and inclusion had become consistent, persistent discussion topics in my newsroom and related classrooms to the point that students could identify and resolve problems without my assistance.

In twenty years of teaching in a department that has, at different times, housed media sequences geared toward advertising, print, and multimedia journalism, public relations, radio, corporate video production, and TV/film, I have seen an assortment of student media organizations grapple with issues of diversity and inclusion. As a result, I have devised a number of strategies to help faculty advisers navigate and, more importantly, prevent issues involving race representation during production processes and within content students create.

Today's media professionals recognize the increasing demographic diversity of the nation, along with the failures to improve representation within our industry. Journalists have worked for more than a half-century to address newsroom inequities and the content creation problems that result. The American Society of News Editors has made little progress on its goal of making racial and ethnic diversity in newsrooms match the population at large (Arrana, 2018). And in 2020, both the advertising and public relations industries released data indicating a lack of progress in diversity hiring. Even when racial minorities were hired, studies found they were typically at a nonmanagement level (Barrett, 2020; Monillos, 2020).

Recent high-profile protests led by initiatives such as the Black Lives Matter movement have resulted in more candor about the lack of progress in hiring minorities, especially Black male professionals. Newsrooms are not inclusive, and Blacks who find places in them typically are not mentored or promoted. As a result, they remain isolated, become frustrated, and often are sent or voluntarily walk away (Arrana, 2018).

A study released in 1990 found a 17 percent minority participation in college newspapers at universities with majors accredited by the Accrediting Council on Education in Journalism and Mass Communications encouraging, but it cautioned that the low numbers in management positions were a cause for concern. The study noted hiring minority faculty; paying special attention to recruitment, retention, and promotion efforts regarding minority students; and training White students to be culturally competent were all effective strategies to improving the inclusiveness of student newsrooms (Wearden et al., 1990). Thirty years later, many of today's media education programs still fail to adequately prepare students for the worlds in which they will work, and student newsrooms reflect the same lack of ethnic and racial diversity as their professional counterparts.

The experiences gained from participation in student-run advertising and public relations agencies increasingly have gained the interest of researchers in the past decade, but much of the work has focused on the technical operation and improvement of these firms with little guidance or evaluation of diversity and inclusion strategies. The *Student-Run Firm Handbook*, produced by the Public Relations Student Society of America (PRSSA, 2019), makes no mention of diversity. Recent research has shown despite emphasis on diversity in the field of public relations, PR students had moderate exposure to diversity and a low level of perceptions about race/ethnicity-related issues in public relations practice (Muturi & Zhu, 2019).

In an interview study on how public relations students and faculty linked leadership and diversity and inclusion success, Bardhan and Gower (2020) found diversity and inclusion are impossible without top-down personal engagement, responsibility, and accountability. The ten undergraduates and ten faculty interviewed said leaders must set the tone for valuing diversity.

Despite resources like *The Diversity Style Guide* produced by Rachele Kanigel of San Francisco State University in 2019, the *Diversity Toolbox* maintained by the Society of Professional Journalists, and the many resources provided in PRSSA's *Diversity Initiative*, student media staffs, leadership, and perspectives remain largely White and disconnected from the experiences of racial and ethnic minorities in the campus community. Student reporters and agency professionals who are Black, Indigenous, and People of Color (BIPOC) are underrepresented in managerial positions, feel isolated, and can become demoralized by their White colleagues' racial blind spots that render them incapable of recognizing the importance of viewpoints or concerns outside of their own experiences (Ingram, 2018).

The lack of racial diversity in college media also has an external impact, as today's more racially and culturally diverse audiences become frustrated and learn to tune out media outlets that neglect to cover diverse audiences while in college. As a result, graduating White student media professionals enter their industries and allow the problems of limited diversity and inclusion to persist because they never learned intercultural communication competence. This competence is defined as the ability to effectively and appropriately communicate in a culturally diverse environment (Chen & Starosta, 1996).

In the book *Pluralizing Journalism Education: A Multicultural Handbook*, Sharon Bramlett-Solomon (1993) described the connection between minority student participation in college media and diversity in the industry. Bramlett-Solomon wrote on the premise that organized recruitment efforts by campus media organizations are necessary to increase minority staffers because minority students feel their presence in campus newsrooms is unwelcome. Their absence in college media results in a lack of skill development and experience that ultimately renders them unprepared to compete for industry jobs. Bramlett-Solomon wrote:

> Campus media jobs give students of color practical preparation for print and broadcast news and can increase their chances of landing a job after college. Organized minority journalism students on campus is one way to get more minority students into the campus newsroom and, in the long run, into the industry. (p. 229)

When I became faculty adviser of the same newspaper where I once served as the first Black EIC in the mid-1990s, we rarely saw BIPOC representation in our newsroom or our coverage in any meaningful way. I decided I would address these issues head-on with the initial goals of empowering my BIPOC students to be present, to pursue leadership roles, and to speak up on issues of diversity. I also wanted my White students to create a more welcoming newsroom culture that enabled my first set of goals and to broaden their news selection and proactively recognize potential diversity problems in their content. I knew none of this would be achievable if we were not able to create a safe place where people could share their (mis)understandings about race, gender, and sexual identity, and that meant first and foremost that I had to be comfortable discussing these issues. I immediately set about creating this culture, and following are some of the techniques I have used to educate and empower my students.

PROVIDE A BLUEPRINT FOR EXPANDING BIPOC COVERAGE

According to a 2017 *College Media Review* article, experiential learning theory has been embedded in collegiate journalism education since the 1800s (Longinow & Welter, 2017). On-site learning through practical field experiences enables student journalists to practice and refine professional and critical thinking skills that are necessary for complex journalistic storytelling. It also provides a vehicle for broadening the personal experiences of students who may have limited exposure with people from different cultures.

My academic department implemented a restructured journalism curriculum in 2010, during my first year as a faculty adviser, that incorporated a closer connection to our student newspaper. The new curriculum included a seven-course multimedia journalism sequence that had a heavy experiential learning component at the newspaper. Our goal was to help students refine skills being developed in classrooms while simultaneously increasing students' participation as reporters, designers, and multimedia content developers and elevating the quality of content produced at the campus's student-run newspaper throughout the semester. The new emphasis on experiential learning provided an opportunity to increase intercultural communication competence, thereby enabling students to improve representation in both the newsroom culture and the content they produced. My mostly White staff and an increased number of BIPOC reporters, present at first as forced course participants but later promoted to paid staff due to their performances, learned to trust and rely on one another as they participated in the editorial process.

By sending students into unfamiliar field experiences that challenged their limited understandings, I hoped to make students better able to identify, frame, and evaluate their coverage of news involving racial and ethnic minorities. Although we successfully improved intercultural communication between journalism students as a result of increased trust, we did not automatically see that competency transfer to our content.

It is no secret that BIPOC communities at predominately White institutions tend to be hidden in plain sight. One of the biggest complaints White students had whenever I initiated the conversation of improving diversity coverage was that they did not know where to look. That is why I started letting my staff know about the stories they were missing. I would talk about well-attended events, such as the Miss Black and Gold pageant held by the Alpha Phi Alpha fraternity or the henna painting and international dinner sponsored by the Muslim Students Association. These were stories I was aware of because I either knew where to look or I was a member of the BIPOC community.

When White staff members would ask me why no one knew about these events, I would gently correct them: "You mean, why didn't *you* know about these events, right? Clearly, *someone* knew about them if there were one hundred people there." This would cause them to turn to their BIPOC reporters and ask if they knew about these events. The response was invariably some form of agreement: "Yes, but we didn't think you'd want to write about it."

What the BIPOC reporters were expressing was a natural distrust of student and mainstream news media that evolves in minority social communities after years of botched, negligent, and absent reporting. Bramlett-Solomon (1993) saw a similar distrust when she organized her Arizona State University BIPOC students into an association to encourage their involvement in student media. Students told her they felt invisible and unwanted, and it was only by meeting and discussing those feelings with student managers that they were able to develop new strategies to improve hiring practices and the telling of minority stories at the campus.

In a 2016 article in *The Atlantic*, *The Brown Daily Herald* news editor Kate Talerico wrote about how college newspapers, like hers at Brown University, struggled with being stonewalled as they tried to cover a wave of student activism that emerged following the death of Michael Brown. She and her peers across the nation noted activists often boycotted student media because of their lack of support for those in marginalized communities, even as they critiqued them and demanded improvement in news media and in their academic communities. Years of distrust, coupled with present-day publications of slanted opinion pieces and stories that appeared to delegitimize activist narratives, worsened the problem, and editors were flummoxed as to how to repair the damage. What is more, if collegiate newspapers failed to take a social justice approach to reporting about activists' concerns, they were seen as participating in what activists identified as institutional bias (Talerico, 2016).

"The Black Lives Matter movement, particularly in the past year, has really helped to elevate, amplify and accelerate the diversity movement," said David Brown, assistant professor of instruction at Temple University (D. Brown, personal communication, January 18, 2021). Brown said the recent "racial reckoning" has had a major impact on the Black Public Relations Society (BPRS) student chapter he advises and in his diversity and inclusion duties to the university's PRSSA chapter and student public relations agency, as well as to the dean of Klein College of Communication and the university president's office. He said students have realized the need to be more diverse and are now reaching out to BPRS and other cultural professional organizations for help connecting with their audiences.

"We found some structural issues in terms of needing to be more diverse, and we determined it would be beneficial to look at those areas where students may not be trained in the discipline but had an interest in communications to find help," Brown said. "Students also recognized they needed to do some things differently in terms of paying for freelancers and making things more economically feasible. The good thing is while I'm helping to facilitate, the students are leading" (D. Brown, personal communication, January 18, 2021).

Both Brown and I have found teaching students to become more diverse professionally requires persistent, ingrained engagement and accountability. Student leadership is constantly changing due to graduation, so efforts must become a part of organizational infrastructure. "What we try to help folks do is say it happens all of the time and it's not going away overnight," Brown said. "Part of what we want to make sure is you never just skim the surface when it comes to [diversity, equity, and inclusion]; you've got to go deep" (D. Brown, personal communication, January 18, 2021).

Efforts to go deep in an agency context include everything from paying attention to where seminars, focus groups, and events are held, to purposefully selecting organizational officers and managers of color, to simply being mindful at the leadership level that mere incremental progress should not always be touted as the best possible outcome. "We've got to get our history right and not rest on progress. We've got to be real and substantive in terms of how much progress has been made and whether that is meaningful," Brown said. "It can be a little frustrating in terms of evolving metrics that matter" (D. Brown, personal communication, January 18, 2021).

In my newsroom, creating an infrastructure of mindful story selection and sourcing requires persistent effort because most young reporters primarily approach their friends or acquaintances when covering news. One magazine executive has noted that it's important for White editors to leave their comfort zones and broaden their circles rather than wait for minority sources to come to them (Arrana, 2018). Meredith Talusan is the executive editor of *Them*, an intersectional queer publication launched by Condé Nast, the global mass media company owned by Advance Publications. In a 2018 article in the *Columbia Journalism Review*, Talusan noted, "To empathize with people who are not like you—to really see them—you have to become their friends" (Arrana, 2018, para. 9).

Efforts to engage more BIPOC sources were not immediately embraced on my campus because leaders were suspicious of the motives behind the offers of coverage. I encouraged my students to persevere, and slowly photos and interviews made their way into print. To support these efforts, I created cultural beats in my upper-level classes so that more experienced reporters were required to enterprise feature stories that showcased the members of these communities. Reporters also identified BIPOC influencers—those unofficial party promoters, political wranglers, and all-around connected persons—to engage in our news and entertainment content as often as possible in hopes that they would cement the newspaper's legitimacy in the community. I also encouraged our staff to have meetups with the influencers and sources they had developed relationships with to discuss specific problems firsthand, and I coached them on how to answer the questions they received.

These tactics worked to a large degree, but there was a wrinkle: Even as reporters found it easier to identify and expand their coverage of BIPOC communities, they also had to answer tough questions regarding what took them so long to acknowledge the communities and why they made so many mistakes. These were the challenges Talerico wrote of, and it was important that our staff respond correctly to retain their progress.

USING SELF-EVALUATION TO MONITOR DIVERSITY

Like professional media organizations, student publications have made many gaffs over the years when it came to trying to cover minority events or issues. Either they covered cultural events in stereotypical ways, or they published offensive visual images or opinions, or they simply stated facts incorrectly. As then Clemson University student media adviser Jackie Alexander said in a Student Press Law Center article in 2015,

> The content is very flat, it's very one-sided, and our diverse students aren't reading us because they don't see themselves or their lives reflected in the newspaper. And if students attempt diverse stories, because there's no one else in the room to say "Hey, that looks off," it runs the risk of stereotypical or downright offensive content. (Jeffries, 2015, para. 4)

I thought the best way for my staff to understand the source of BIPOC distrust and how to overcome it was for them to conduct a thorough and regular review of their work. At one time, I scheduled presentations from several university offices and student organizations who represented populations related to race, ethnicity, nationality, and ability. They were asked to specifically share instances when the newspaper had reported on their organizations, services, or events in good or problematic ways and to explain what was important to them for future coverage.

I also implemented a critique of our print product during our weekly staff meetings, and it is something we continue today. In the first critique, I listened as students discussed how their page design, story selection, and headlines could have been improved. When they were done, I asked them to tell me what was missing from their content: No one had noticed there was not one picture of a student of color outside of the Sports section. They discussed being more inclusive, and the next week, we noted a purposeful effort to include a Black student in a standalone photo. From there, regular reviews helped us fill the gaps and become more inclusive.

For my editors, the regular critiques kept diverse coverage in the forefront, and they began to proactively work with reporters, photographers, and designers to ensure newsgathering resulted in improved representation of racial and ethnic minorities. They also began to question problematic content before publication. In one example, I was finishing class one day when the EIC walked into the room and requested advice. He was working on a story about how a White supremacy group had placed flyers on cars around campus overnight. He wanted to run the story but had no art other than the flyer and screenshots from the organization's website, and he did not want the newspaper to be seen as promoting the organization in any way.

It was a big moment for this editor, who hailed from an extremely rural, conservative, nondiverse community, to seek advice regarding whether he would be publishing potentially offensive content. It meant the critiques and conversations with different communities were helping to embed the importance of diversity and inclusion, as well as the responsibility the staff had to treat sensitive topics with care. Over time, we began to see more and better coverage of not only events but also enterprise reporting about BIPOC concerns on campus. We also discovered editors became more conscientious about proofing these stories to prevent errors that might cause communication setbacks.

IMPLEMENT EFFECTIVE STAFF TRAINING

One of our departmental goals is to destigmatize diversity conversations among our students, and another is to empower them to be strong advocates in their professional lives for inclusive and accurate representation of minorities. As the lone racially identifiable professor in the department, it was probably inevitable that I would be heavily involved in both of these efforts, and I have made diversity an integral part of my research agenda and professional development. To that end, I have pursued formal training and continuing education on diversity issues whenever possible. In 2019, for example, I attended the Train the Trainers program hosted by the Freedom Forum Institute's Power Shift Project and became certified as a Workplace Integrity trainer.

The Workplace Integrity curriculum was designed by Jill Geisler, the Bill Plante Chair in Leadership and Media Integrity at Loyola University Chicago, in her role as a Freedom Forum Institute fellow in women's leadership. The three-part training focuses on critical thinking, courageous conversations, and cultures of respect and trust. It works to help organizations stop addressing diversity efforts as compliance issues, which focus on avoiding lawsuits, and move to integrity approaches, where organizations embrace equitable and nonharassing cultures as a value.

The new certification was the impetus I needed to formalize diversity training sessions I had instituted for our student media managers two years earlier. Then I simply focused on the need for inclusive language and a supportive newsroom culture. I continued sharing my blueprint for identifying stories in minority communities, and we brought in specialists to help our editors better understand the need to adjust processes in multimedia activities, like lighting for photos and videos to account for differences in skin tone.

After participating in the Workplace Integrity training, I understood more formal training was necessary to teach my students how to initiate conversations when they witness or experience harassing and discriminatory behaviors and to be intentional about efforts to create civil, non-harassing, equitable workplaces. Using the formal training to develop a value-driven approach to diversity may be the most difficult of the diversity efforts I have attempted with my staff because it requires students to move beyond mere acceptance of difference. Rather, it requires students—specifically for our staff, primarily White students—to embrace allyship; they must be prepared and trusted to set aside their privilege and "act on behalf of equity" (Geisler, 2020, para. 5).

It may be too soon to know how effective the formal training has been with my students. However, I feel confident in saying it adds an important layer to a process I have spent a decade building.

FINAL THOUGHTS

Whether inside or outside of the classroom context, I believe the layering of techniques is what's required to have an integrated, consistent, persistent approach to diversity and inclusion in student media. My process works for me because I have given students a safe place to grow their understanding of past problems, present challenges, and future benefits. I have developed a program where students invest in each other and are open to the improvements diversity can bring to their content production. The newsroom culture has radically changed from what it was before, and the content is richer and more representative of the audiences they serve. They still make mistakes, as all media organizations do, but my joy is seeing my students critique themselves, proactively recognize potential or actual diversity problems in their content, and initiate change.

REFERENCES

Arrana, G. (2018). Decades of failure. *Columbia Journalism Review*. https://www.cjr.org/special_report/race-ethnicity-newsrooms-data.php.

Bardhan, N., & Gower, K. (2020). Student and faculty/educator views on diversity and inclusion in public relations: The role of leaders in bringing about change. *Journal of Public Relations Education*, 6(2), 102–41.

Barrett, S. (2020, June 19). No more excuses. PR firms have to make progress on diversity. *PR Week*. https://www.prweek.com/article/1687139/no-excuses-pr-firms-progress-diversity.

Bramlett-Solomon, S. (1993). Organizing minority student journalists to enhance diversity in the college newsroom. In C. Martindale (Ed.), *Pluralizing journalism education: A multicultural handbook* (pp. 225–29). Greenwood Press.

Chen, G. M., & Starosta, W. J. (1998). A review of the concept of intercultural awareness. *Human Communication*, 2(1), 27–54.

Geisler, J. (2020, August 24). To be an ally, you can't just hold others to account. Journalism Institute. https://www.pressclubinstitute.org/2020/08/24/to-be-an-ally-you-cant-just-hold-others-to-account/.

Ingram, N. (2018, July 25). Campus newsrooms rethink their approach to race. *The Christian Science Monitor*. https://www.csmonitor.com/EqualEd/2018/0725/Campus-newsrooms-rethink-their-approach-to-race.

Jeffries, T. (2015, November 11). A lack of diversity in student media sparks frustration, debates across the country. Student Press Law Center. https://splc.org/2015/11/lack-of-diversity-in-student-media-sparks-debates/.

Longinow, M., & Welter, T. (2017). Using narrative media instruction and experiential learning to build cultural competency in future journalists. *College Media Review*, 55, 1–54.

Monillos, K. (2020, June 23). "Long road ahead": Ad agencies are releasing data—and admitting their shortcomings. Digiday. https://digiday.com/marketing/long-road-ahead-heres-a-look-at-the-agency-diversity-data-released-so-far/.

Muturi, N., & Zhu, G. (2019). Students' perceptions of diversity issues in public relations practice. *Journal of Public Relations Education*, 5(2), 75–104.

PRSSA. (2019). *The student-run firm handbook: 2019–2020*. Public Relations Student Society of America. https://prssa.prsa.org/wp-content/uploads/2019/07/Student-run-Firm-Handbook.pdf.

Talerico, K. (2016, June 30). When student activists refuse to talk to campus newspapers. *The Atlantic*. https://www.theatlantic.com/education/archive/2016/06/when-student-activists-refuse-to-talk-to-campus-newspapers/486326/.

Wearden, S., Hipsman, B., & Greenman, J. (1990). Racial diversity in the college newsroom. *Newspaper Research Journal*, 12(3), 80–85.

PERSPECTIVE: COVERING RACE PANIC STORIES AND DIVERSITY FLARE-UPS

Cristina L. Azocar, San Francisco State University

Professor Buck's blueprint for expanding diverse storytelling can easily be adapted to any journalism program. When students are empowered to tackle problems with consistency and persistence, they can take the lead and pass on their knowledge so that future college publication staffs are better equipped to deal with issues when they arise. But first, that program needs to ensure it has the leadership to enact it. Many of our White colleagues are waking up to how the years of neglect of campus coverage of those in Black, Indigenous, and People of Color (BIPOC) communities has left deep distrust in news media. But without BIPOC leadership, I do not see how the deep, long-lasting cultural changes required will transpire.

As president-elect of the College Media Association, Professor Buck is among a handful of BIPOC college campus media advisors at traditionally White institutions. The Accrediting Council on Education in Journalism and Mass Communications (ACEJMC) recently revised its standards, including a major revision of the diversity and inclusiveness standard (see Moody-Ramirez, this volume), which up until 2018 was one of the two accreditation standards on which programs were most often found to be noncompliant (the other is assessment). Under the new ACEJMC standards that take effect in 2022–2023, the diversity standard is much more rigorous. Still, no unit will lose its accreditation if it is noncompliant on just the diversity standard. I do not see changes on the horizon until White people realize that diversity is a White problem with which White people need to deal. Campus journalism operations need to not be afraid to call out racism and not be afraid of White fragility. And they also need to shift their perspective to what stories are important. Those of us who identify as BIPOC find that it falls on us to initiate and create the path for change for those White people and their White institutions. So leadership is key. Once all journalism programs live in Professor Buck's reality, then we may really start to see change.

In the meantime, however, we can use her template to bypass racial panics and diversity flare-ups by getting ahead of them and acknowledging they are a White problem. The layering techniques she suggests to develop an integrated, consistent, persistent approach to diversity and inclusion of newsrooms help student staff reframe race panic and diversity flare-up stories. To reiterate, race panic and diversity flare-up stories are in reaction to White racism. White people are the cause of race panics and diversity flare-ups. White reporters, editors, publishers, and the entire structure of mainstream news media are responsible for the stories that create race panics and diversity flare-ups, and they are responsible for their proliferation. Before delving into how to reframe stories, I will quickly discuss what race panic and diversity flare-ups are and provide some past and current examples.

Racial Panics

Racial panics fall under Cohen's (1972) definition of moral panics: conditions, episodes, and persons or groups of persons that emerge to become defined as a threat to societal values and interests. The news media have played a significant role in constructing and amplifying moral panics (Critcher, 2003; Jewkes, 2015). Racial panics are isolated events without context of the social practices, institutional policies, and historical legacies that they are rooted in (Lehrman & Wagner, 2019).

For example, in the early 1990s, states pushed tougher laws for "super predators." These remorseless, predatory teenage criminals were going to take over the streets unless they were given harsh jail sentences and tried as adults. Unsurprisingly, Black males were the main targets of the media attention surrounding super predators as they were in the "knockout game." This phenomenon, starting in 2013 in Brooklyn, accused young Black assailants of randomly picking unlucky targets and trying to knock them out with just one punch.

Other examples of racial panics abound: Hordes of Mexicans attempting to rush the U.S.-Mexican border and take American jobs. Muslims hiding in suburban neighborhoods creating hidden dens of extremism. Asian Americans taking seats from White students at elite universities. Native Americans threatening economic development by blocking progress. The news media tend to rely on anecdotal information, examples from social media, and dubious statistics when reporting these stories.

White people never produce racial panics, although they should. More White males commit more acts of terror on people of color than people of color do on Whites. Native people did not give White people disease-infected blankets. Black people did not lynch White people. Japanese Americans did not round up German Americans and put them in concentration camps. BIPOCs do not call the police on large gatherings of White people when they wander outside their allowed space. The murder of White people by police are not livestreamed. And on campuses, a racial panic is not declared when White students fly Confederate flags at sports events or when they shout racial slurs at students.

Diversity Flare-Ups

Campus diversity flare-ups are often caused by a series of acts and the protests that follow them that underscore racial tensions on college campuses and highlight administrations' cluelessness about racism by White students and faculty on their campuses. In 2015, the University of Missouri's president resigned after being accused by activists of not addressing racist and bigoted incidents. This included the undergraduate student body president being called the n-word, a White student climbing onto a stage and shouting slurs as Black students rehearsed a skit, and when a swastika was drawn on a wall with human feces (Svrluga, 2015). The chancellor also resigned.

At Syracuse University in 2019, ten incidents, including graffiti targeting Black, Asian, and Jewish students and a verbal attack on a Black female student by fraternity members, were followed by a week-long student sit-in. A Council on Diversity and Inclusion was instituted in late 2020 to provide feedback about the campus climate. In the same year, at Arizona State University, the provost revoked a job offer to the dean of journalism after more than four thousand students signed a petition accusing her of microaggressions and a history of racist, homophobic, and body-shaming comments (Myskow & Hansen, 2020). Just as White people are to blame for moral panics, they are also to blame for diversity flare-ups. When BIPOC expose these flare-ups, which they always do, the White responses are shrouded in "well-intentioned" apologies, and the appropriate leadership reacts with shock that this occurred in their community (neighborhood, campus, workplace, church, etc.).

Reframing Racial Panics and Diversity Flare-Ups

Similar to what Audre Lorde (1984) explained in her essay "The Master's Tools Will Never Dismantle the Master's House," the news media couch moral panics and diversity flare-ups in terms that protect White people from their roles in perpetuating racism. The news media also protect themselves in the same way. But what is a college newspaper to do when the majority of college media advisors are White? When the goal for the graduates of college journalism schools is to work in mainstream news media? When the world they leave is the one expected of them to perpetuate?

If an issue around race starts bubbling up on campus, instead of covering the panic, the story should be written using real statistics and quotes from thought leaders on the issue behind the story. And even before then, BIPOC reporters are bound to know what types of stories they see too many of and they can work to counter them. For example, racial panic stories often revolve around crime, which we know from government reports is statistically decreasing. If an episode occurs, ignore the tendency to report on it. Instead report on the statistics. How is the campus working to keep its community safe and what classes are available for students to protect themselves? Remember that many instances are only single ones that only become issues because news media make them issues. Unfortunately, social media allows single incidents to explode into moral panics at a quicker pace. There needs to be a response developed around that too—"check out this story on the decrease of crime on college campuses." Most importantly, students need to actively avoid perpetuating the notion of racial panics.

References

Critcher, C. (2003). *Moral panics and the media.* Open University Press.

Cohen, S. (1972). *Folk devils and moral panics: The creation of the mods and rockers.* St. Martin's Press.

Jewkes, Y. (2015). *Media and crime.* Sage.

Lehrman, S., & Wagner, V. (2019). *Reporting inequality: Tools and methods for covering race and ethnicity.* Routledge.

Lorde, Audre (1984). The master's tools will never dismantle the master's house. In A. Lorde (Ed.), *Sister Outsider: Essays and Speeches* (pp. 110–14). Crossing Press.

Myskow, W., & Hansen, P. (2020, June 5). Incoming Cronkite dean has alleged history of racist, homophobic comments toward students. *The State Press.* https://www.statepress.com/article/2020/06/spcommunity-incoming-cronkite-dean-has-alleged-history-of-racist-homophobic-comments-toward-students#.

Svrluga, S. U. (2015, November 9). Missouri president, chancellor resign over handling of racial incidents. *The Washington Post*. https://www.washingtonpost.com/news/grade-point/wp/2015/11/09/missouris-student-government-calls-for-university-presidents-removal/.

9

Embracing a Pedagogy of Pain

Meta G. Carstarphen, The University of Oklahoma

On May 31, 1921, one of the most dramatic acts of violence against American citizens erupted in Tulsa, Oklahoma. In less than twenty-four hours, a thirty-five-city-block area comprising the African American enclave of Greenwood was destroyed, with estimated losses of hundreds of homes, scores of businesses, and as many as three hundred dead (Tulsa Historical Society and Museum, n.d.).

Greenwood, dubbed "The Black Wall Street," was recognized as the most prosperous African American–owned town in the United States and prospered in a self-contained enclave within the growing city of Tulsa. Newness enveloped this place, as Greenwood residents aimed to grow right along with the developing fortunes of the new state of Oklahoma, which was officially recognized as such in 1907. Nearly all of it dissipated in the angry smoke and fire of riotous White citizens. White-owned daily newspapers at the time contributed to the horror through deliberate omissions and underreporting about this incident that attracted widespread coverage outside its borders (Krehbiel, 2019). Decades upon decades later, Oklahoma students were still able to complete all the requirements of a high school diploma without reading one documented word about this horrific event that happened literally in their own backyards.

The year 2021 marked a momentous anniversary for the Tulsa Race Massacre, as it came to be known. As with any historic remembrance, the Tulsa Race Massacre could be easily incorporated within a topical discussion, an assignment, and/or a reading in any standard journalism and mass communication class. This kind of glancing but important recognition would be reflexive in most of our classes, but what might it look like if students were invited to examine such a weighted and historic topic for an entire semester? How might students wrestle with the traumatic weight of the past and balance it against the socially fraught conversations of contemporary times? And, most importantly, what would be the value to students and instructors of such a course?

This chapter considers these questions against the backdrop of preparations for a spring 2021 course devoted to examining this event. Called "The Tulsa Massacre: 100 Years Later," the proposal for this one-time course offered a chance to provide students with an innovative, multiperspective, and cross-disciplinary understanding of the Tulsa Race Massacre and some of the event's consequences. Specifically, this chapter focuses on (a) highlighting a conceptual rationale for teaching difficult subjects such as this one to journalism and mass communication students, (b) preparing to guide students through potentially highly sensitive readings and conversations about racial violence, and (c) presenting strategies that faculty members engaged in this kind of teaching can use to navigate through the challenges that may occur in their own professional and personal spaces.

MAPPING A PATH: COMPONENTS AND ASSESSMENTS

Our course blossomed into a team-taught class that began from a conversation with my colleague, Karlos K. Hill, chair of the Clara Luper Department of African and African American Studies at the University of Oklahoma where I teach. Soon after, we met for a relaxed, evening chat in late 2019 with another colleague, Rilla Askew, a faculty member with the University of Oklahoma's Department of English. Our dreams were bold and ambitious. We wanted to have students explore the consequential events of the Tulsa Race Massacre through the perspectives of three disciplines: history, journalism/media, and creative writing. As our conversations continued, we decided to add a digital humanities site drawn from our class activities and student work. Our fourth colleague, John Stewart, who is a specialist in digital learning, joined our team as well.

One of the earliest choices to make was whether we wanted to design a class for a potentially large lecture room or for a smaller, seminar-style experience. We landed somewhere neatly between these polarities with a projected student enrollment of forty-five, with some limited spots for graduate students. In our planning, we imagined having a traditional classroom setting, with guest speakers and vigorous group interactions. However, the realities of offering this class during the COVID-19 pandemic led us to temper our initial planning. Adjustments included reducing the potential enrollment to a total maximum of forty to allow for socially distanced seating in our chosen classroom, adapting a "hybrid" class format to allow for some online delivery as needed, and hosting some virtual presentations in lieu of large face-to-face events open to the general public.

Still, despite these adjustments, the course design for "Tulsa Race Massacre: 100 Years Later" remained consistent with the original vision. The limited enrollment remained open to all majors, still accommodating the planned online discussions and hands-on activities. Each of the three subject areas have four weeks of planned content in the following order: African Americans/history, journalism/media, and English/creative writing. Students will work through historic documents, news reports, and texts to critique the ways history was and still is reported. Ending with a creative writing experience will allow students an outlet for their own ideas. Finally, the course will punctuate the pacing (and intensity) of these units with a "check-in" about digital humanities and their ability to weave together narratives using multiple media, narratives, perspectives, and time frames. Regardless of their majors, students could find within this robust classwork a bridge to future conversations and careers. Designing the assessment of student performance is both collaborative and individually discipline specific. At the end of each of the three subject units, students will get to complete a final assessment of what was presented in history, journalism, and creative writing. We will rotate grading responsibilities according to our areas of expertise. Small teams will complete their digital humanities projects at the end of the course. Last, in lieu of a final exam, all students will respond to simple prompts with their own personalized presentations: What did you learn? What will you do with what you learned? How will you share it?

AVOIDING THE PARACHUTE

My opportunity will be to guide students from these diverse majors and academic backgrounds into a media literacy discussion that probes the role and influence of media. Rather than locating this discussion within the confines of normative theory and safe topics, students will be asked to consider these questions as part of a complex and controversial event. Even as I guide the students to analyze previous media reports through archives and other historical resources, I will ask them to make comparisons and analyses of contemporaneous representations. These now include ongoing journalism reports about events related to the yearlong commemoration, the unresolved issues about reparations for the descendants of the original victims, and the search for forensic evidence of mass graves from the event. We will also consider the emerging popular media portrayals of the Tulsa Massacre, such as in the 2019 HBO series *Watchmen* and the 2020 season debut of *Lovecraft Country*, also on HBO.

Yet for all of the compelling, persuasive reasons to leverage this moment in time as a structured "teaching moment," there are perils for both me and my students. I am African American, a female with the rank of professor, and I should not exist. In many journalism and mass communication programs, I or someone like me does not (yet) exist. When I pursue teaching content that unravels the lived experiences of people who may be invisible in the standard pages of learning, I am unpeeling layers of self.

My professional life as a feature writer and as a public relations specialist informs my experience with journalism's professional protocols. The work is sticky and at times confounding. We want truth but we are always in a hurry for it. We represent power but we want to speak for the powerless.

Journalism and its related disciplines in media production and strategic communication can be intensely defined by time and circumstance. Breaking events control the decision making for news organizations, while a misspoken statement can halt an organization's marketing and brand strategies unexpectedly and suddenly. These realities create circumstances where media professionals are expected to "parachute" into such controversies and accurately report about them or communicate about them. Our curricula encourage this behavior. Perhaps we create brief assignments about mock crises or dedicate a lecture to a social issue. We may assign students to learn about changes in professional protocols that reflect shifting cultural or social mores and quiz them, as when the *Associated Press Stylebook* updates its guidelines on race-related coverage or usage of gender-neutral terms. However, the professional challenges facing them in their future work may be indeed more complicated than they have been prepared to face. One way to help our future practitioners is for them to intentionally and strategically engage the past.

One of the immediate challenges in having students revisit a historical event is to recreate known facts about what happened. One of the lingering benefits, though, is having the benefit of hindsight and informed critiques in the form of scholarly literature and professional observers about the omissions of the historical record. Thus, by intentionally inviting students to understand how an event happened and how it was reported and compare such coverage with subsequent critiques, we can invite students into unparalleled opportunities for critical thinking and reflection. Moreover, one important potential observation about historical memory seems congruent with our understanding of best practices in our field. Our media excellence and independence thrive upon the ability to include multiple voices and perspectives.

Similarly, history is not unilateral narrative. But when we train our students to cover historical events, we unwittingly encourage them to drop into events and locales with parachutes, prepared for quick entry and quicker departures. We tell them—directly or by implication—that official sources are the most reliable and that historical documents may be beyond scrutiny.

In her critique of a "universal history," Emma Rothschild (2008) discusses how scholars confronted the challenge of building a history of a global institution, the United Nations. Although the UN's official documents framed a starting logic about to how to approach constructing a historical narrative, this history proved to be far more complex. The history built upon documents could be interpreted through multiple "new" histories, including through the recorded lives of individuals, through the multiplicity of languages and their usages, through the political and social issues debated, and more (p. 396).

Journalists and media communicators frequently use the materials of archives and from official records as a starting point for an inquiry or even the framework for understanding a story. Therefore the history of how the archive was developed is as important as what it contains because such an account reveals how knowledge was constructed and how it became known. Knowing this history and questioning it allows us to peer into the subtle, hidden designs of power because there is a significant type of power that allows decisions to be made about what is worth preserving, upholding, and canonizing in the confines of public sites of memory. These include museums, archives, libraries, and monuments, as well as the memories—however ephemeral—of survivors, witnesses, and ancestors.

In the case of the 1921 Tulsa Race Massacre, this power to build and preserve knowledge has strong resonances for what students will be asked to consider. Most recently, Tulsa-based journalist Randy Krehbiel published a meticulous study of how the White-owned Tulsa newspapers covered the massacre in 1921 and over the decades since, documented discrepancies between what happened, what was printed, and what has been preserved. One example was an article in the *Tulsa Tribune* originally published with the front-page headline "Nab Negro for Attacking Girl in an Elevator" that was torn from a final edition version before being submitted for microfilming (2019, pp. 64–65). Many historians believe that this article with its inflammatory headline was one of the factors contributing to the rapid mobilization of hundreds, which eventually grew to thousands, of Whites who descended upon Greenwood on March 31, 1921.

This example offers just a snapshot of the complexities of getting students to understand the construction of history and the documents upon which such accounts are built. This discussion and others similar to this can provide such a rich opportunity for teachers of journalism and mass communication courses and for their students. It may seem counterintuitive that those of us tasked with teaching the communicators of the future should take time to look at the past. Yet this allows us to impress upon our students that words, videos, images, ads, news releases, and social media that they create will inevitably become the foundations of historical narratives for future generations. Last, the methodical ways in which students will build and understand knowledge moves them beyond intuition into embracing the role of theory in professional work (Vocate, 1997).

EXPLORING A PEDAGOGY OF PAIN: USING PAST AS PROLOGUE

The central proposition for our students is simple. Imagine the spaces we occupy as sites of learning, including places that go beyond the classroom. These include libraries, archives, and individuals connected to our subject, and even the physical location of a historic event. What stories would students tell about them? Even as history constructs this as an episode behind us, the 1921 Tulsa Massacre remains as an active acknowledgment in a palpable way of the "blindnesses" of contemporaneous reporting and knowledge generation that would serve our students well. This service could not be better rendered than as we struggle, even in the twenty-first century, to bring home the vital necessary of diverse storytelling.

What I am referring to as a "pedagogy of pain" recognizes that the tumult of the world outside the classroom cannot separate itself from its students, professors, and instructors, or even its curriculum. The veneer of objective and dispassionate knowledge is thin. For students of color and professors of color, teaching in the context of social injustice, political affronts, and physical threats and violence wear on the resilience of learning. Sometimes the assault is like a drip. Sometimes it is like a tsunami. In between these spaces reside learning opportunities. What does it look like to walk headlong into a tumultuous event, a topic fraught with trauma, as an intentional learning opportunity? It means that such a pedagogical moment will not be meaningful without three factors: (a) a point of entry, (b) provisions for safe passage through the instructional opportunity, and (c) a culmination that allows students to be successful in mastering content and emerging to be more resilient learners as a result of the experience.

For my point of entry, I made a decision to engage a little more than usual with students during the registration period for this course.

Mindful of our enrollment limits, we divided the ways students could enroll across three disciplines: AFAM, ENG, and JMC. For my portion of the class, I was able to add an instructor's permission requirement, allowing me to engage with students prior to their enrollment. As part of a brief email exchange, I encouraged students to take a brief, eight-question survey, where I could learn more about them and share more details about the class.

An important question for me to ask in the middle of the survey was why the student was interested in the class. Some of the responses were tied to their majors, but most were surprisingly personal:

- *I grew up in Oklahoma and never learned about this in school. I want to learn more.*
- *As an African American I feel this is part of my history.*

Two key questions for me ended the survey. In question number seven, I described the topics in the class as covering "violence, trauma, and racial strife" and asked about their comfort with this possibility. Some students answered with brief responses and with some bravado:

- *It is a reality of our history.*
- *I've studied topics like these before.*
- *Comfortable.*
- *It is expected just from the name of the class.*

Others were less certain:

- *I have moderate experience with these topics but I am ready to learn more!*
- *I will ask for help if I need it.*
- *This issue is sensitive to me . . . I believe an environment in which discussion is encouraged would be ideal.*

I ended the survey asking students to brag a bit—asking them to share their additional skills and talents that they felt would add to the class. My intent was to invite them to invoke their own sources of resiliency and talent as they enrolled in this class. Along the way, I discovered a great variety of gifts among them, including strong writing, organizational skills, digital skills, and personal networks in Oklahoma that might add to the sense of community the class will strive to build.

As a faculty team, we had to do some planning of our own beyond assignments, dates, and speakers. Two of the most significant conversations we had evolved around class climate and language. With a shared understanding that the material they will look at will be difficult, we have pledged to build spaces within our class for listening and support. One structural element we will have will be a weekly open-ended online discussion post. Students will be able to respond to source content as it unfolds and we will be able to measure class climate along the way. We will be able to determine if questions or discussions need to be addressed during the formal class meetings as well.

The second most important discussion was about racial language and what our stance was going to be about it before we faced the students. The historic documents we will look at will have examples of racial epithets being used with abandon. In one specific example, *The Tulsa Tribune* published an editorial days after Greenwood was destroyed disparaging the town with a racial epithet ("N****rtown") and declaring a resolve to keep Greenwood from rebuilding (Johnson, 2020, pp. 81–82). As a team, we decided that, regardless of the readings, we would embrace a class practice that would ban the use of racial epithets in our discussions and writings. As instructors, we will model how to refer to such usage without incorporating it in our own speech and discussions. We expect college students to read and understand what they are reading with maturity and respect. No one needs to prove anything by saying offensive language aloud.

WHEN THE HISTORY YOU TEACH IS YOUR OWN

For faculty of color especially, the conversation about racism and social justice in the academy can be fraught with emotional, mental, and intellectual challenges. We are often expected to be the translator of such events and their meaning, sometimes in the face of vocal skeptics. We might encounter resistance from our students and a devaluation of our intellectual effort on race and racism, suggesting that our silence is more valued than our knowledge. It is certainly a truth that exploring such topics can tap into personal pain, family legacies, and social stigma in ways that our colleagues may never have experienced or understood. Maria Yellow Horse Brave Heart is an early scholar who identified the phenomenon of "historical trauma" as a way of describing pain experienced by generations of a group that has suffered great tragedy and loss. Although her research draws from the specific historic contexts of the Lakota Sioux, her analyses can offer relevance to the experiences of those victimized by racism and violence.

I experienced this acutely when, many summers ago, I participated in an academic workshop about using archives for research and teaching. I was the sole African American participant in a group of about twenty-five scholars. When one presenter discussed how he used civil rights archives, touching upon stories of violence and lynching used to suppress voting in the Deep South, I became overwhelmed with sensations. I was physically uncomfortable—enough to leave the room before the presentation ended. While I have no stories in my immediate family and known relatives about lynching, I felt the trauma of such violence as if I had. This experience, and others similar to it, prod me to remember that all of us will need to allow spaces to read, reflect, comment, and pause as we navigate through this semester-long experience about the 1921 Tulsa Race Massacre.

I feel extremely fortunate that the colleagues I have chosen to work with are like-minded. While all of our experiences, life stories, and identities are different, we have arrived at a similar point in understanding the value and legacy of the story of the 1921 Tulsa Race Massacre. We know the importance of sharing this story with our students, and in doing so carefully. Yet I intend to fortify my own position as a scholar of color with what Ersula Ore (2017) so deftly describes as a *pedagogy of care*. Through an extended example and position that focuses on language and choice, Ore describes a strategy of "pushback," which is an active and aggressive response to "injustice by consciously disrupting acts of implicit racism *as they operate* [emphasis added]" (p. 21). In other words, *pushback* is a position that is intentional and planned, allowing faculty members of color, especially, to prepare for challenges to their authority, their intellectual currency, and their being in the moment of the challenge. Pushback prepares faculty to care for themselves as they continue to do the work they have chosen.

I think of pushback as congruent with the work we have trained to do as journalists and media professionals because its effectiveness lies in the power to ask a simple question and to wait for its answer. In the scenarios I imagine, this pushback question is always a "why," as in:

- *Interesting.* **Why** *do you think that?*
- *Oh?* **Why** *do you say that?*
- *Really?* **Why** *do you think that is?*

These "imaginary" responses become realized in the moment of discourse. In scenarios where these conversations might arise, they offer a different path of engagement. For one, I am relieved of the false burden of overexplaining or rationalizing because I learn to wait, together, in silence with the questioner. Second, and more importantly, this moment pivots from a potential emotional trigger to a learning opportunity. The person asking the question has to reflect upon the reason for his or her question and, in doing so, become aware of a bias that may have framed the question in the first place. When the exchange ends, whether after

Figure 9.1. University of Oklahoma Public Relations Student Society of America

an extended frank conversation or after an awkward, quick pivot to the weather, I have a path forward.

LEARNING OPPORTUNITIES BEYOND THE COURSE

In addition to our course, the University of Oklahoma has events, symposia, a library exhibit, and more to commemorate this anniversary. My work on this course allowed me to open up discussions with colleagues in my college for potential collaboration and cocurricular activities. Examples include a commitment from our student chapter of the Public Relations Society of America to follow the development and delivery of the class with a social media campaign across multiple platforms. This same group of students designed a logo for our course and is assisting with other promotional assets, such as flyers and posters. Another class will video class sessions and guest speakers, helping us to make the content available more broadly. Other colleagues in our college may develop assignments compatible with advertising, social media, and reporting classes along the topic of the Tulsa Race Massacre 100-year anniversary and the various community-based organizations involved.

It is ironic, perhaps, but supremely satisfying that the opportunity to bring historic pain into the classroom in a systematic way will open up opportunities for so many of our students to make their studies socially and culturally relevant. As scholars of color, just imagine how our stories, histories, and sensibilities could change the academy and the professions we represent with more of the same. We should lean in to, not away from, our identities, understanding them as gifts instead of obstacles in the classrooms we inhabit.

REFERENCES

Brave Heart, M. Y. H. (2000). Wakiksuyapi: Carrying the historical trauma of the Lakota. *Tulane Studies in Social Welfare, 21–22*, 245–65.

Johnson, H. B. (2020). *Black Wall Street 100: An American city grapples with its historical racial trauma.* Eakin Press.

Krehbiel, R. (2019). *Tulsa 1921: Reporting a massacre.* University of Oklahoma Press.

Ore, E. (2017). Pushback: A pedagogy of care. *Pedagogy: Critical Approaches to Teaching Literature, Language, Composition, and Culture, 17*(1), 24.

Rothschild, E. (2008). The archives of universal history. *Journal of World History, 19*(3), 375–401.

Tulsa Historical Society and Museum (n.d.). 1921 Tulsa Race Massacre. https://www.tulsahistory.org/exhibit/1921-tulsa-race-massacre/#flexible-content.

Vocate, D. R. (1997). Teaching communication theory in the professional school. *Journalism & Mass Communication Educator, 52*(2), 4–14.

PERSPECTIVE: CONFRONTING COLOR-BLINDNESS

Keonte Coleman, Middle Tennessee State University

Research has shown the number of accredited and nonaccredited journalism and mass communication programs offering special courses on media diversity has been increasing steadily for the past two decades. Biswas and Izard's (2010) survey of 105 programs found while most prefer teaching diversity throughout the curriculum, the number of ACEJMC-accredited programs with at least one course on media diversity increased from 60 percent in an early study to 74 percent. Most recently, in a 2015 survey, 83 percent of programs offered at least one separate/dedicated course on diversity, with gender, diversity in general, and race/ethnicity as the topics most often highlighted (Biswas et al., 2017). I teach two of these courses at Middle Tennessee State University. Teaching media diversity courses focused on race, gender, class, and sexual orientation has the power to reconstruct students' limited, bigoted, and/or prejudiced knowledge before they serve communities as media professionals.

Situating Yourself Creates Trust

I start each semester of my media studies courses focused on diversity, equity, and inclusion the same way. I tell the students about three stages of my life: my educational background as a student, my professional background as a journalist, and my academic background as a faculty member and higher education administrator. Details about my upbringing, current family, and personality are woven throughout the stages of my life. I have found that being vulnerable to the students and admitting areas where I have been ignorant or insensitive in relation to the topics we will cover shows that we are all works in progress. I want them to see all of me. I need them to notice that I am a Black man, Southerner, husband, father, leader, scholar, journalist, ally, sports fan, gamer, and mentor. I provide detailed information about my life so they will understand that I am not going to ask anything of them that I am not willing to share myself.

Combat Color-Blindness and Classless Society Narratives

I want my future media practitioners to break away from the false narrative of a color-blind society in which individuals claim not to see differences in others. They should see and respect differences and identify similarities to help foster a more diverse, equitable, and inclusive media industry. Students must also be made aware that a class system exists in the United States and obtaining the American Dream is not always as easy as "working hard" and "pulling yourself up by your bootstraps."

Establish Clear Rules

I make it clear that we will consume and comment on issues that many have not fully considered or talked about in mixed company. I pledge to work at maintaining a safe space for the free flow of ideas. This only happens if everyone agrees to be respectful of each other and follow a few rules.

- **Keep it in the bubble:** What is said in the classroom stays in the classroom, so students feel comfortable sharing their experiences.
- **No derogatory language:** Derogatory/slang terms are forbidden because they hurt feelings and become distractions.
- **Professor directs the discussion:** I am the discussion traffic cop directing who speaks and when while keeping the conversation directed at me. A civil conversation can turn chaotic when students talk to each other about sensitive topics, so it is best if they engage with the professor, even when responding to classmates' comments.
- **Complete assignments before class:** Everyone needs to complete readings and personal reflections before class to facilitate informed conversations. This provides students time to ponder their feelings before discussing sensitive topics in class.

Demographically Different Students Respond Similarly

I have been a full- or part-time faculty member at four institutions of higher learning in the American Southeast for more than ten years. They are a mixture of HBCUs, PWIs, public, private, religious, small, large, teaching-focused, and research-focused institutions. Whether

I am talking to a room filled with all women, all Black students, majority White students, or an equal mixture of men and women from different ethnic and racial backgrounds, broaching issues of class, gender, race, and sexual orientation is always difficult.

It is interesting seeing a roomful of students realize that much of who they are is a product of the socialization that has occurred via parents, siblings, friends, religion, school, and media. The students are equally surprised to learn that they all benefit from some form of privilege and usually take that privilege for granted. These discussions have to be layered throughout the semester and revisited whenever a new topic is introduced to drive home the message that our points of privilege vary based on different factors, and how we are socialized affects how we handle the sensitive topics in the course.

There is always a collective "aha" moment where the class realizes that their worldview is not like everyone else's. Using the example of how a Christian-based holiday, Christmas, is the only religious federal holiday in the United States always starts fascinating conversations. Most of my students observe the holiday even if they are not religious, but there are a few who talk about feeling ostracized during the Christmas season because their families do not observe the holiday. It is shocking for many students to learn that everyone does not celebrate Christmas, and it is appalling for the students who do not celebrate it to realize that the majority assumes they do.

Allowing students to talk through how they do or do not celebrate the holiday also uncovers class and cultural differences. I have them think about what happens if they marry someone with different holiday values because many care deeply about passing along their traditions to their future families. At this point, the students are starting to question some parts of their upbringing. This is the perfect time to introduce the course topics.

Introduce First-Person Accounts

Spend time curating personal accounts from documentaries, news interviews, and panel discussions to present various perspectives to your students. I like to use issues like the wealth gap, redlining, and the GI Bill to discuss the class divide in America. I found videos hailing the GI Bill as one of the ways the U.S. government helped create generational wealth. White veterans talked about being able to get assistance checks, jobs, higher education, and home loans. But a different video highlighted how Black veterans were not allowed the same opportunities because their states' policies discriminated against them. Watching the videos and seeing how the system favored one group over another always resonates with students. I use the same method to address gender, race, and sexual orientation issues.

Empower Students to Reflect

I am asking students to digest information that conflicts with foundational beliefs taught to them by people they love and trust, so asking them to reflect on their experiences is essential. I constantly check the temperature in my classroom by having students complete reflection papers. They must tie information from the text, documentaries, and our discussions to their lives. I do not want them to tell me what they *think* about the topics but to relate their personal experiences with them. This means I have quite a bit of reading to do, but it is worth it to see the students really open up. They normally reveal more in writing than during class discussions.

Encourage Students to Engage

To encourage students to share their reflections, I have them give one- to two-minute oral presentations on their reflection essays. This is enough time for the students to summarize their papers and share personal anecdotes that connect with the topic. It also provides a space for reserved students to share without being put on the spot. These sessions spark more conversation than the lecture discussions because now the students have fully digested the information. I do not allow visual aids because I simply want the students to express what resonated with them most. This assignment, along with discussion boards, helps the students learn from each other's experiences in tangible ways.

Conclusion

By the end of the semester, students tell me that I have ruined their absent-minded media consumption because they are noticing unjust portrayals of marginalized groups. They are questioning why they have never been taught that marginalized communities are often impacted negatively by policies and laws that benefit those in privilege. I have had students put what they have learned into action through journalism publications. More personally, students begin to share lessons learned with their families and friends. This can elicit mixed reactions, so I warn students not to make it their duty to change others' mindsets. I tell students that we are all ignorant about many topics, but once we know better, we should do better. After the course, they know that the world is bigger than the bubble they were raised in, so they should always be mindful of diversity, equity, and inclusive practices to ensure that they are painting accurate pictures of the communities they are serving.

References

Biswas, M., & Izard, R. (2010). 2009 Assessment of the status of diversity education in journalism and mass communication programs. *Journalism & Mass Communication Educator, 64*(6), 378–94.

Biswas, M., Izard, R., & Roshan, S. (2017). What is taught about diversity and how is it taught? A 2015 update of diversity teaching at U.S. journalism and mass communication programs. *Teaching Journalism and Mass Communications, 7*(1), 1–13.

10

Guiding Research in Issues of Diversity and Difference

Troy Elias, University of Oregon

A common reality for tenure-track professors at research universities across the United States is that the quality and quantity of research that faculty publish are often enhanced by contributions made from their motivated graduate and undergraduate advisees. Faculty provide students with foundational knowledge and skills training (Johnson et al., 2019), but they also provide mentoring, which helps prepare students in their postgraduate careers. Mentorship is particularly valuable for those who go on to become future faculty as they are able to learn from observation how to achieve balance and to succeed in their own eventual advising, service, and teaching requirements (Breen & Barbuto, 2010).

My research investigates the role that media play in shaping differences in environmental concern across racial, ethnic, and cross-national groups (Elias et al., 2019; Elias & Hmielowski, 2020). My studies in this line of research seek to uncover insights that may help guide international and domestic climate change organizations, brands, and journalists better understand the value of an inclusive approach to climate change mitigation (Elias et al., 2018) and also seek to identify effective ways in which these entities can incorporate and communicate with communities of color. The issues that I research are also predicated on the fulcrum of privilege. Overall, these constructs and social issues represent the cornerstones of all of my work.

Apart from my research, they also inform my pedagogy and largely direct my service commitments. A major component of these studies, however, has been the contributions made by graduate students in exploring these topics. It is my belief that as the United States becomes increasingly diverse, educators and scholars need to intensify our commitment to researching and teaching issues of diversity and difference for the next generation of future faculty, in particular, to be sufficiently equipped (see Thomas & Jones, 2019).

Given my research stream, I tend to advise students with similar interests in diversity, equity, inclusion, and media, and I do so in a variety of capacities. For instance, I am the faculty advisor for the University of Oregon chapter of the National Association of Black Journalists. These students are currently producing a digital publication that revolves around issues faced by students of color on campus and communities of color around Oregon. A critical component of their work involves choosing stories and sources that bring to light nuanced and complex perspectives missing from mainstream media's narratives about communities of color.

The increasing diversity within audiences today and their attendant interests make it critical that students in a journalism department understand how to research and communicate topics of diversity and difference (Elias, 2019). Naturally, interviewing plays a vital function in the process of storytelling, but so too do other forms of research. For instance, our students supplement information acquired from sources with insights from secondary research. Our students commonly include data and other forms of information on national, regional, and local trends obtained via survey and/or experimental study data. I have worked with undergraduate students who have sought to conduct their own surveys, focus groups, and experiments in instances where secondary research does not adequately address their needs.

There have also been a number of occasions where I have worked with students pursuing undergraduate honors theses in topics that align with some aspects of my work. In addition to advising undergraduate research, and perhaps most commonly, I have worked with graduate students in an official role as their advisor for their master's projects and theses and with PhD students on their dissertations. Additionally, there are times when I have coauthored studies with graduate and undergraduate students who I did not formally advise. Advising student research across a variety of classifications is, of course, not uncommon. In fact, the impact of faculty advising and mentoring of students along their research paths has long been a topic of great significance in academia (for example, Breen & Barbuto, 2010; Brewer et al., 1999; Hayward et al., 2017; Rugg & Petre, 2004).

Productive faculty in higher education frequently benefit by having students aid them in the creation of new knowledge. Novel results and findings can then be applied in practice to unique social problems and also can be implemented into teaching, ultimately improving professors' pedagogical practices. The primary ambition of universities and colleges in the United States is to create and transmit knowledge and is guided by the common good (Ballengee, 2020). Knowledge production, facilitated primarily through faculty members working attentively with graduate and, in some cases, undergraduate students, represents the foundational pillars of academic activities for these institutions (Carter et al., 2015; Rugg & Petre, 2004).

HOW DO STUDENTS BENEFIT FROM PARTICIPATING IN RESEARCH?

Existing scholarship has shown that undergraduate students profit in terms of improved communication, teamwork, leadership, and research skills (Carter et al., 2015; Kremmer & Bringle, 1990); clarification and confirmation of their career plans (Seymour et al., 2004); enhanced preparation for their future careers and for graduate school (Alexander et al., 1998); shifts in attitudes toward working as a researcher (Seymour et al., 2004); and the attainment of a variety of professional goals (Pawlow & Sleeper, 2018). It is not much of a reach to see how many of these advantages and benefits also extend to master's students who also are engaged in research. Relative to doctoral students, a PhD is a demonstration of mastery of one's subject, research competence, and the capacity for independent research. Many doctoral students go on to serve in academia or to consult on research in a variety of industries (Rugg & Petre, 2004). Extant scholarship has shown that one factor that benefits graduate students in terms of their research productivity in the years after they graduate is the students' research productivity during their graduate program (Brewer et al., 1999). Therefore mentoring students on how to ask and address important research questions, training students well in terms of research methods, exposing them to quality research, and accentuating the importance of research in the classroom are central to graduate students' professional success and postgraduate productivity (Brewer et al., 1999). For graduate students, faculty advising has implications for their pace of progress through a program, their ability to become competent researchers and teachers with transferable skills, and the type of job they will be able to attain after graduation (Ohio State University, School of Communication, n.d.; Yale Graduate Program Handbook, n.d.).

While much has been written regarding best practices and/or benefits of advising graduate and undergraduate students in research initiatives, the literature specifically dedicated to providing insight on how to guide students in researching issues of diversity and difference is relatively sparse. In the following paragraphs, I share my approach and my perspective, which are by no means exhaustive. Hopefully they contribute to ongoing thoughtful discourse on this topic and add to students' and faculties' existing repertoire of strategies.

GUIDING STUDENTS ON HOW TO RESEARCH ISSUES OF DIVERSITY AND DIFFERENCE

Before discussing strategies to help guide students in researching diversity, it is perhaps most helpful to address the elephant in the room directly. Research has shown that a diverse faculty plays an important role in achieving inclusive institutions (U.S. Department of Education, 2016). For example, faculty members' curricular decisions and pedagogy, including their individual interactions with students, can foster inclusive climates.

It is also vital to note that diversity is much more multifaceted than mere race and ethnicity. At the same time, within the social sciences, as in most of academia, the research has shown faculty mentors, staff, and students were predominantly White (Johnson et al., 2019; Lam, 2015). Based on data compiled by the U.S. Census and the Bureau of Labor Statistics, 80.8 percent of social scientists were White, 5.5 percent were Black or African American, 5 percent were Asian, and 6.5 percent were Hispanic (Lam, 2015). Students from marginalized and/or underrepresented groups constantly confronted the assumption that they did not belong in higher education and had to invest time and energy reacting to barriers and microaggressions, which diverted their energy and attention away from their studies and research (Johnson et al., 2019).

At the same time, an assortment of issues existed that facilitate the collision of myriad cultures and people across the United States. These issues often have great significance to students from marginalized communities. These topics include, but are by no means restricted to, religion-driven culture wars, climate change amelioration, a global coronavirus-based pandemic and concomitant economic crisis, natural disasters and mass migration, LGBTQ activism, and misinformation propelled by social media, which has, arguably, facilitated an increased lack of observance of basic facts. In the United States specifically, there is also widespread concern around racial and ethnic inequality, including rising distress over the murders of unarmed Black men and women at the hands of police officers and White individuals who take the law into their own hands (for example, George Floyd, Breonna Taylor, Atatiana Jefferson, and Ahmaud Arbery). Regardless of a faculty member's racial or ethnic background, students need their mentorship and guidance. A lack of satisfactory mentoring has been linked to a number of poor consequences, including a loss of interest in graduate school, misconceptions about graduate school, and derailment from graduate school ambitions (Cooper et al., 2019; Thiry et al., 2011).

Guiding students in terms of their research is challenging. Fortunately there are a number of steps, derived from a variety of fields (for example, social sciences; science, technology, engineering, and mathematics [STEM]; and education), that may be helpful. For instance, existing research from both education and STEM indicated that before research can be achieved, student well-being ought to be prioritized. To help students publish and be successful, research has shown that an effective approach is to start by understanding students' career objectives and, working in conjunction with them, outline a plan that will help them to prepare and be successful (Breen & Barbuto, 2010). This process inherently involves active listening, empathy, and cultural sensitivity. It is also important to understand additional barriers to students' success. As such, the first step in guiding students on how to research issues of diversity and difference starts with faculty commitment to their own students.

Mind the Store: Listen, Respect, and Care

Most of us get into academic positions and have very little experience advising students, but we are expected to do a great job regardless (Monk, 2015). What is clear is that before we can work with students to produce great research on issues of diversity, we first need to ensure that our students are in a good space. It is my belief that before educators can help students meaningfully start illuminating problematic societal diversity issues via their research, issues that are central to those students need to be addressed and ameliorated.

Schlosser et al. (2010) have contended that a competent advisor will be self-aware with regard to personal racial and cultural identity, cultural biases, and privilege. Competent advisors, they argue, are also careful to consider and at times address advisees' cultural characteristics including racial identity, gender, and sexual orientation, and they must be genuinely interested in and committed to the personal and professional experiences of all students, including people of color, women, and LGBTQ+ individuals. As a result, the first step of guiding students on researching issues of diversity originates with the advisor and involves active listening, empathy, and cultural sensitivity.

In partial support, data from the National Survey of Student Engagement has suggested that factors that make for successful advising involve listening, respect, and caring (Flaherty, 2020). These data were not inclusive of perspectives from graduate students; however, it seems reasonable to assume that this approach would also be effective with students at that level, if not more so. Furthermore, Johnson et al. (2019) contended that this may be an effective approach even when faculty do not share identities with students from marginalized groups. They posited that in such cases, faculty can create successful learning environments by frequently checking in with students and explicitly stating support and defending aspects of students' professional and personal lives that leave them vulnerable. They also must be open about their own experiences and trajectory and provide visual cues, such as photos, art, and posters, that show support for issues related to the students' identities, as well as through promoting events centering on marginalized people.

In short, guiding students along the path of researching diversity involves following through on these issues via a variety of touchpoints and letting students from diverse and marginalized backgrounds see that commitment being manifested. There is one glaring caveat. Faculty need to provide support and empathy, but students still need to be resilient and independent. While advising is one of the most important roles for faculty during students' degree programs, and their support is critical to student success (Barnes & Austin, 2009; Johnson et al., 2019; Monk, 2015), it is important that students gain the perspective that their advisor's job is to help them navigate rough patches, but students still need to be able to overcome adversity. Achieving academic success necessitates diligence among all concerned: students, faculty advisors, and institutions (Breen & Barbuto, 2010).

CRITICAL REFLECTION

As a faculty member, I have found critical reflection and introspection useful in identifying privileged spaces and positions in which I find myself. I then attempt to use this insight to guide my research. As an example, I am a middle-class, able-bodied, cisgender, Black male academic of Afro-Caribbean ethnicity. My gender and sexual orientation afford me a certain degree of privilege. Hence, I have used my research to explore racial and ethnic differences in sexual prejudice directed toward lesbian/gay/bisexual people of color (LGB-POC) (Elias et al., 2016). My experiences living in ethnic communities in the Caribbean, the Deep South (for example, South Carolina and Florida), as well as the Midwest and the Pacific Northwest have led me to believe that media portrayals of racial minorities' attitudes and behaviors toward LGB individuals are often oversimplified. In this particular study, via purposive sampling, my coauthors and I examined African American, Hispanic, and non-Hispanic Whites' self-reported likelihood of subjecting LGB-POC to microaggressions. The results of our study revealed that while African Americans hold significantly less favorable attitudes toward same-sex relationships than White individuals (but not Hispanics), they express significantly lower likelihoods of engaging in LGB-directed microaggressions than both White individuals and Hispanics. In fact, as White individuals' ethnic identity gets stronger, their likelihood of engaging in microaggressions directed to LGBs of all ethnicities increases, an effect that was not found for African American or Hispanic individuals. In short, my platform allows me to check my privilege and conduct research for what I believe is communal good. More importantly, many of my studies, including the previous example, have been driven by my work with graduate and/or undergraduate students who have helped make the final drafts better. It is also important to be open to ideas or suggestions from graduate students in terms of topics around diversity to research based on issues that may likewise be central to their identities.

THE FINE POINTS OF WRITING RESEARCH AND THE BIG PICTURE

Part of conducting research on issues of diversity and difference is, of course, writing social science papers. There are a number of papers and book chapters that provide assistance to neophyte researchers on how to write empirical research (for example, Bain et al., 2016; Milardo, 2015; Sabatelli, 2010; White, 2005). This is a skill required by virtually all student researchers in the field of communication. Writing is central to students in terms of developing critical thinking skills, getting hired, salary implications, appeal as candidates for other jobs, and tenure and promotion decisions. Publications are commonly used measurements for determining appropriateness for hiring, tenure, and promotion and are essential for promising new scholars, who are often expected to publish at rapid paces (Mustaine & Tewksbury, 2013).

It bears noting, however, that if students embark on this career path of writing papers based on issues of diversity, they are likely to encounter structural barriers that exist beyond the mere mechanics of writing. For instance, Chakravartty et al. (2018) found that non-White scholars continue to be underrepresented in publication rates, citation rates, and editorial positions in communication studies. There is evidence of similar findings in other fields as well, including cognitive, developmental, and social psychology with additional implications for Black women (Buchanan, 2020; Roberts et al., 2020; Williams, 2020a, 2020b). Roberts et al. (2020) found that White journal editors—whose gatekeeping function positions them to govern what is worthy of publication—tend to be less likely than journal editors of color to publish research that highlights the role of race in human psychology. And so it is important to understand the choices students researching diversity may have to make in terms of choosing a journal that reflects a certain discourse community as opposed to journals that may have higher impact factors or that may be more well known.

These are not necessarily mutually exclusive conditions. However, these situations may arise and warrant candid conversations with students on a case-by-case basis. Some scholarship has argued that a good approach is for authors to consider the readership that they wish to reach and that they read regularly as they will know its scope and its readership (Bain et al., 2016). It should be noted that in no instance should students not be advised to seek the best journals possible, but they should absolutely be made aware that there are certain structural barriers in existence that may hinder their chances to publish in a timely manner, such as their careers require. This is a sad reality that has now received empirical support.

CONCLUSION

In conclusion, one way to help guide students interested in researching diversity and difference is to start by understanding their career objectives and, working in conjunction with them, outline a plan that will help them prepare and be successful (Breen & Barbuto, 2010). This process incorporates listening, empathy, and cultural sensitivity. Cultural reflection is also an effective strategy to unearth potential topics for research. For more on this, Thomas and Jones (2019) published an article called "Critical Reflexivity: Teaching About Race and Racism in the Advertising Classroom." In this manuscript, they used an even more advanced approach to critical reflection and applied it to the constructs of race and racism specifically. Their manuscript is an excellent resource with a critical paradigm to foster critical reflexivity from which other issues of diversity may potentially be scrutinized for teaching and research purposes. Finally, candid conversations about the research process, including publication opportunities and challenges, are essential to the success of students entering this field and seeking to contribute to the literature.

REFERENCES

Alexander, B. B., Foertsch, J. A., & Daffinrud, S. (1998). *The Spend a Summer With a Scientist Program: An evaluation of program outcomes and the essential elements of success.* University of Madison–Wisconsin, LEAD Center.

Ballengee, J. (2016, December 16). Academic freedom and responsibility. Inside Higher Ed. https://www.insidehighered.com/views/2020/12/16/academic-freedom-and-diversity-higher-education-opinion.

Bain, B. J., Littlewood, T. J., & Szydlo, R. M. (2016). The finer points of writing and refereeing scientific articles. *British Journal of Haematology, 172,* 350–59.

Barnes, B. J., & Austin, A. E. (2009). The role of doctoral advisors: A look at advising from the advisor's perspective. *Innovative High Education, 33*(4), 297–315.

Breen, J. A. M., & Barbuto, J. E. (2010). Doctoral advising, research productivity and the academic balancing act: Insights from Michael A. Hitt, Edwin A. Locke, Fred Luthans, Lyman W. Porter, and Anne Tsui. *Organization Management Journal, 7*(3), 182–91.

Brewer, G. A., Douglas, J. W., Facer II, R. L., & O'Toole Jr., L. J. (1999). Determinants of graduate research productivity in doctoral programs of public administration. *Public Administration Review, 59*(5), 373–83.

Buchanan, N. T. (2020). Researching while Black (and female). *Women & Therapy, 43*(1–2), 91–111.

Carter, D. F., Ro, H. K., Alcott, B., & Lattuca, L. R. (2015). Co-curricular connections: The role of undergraduate research experiences in promoting engineering students' communication, teamwork, and leadership skills. *Research in Higher Education, 57*(3), 363–93.

Cooper, K. M., Gin, L. E., Akeeh, B., Clark, C. E., Hunter, J. S., Roderick, T. B., Elliott, D. B., et al. (2019). Factors that predict life sciences student persistence in undergraduate research experiences. *PLOS ONE* 14: e0220186.

Chakravartty, P., Kuo, R., Grubbs, V., & McIlwain, C. (2018). #CommunicationSoWhite. *Journal of Communication, 68*(2), 254–66.

Chambers, J. P., Kreshel, P. J., Richards, J. I., & Timke, E. (2019). Roundtable on teaching an advertising & society course. *Advertising & Society Quarterly, 20*(4).

Chambliss, D. F. (2014). *How college works.* Harvard University Press.

Elias, T. (2019). Interviewing and diversity: The importance of topics and sources of diversity. In P. Laufer (Ed.), *Interviewing: The Oregon Method* (2nd ed.). School of Journalism and Communication Center for Journalism Innovation and Civic Engagement.

Elias, T., Blaine, M., Morrison, D., & Harris, B. (2019). Media use, cross-national samples, and the theory of planned behavior: Implications for climate change advocacy intentions. *International Journal of Communication, 13,* 3694–718.

Elias, T., Dahmen, N., Morrison, D., Morrison, D., & Morris, D. (2018). Understanding climate change inactivity across Hispanic, African American, and Anglo racial/ethnic groups. *Howard Journal of Communications, 30*(1), 38–56.

Elias, T., & Hmielowski, J. (2020). Media use, race, and the environment: The converging of environmental attitudes based on self-reported news use. *Environmental Values.* Advance publication online.

Elias, T., Jaisle, A., & Morton-Padovano, C. (2016). Ethnic identity as a predictor of microaggressive behavior towards Blacks, Whites, and Hispanic LGBs by Blacks, Whites, and Hispanics. *Journal of Homosexuality, 64*(1), 1–31.

Elias, T., Phillips Honda, L., VanRysdam, M. K., & Chun, J. (2016). A mixed methods examination of 21st century hiring processes, social networking sites, and implicit bias. *Journal of Social Media in Society, 5*(1), 189–228.

Flaherty, C. (2020, December 14). Advising in the time of COVID. Inside Higher Ed. https://www.insidehighered.com/news/2020/12/14/study-abcs-advising-are-listen-respect-care.

Greer, T. M., and K. Chwalisz. (2007). Minority-related stressors and coping processes among African American college students. *Journal of College Student Development*, 48(4), 388–404.

Grillo, G. (2015, April 23). The advertising industry needs diverse leadership to thrive. *AdAge*. https://adage.com/article/agency-viewpoint/advertising-industry-diverse-leadership-thrive/297998/.

Hayward, C. N., Laursen, S. L., & Thiry, H. (2017). Why work with undergraduate researchers? Differences in research advisors' motivations and outcomes by career stage. *CBE Life Sciences Education*, 16(1), 1–11.

Jaschik, S. (2020, December 7). Doubts about going to college. Inside Higher Ed. https://www.insidehighered.com/admissions/article/2020/12/07/more-third-prospective-college-students-are-reconsidering-higher.

Johnson, K. M. S., Briggs, A., Hawn, C., Mantina, N., & Woods, B. C. (2019). Inclusive practices for diverse student populations: Experimental biology 2017. *Advances in Physiological Education*, 43(3), 365–72.

Kremmer, J. F., & Bringle, R. G. (1990). The effects of an intensive research experience on the careers of talented undergraduates. *Journal of Research and Development in Education*, 24(1), 1–5.

Lam, B. (2015, June 29). The least diverse jobs in America. *The Atlantic*. https://www.theatlantic.com/business/archive/2015/06/diversity-jobs-professions-america/396632/.

Milardo, R. (2015). *Crafting scholarship in the behavioral and social sciences: Writing, reviewing, and editing* (1st ed.). Routledge.

Monk, D. (2015, March 20). Reflections on advising graduate students. Inside Higher Ed. https://www.insidehighered.com/advice/2015/03/20/steps-help-professors-better-advise-graduate-students-essay.

Mustaine, E. E., & Tewksbury, R. (2013). Exploring the black box of journal manuscript review: A survey of social science journal editors. *Journal of Criminal Justice Education*, 24(3), 386–401.

Ohio State University, School of Communication (n.d.). *Graduate school handbook*. Retrieved February 15, 2021. https://gradsch.osu.edu/handbook/all.

Pawlow, L., & Sleeper, K. (2018). Multifaceted undergraduate research program assessment plan: Benefits, challenges, and utility. *Scholarship and Practice of Undergraduate Research*, 1(3), 5–15.

Roberts, S. O., Bareket-Shavit, C., Dollins, F. A., Goldie, P. D., & Mortenson, E. (2020). Racial inequality in psychological research: Trends of the past and recommendations for the future. *Perspectives on Psychological Science*, 15(6), 1295–309.

Rugg, G., & Petre, M. (2004). *The unwritten rules of PhD research*. McGraw Hill/Open University Press.

Sabatelli, R. (2010). Writing for a scholarly journal. *NCFR Report*, 55, F2–F5.

Schlosser, L. Z., Lyons, H. Z., Talleyrand, R. M., Kim, B. S. K., & Johnson, W. B. (2010). A multiculturally infused model of graduate advising relationships. *Journal of Career Development*, 38(1), 44–61.

Seymour, E., Hunter, A.-B., Laursen, S. L., & DeAntoni, T. (2004). Establishing the benefits of research experiences for undergraduates in the sciences: First findings from a three-year study. *Science Education*, 88(4), 493–534.

Thiry, H., Laursen, S. L., & Hunter, A-B. (2011). What experiences help students become scientists? A comparative study of research and other sources of personal and professional gains for STEM undergraduates. *Journal of High Education, 82*(4), 357–88.

Thomas, K. D., & Jones, N. (2019). Critical reflexivity: Teaching about race and racism in the advertising classroom. *Advertising & Society Quarterly, 20*(2).

U.S. Bureau of Labor Statistics. (2020). Labor force statistics from the current population survey. https://www.bls.gov/cps/cpsaat18.htm.

U.S. Department of Education. (2016). *Advancing diversity and inclusion in higher education: Key data highlights focusing on race and ethnicity and promising practices.* Washington, DC.

Walls, J. K., & Hall, S. S. (2018). A focus group study of African American students' experiences with classroom discussions about race at a predominantly White university. *Teaching in Higher Education, 23*(1), 47–62.

White, L. (2005). Writes of passage: Writing an empirical journal article. *Journal of Marriage and Family, 67*(4), 791–98.

Williams, M. T. (2020a). Microaggressions: Clarification, evidence, and impact. *Perspectives on Psychological Science, 15*(1), 3–26.

Williams, M. T. (2020b). Psychology cannot afford to ignore the many harms caused by microaggressions. *Perspectives on Psychological Science, 15*(1), 38–43.

Yale Graduate Program Handbook (n.d.). Graduate School of Arts and Sciences programs and policies 2020–2021. http://catalog.yale.edu/gsas/.

PERSPECTIVE: MENTORING STUDENTS OF COLOR

Maria De Moya, DePaul University

A student's experience is significantly impacted by the support he or she receives during his or her studies. The support we provide as faculty members often extends outside the classroom with relationships we form with students with a focus on their growth, career advancement, psychological well-being, and/or professional development (for example, Crisp & Cruz, 2009). Having achieved a level of professional and personal success as mentors, we are "willing and able to share covert and overt practices that have assisted him or her in becoming successful" (Kalbfleisch, 2002, p. 63).

As the number of students of color in our classrooms continues to increase, our mentorship is in demand. The most recent survey of journals and mass communication U.S. enrollments (McLaughlin et al., 2020) found that students of color represented approximately 35 percent of the undergraduate and master's students in journalism and mass communication and nearly one in four of the doctoral students. For these students, navigating the classroom in the college or university can be especially challenging.

The Experience of Students of Color

Students of color are commonly exposed to racial prejudice in the classroom during their college education (Boysen, 2012; Curtis-Boles et al., 2020; Hubain et al., 2016). Students experience a variety of microaggressions including isolation, invalidation, tokenism, and the pressure to advocate for their cultural group and correct misinformation or misconceptions (Curtis-Boles et al., 2020). Although not a remedy for all these ills, positive mentoring experiences can lead to higher grades, greater self-efficacy, clearer academic goals, and lower attrition rates in students of color (Tsui, 2007).

Mentoring around research can be especially beneficial to students of color, who are more likely to be assumed to be less capable or only provided opportunities to conduct research on culture or race-related issues (Joseph & Hirshfield, 2011). Students who intend to enter academia will be challenged by the expectations of many of the PhD programs to present and/or publish research papers before graduation (Christ & Broyles, 2008). This is in addition to being able to demonstrate the ability to teach and render service at both the academic and professional level (Royal & Smith, 2019). Their mentors can ease the burden of these expectations by providing them with the benefit of their own experience.

My Experience Mentoring Around Research

Most of my mentoring relationships have started with a student approaching me after class or during office hours to discuss their experience as someone different from the perceived archetypical public relations or advertising professional. They see in me (a woman, an immigrant, and Latina) someone who might have cultural similarities and shared experiences. I am also someone with whom they can discuss their fear of how bias shapes their experience as students and potential professional or research opportunities.

One of the areas in which this work can be most straightforward is in research. Through the quality of their work, students can demonstrate how they develop knowledge, understand publics, and apply their analytical skills. Whether their research interests are aligned with popular subjects in our field or related to neglected research areas, our students can bring the unique perspective offered by their experience as underrepresented, often marginalized, individuals. To be clear, this does not require a focus on race or cultural research (unless that is their area of interest). Instead what is required is their willingness to look at research problems in different ways.

Designing research—be it to inform communication strategies or to advance theory—to consider the questions of power, privilege, and difference that shape much of their learning experience can lead to developing new and deeper knowledge. If our advice focuses solely on methodology or finding the right answers to practical questions, we risk overlooking the experiences and voices of people who have been understudied and dynamics we need to understand.

Mentoring Future Scholars

As a PhD student, I was fortunate to have in Juan Carlos Molleda a mentor who encouraged me to pursue my own scholar research interests. As a Latino and immigrant himself, Molleda had the type of similar experience the research has shown informs one's approach to mentoring graduate students (Pardun et al., 2015). He was able to understand my vocation to research issues closer to my heart. As a result, my research trajectory has focused on issues that are deeply important to me, such as ethnic advocacy and immigration (for example, De Moya, 2018; De Moya & Bravo, 2016; Rendon et al., 2019).

Four Principles for Mentoring Future Scholars

The focus on research can be a potential way to maximize our support and the impact of our mentoring, especially if grounded in our understanding of the needs and challenges that our students faced. In my own exchanges, I lean on four guiding principles to inform my mentoring of students as they conduct research relevant to their own experience and especially when questioning issues of power, difference, and diversity. Here I detail these guidelines and my rationale behind each one.

Questioning Established Knowledge

In addition to focusing on testing and developing theory, we should challenge students to consider potential limits and weaknesses of these theories. For example, there is little discussion of the homogeneity of the theorists that conducted this foundational work or the scope—or lack thereof—of their focus, such as in the case of public relations and advertising, the concern with supporting business goals. I try to encourage students to, as Shah put it, "examine the very concept of knowledge and how it is determined through a regime of power and privilege rooted in racial hierarchy" (2004, p. 15). This can lead to a deeper understanding of those theories that stand up to their scrutiny while empowering new researchers to address the opportunities for further exploration they have identified in their independent research agendas. The alternative would be perpetuating othering practices and supporting knowledge production systems that marginalize certain groups (Shah, 2004).

Value Understanding over Knowing

Often students might know facts without understanding their meaning or discuss what they know without being able explain why something is true. However, understanding means being able to apply, analyze, synthesize, and evaluate knowledge (Wiggins & McTighe, 2005). A focus on understanding leads students to apply their knowledge creatively and to new settings. For example, in

Carstarphen's chapter (this volume), she describes the process of creating a class about the 1921 Tulsa Race Massacre in which the instructors encouraged students to explore scholarly work and professional observations and critiques, identifying omissions in historical records to glean not only what happened but how it happened, how it was reported, and why.

Consider how this applies to their research. Even when recognizing that understanding through research is framed by the chosen methodology (Holden & Lynch, 2004) we can assist students in looking beyond the limited scope of a specific research project to identify and acknowledge the dimensions of the question that could be answered by other methods or in other contexts, even if they are not the researchers who will undertake this research. The vulnerability of pointing to these gaps in our own understanding can become an opportunity for different and creative applications of future research.

Recognizing Their Position as Researchers

The idea of being always objective and leaving yourself out of the research can be counter-productive. The truth is that our experiences inform our research. Black, Brown, Native, Asian, and LGBTQ scholars might be advised to avoid apparent bias in their research by not focusing on their own community. But as Nzingaa et al. (2018) explained, we should help researchers understand and explore the research traditions that have been segregated or ignored due to political, social, or cultural systems. We, and our students, need to understand that an engaged research stance can lead to trustworthy and good research. In every stage of their research, our students can explore how their ethnicity, race, class, gender, or other differences in their identity have influenced the design and/or direction of their research and teaching. Researchers should be encouraged to disclose this information in their research, not necessarily as a limitation but as drive and motivation for seeking understanding.

Our Stance as Mentors: Keeping Intellectual Humility

This last guideline applies not only to our mentees but to mentors as well. We should always strive for intellectual humility. This requires a willingness to grapple with difficult ideas and reflect on, and seek, deeper understanding with the aim to move toward a more informed engagement with the subject of study (Sensoy & DiAngelo, 2017). For students, the lack of humility can come from the idea that they are studying subjects that are value laden or subjective. For mentors and scholars, it can derive from our experience and familiarity with the subject. In either case, this leads to considering knowledge established, or static, placing knowledge on par with opinions, and closing ourselves to new learning.

We model intellectual humility by questioning our own assumptions. When we use our research as models and examples, we can own up to ways it could be stronger or even not meeting the research goal. For example, we could explain our choice of research setting, method, or scope and suggest how the same (or different) questions can be furthered by other methods or perspectives. Reflecting on these four principles is one of the ways I prepare myself to support students of color in their research. I firmly believe that as faculty members, we must be ready and prepared to guide students through the sensitive readings and conversations they will encounter in their work without allowing them to shy away from concepts that they find unclear or abstract but that are relevant to their scholarship.

References

Boysen, G. A. (2012). Teacher and student perceptions of microaggressions in college classrooms. *College Teaching, 60*(3), 122–29.

Christ, W. G. & Broyles, S. J. (2008). Graduate education at AEJMC schools: A benchmark study. *Journalism & Mass Communication Educator, 62*(4), 376–401.

Crisp, G., & Cruz, I. (2009). Mentoring college students: A critical review of the literature between 1990 and 2007. *Research in Higher Education, 50*(6), 525–45.

Curtis-Boles, H., Chupina, A. G., & Okubo, Y. (2020). Social justice challenges: Students of color and critical incidents in the graduate classroom. *Training and Education in Professional Psychology, 14*(2), 100–108.

De Moya, M. (2018). Protesting the homeland: Diaspora dissent public relations efforts to oppose the Dominican Republic's citizenship policies. In A. Adi (Ed.), *Protest public relations: Communicating dissent and activism* (pp. 106–27). Routledge.

De Moya, M., & Bravo, V. (2016). The role of public relations in ethnic advocacy and activism: A proposed research agenda. *Public Relations Inquiry, 5*(3), 233–51.

Holden, M. T., & Lynch, P. (2004). Choosing the appropriate methodology: Understanding research philosophy. *The Marketing Review, 4*(4), 397–409.

Hubain, B. S., Allen, E. L., Harris, J. C., & Linder, C. (2016). Counter-stories as representations of the racialized experiences of students of color in higher education and student affairs graduate preparation programs. *International Journal of Qualitative Studies in Education, 29*(7), 946–63.

Joseph, T. D., & Hirshfield, L. E. (2011). "Why don't you get somebody new to do it?" Race and cultural taxation in the academy. *Ethnic and Racial Studies, 34*(1), 121–41.

Kalbfleisch, P. J. (2002). Communicating in mentoring relationships: A theory for enactment. *Communication Theory, 12*(1), 63–69.

McLaughlin, B., Gotlieb, M. R., & Cummins, R. G. (2020). 2018 Survey of journalism & mass communication enrollments. *Journalism & Mass Communication Educator, 75*(1), 131–43.

Molleda, J. C. (2001). International paradigms: The Latin American school of public relations. *Journalism Studies, 2*(4), 513–30.

Molleda, J. C., Connolly-Ahern, C., & Quinn, C. (2005). Cross-national conflict shifting: Expanding a theory of global public relations management through quantitative content analysis. *Journalism Studies, 6*(1), 87–102.

Nzingaa, K., Rapp, D. N., Leatherwood, C., Easterday, M., Rogers, L. O., Gallagher, N., & Medin, D. (2018). Should social scientists be distanced from or engaged with the people they study? *Proceedings of the National Academy of Sciences, 115*(45), 11435–441.

Pardun, C. J., McKeever, R., Pressgrove, G. N., & McKeever, B. W. (2015). Colleagues in training: How senior faculty view doctoral education. *Journalism & Mass Communication Educator, 70*(4), 354–66.

Rendon, H., De Moya, M., & Johnson, M. (2019). Dreamers or threat: Bilingual frame building of DACA immigrants. *Newspaper Research Journal, 40*(1), 7–24.

Royal, C., & Smith, S. (2019). Redefining doctoral education: Preparing future faculty to lead emerging media curriculum. *Teaching Journalism & Mass Communication, 9*(2), 1–11.

Shah, H. (2004). Reading and using mass communication research on the "other": Whiteness, folk wisdom, and objects of research. *Multicultural Perspectives, 6*(2), 1–16.

Sensoy, O., & DiAngelo, R. (2012). *Is everyone really equal? An introduction to key concepts in social justice education.* Teachers College Press.

Tsui, L. (2007). Effective strategies to increase diversity in STEM fields: A review of the research literature. *Journal of Negro Education, 76*(4), 555–81.

Wiggins, G., & McTighe, J. (2005). *Understanding by design.* Association for Supervision & Curriculum Development.

Afterword

Of Insurrection, Injustice, and a Racial Reckoning

Deb Aikat, University of North Carolina at Chapel Hill

Current events often define the teaching of race and diversity. January 6, 2021, will go down in U.S. constitutional history books as one of the darkest hours of Western liberal democracy. U.S. president Donald Trump incited an insurrection at the Capitol that changed the country forever. The storming of the building complex by Trump supporters put senators and representatives under siege for several hours, led to the death of five people (including a police officer), left numerous people injured, and parts of the Capitol were damaged and vandalized. A week later, Trump became the first president in U.S. history to be twice impeached.

The January 6, 2021, "Save America" rally and the subsequent insurrection at the Capitol revealed that some parts of White America are earnest about paying the "price of the ticket" to maintain and defend the privileges of whiteness. In some important ways, the attack on the U.S. Capitol was also about race. Interpreting the siege through the lens of the research literature on race and identity in American politics, Stanford University professor Hakeem Jefferson (2021) observed, "This is, like so much of American politics, about race, racism and White Americans' stubborn commitment to White dominance, no matter the cost or the consequence" (para. 2).

In a thoughtful tweet on January 7, 2021, U.S. president-elect Joe Biden expressed concern over police inaction against the insurrectionists who stormed the U.S. Capitol the previous day, with strong words: "No one can tell me that if it had been a group of Black Lives Matter protesters yesterday that they wouldn't have been treated very differently than the mob that stormed the Capitol." Biden (2021) tweeted, "We all know that's true—and it's unacceptable." Biden's race perspective reflected a simple truth: when it comes to race, a common challenge is the conflict between marginalized (or critical) and structurally dominant narratives (those that represent the status quo or an oppressive or more powerful position). Both Jefferson's and Biden's comments exemplify the marginalized or critical narrative. As educators, we should prepare ourselves to navigate the conflict between dominant narratives (DNs) and critical counter-narratives in a way that will lead to learning for all students and foster belonging for students who identify with marginalized groups.

DISPUTING THE DOMINANT NARRATIVES WITH COUNTER-NARRATIVES

Relevant to the importance of countering DNs, educators enjoy a privilege. The university context motivates all of us to engage in an open discussion to counter and question DNs. Morales (2020) feels the university context may facilitate sharing of narratives counter to the DN through student organizations, peer groups, culture courses, community interactions, and social networks. When students of color speak up in response to racial microaggressions, they tend to feel overburdened with having to educate the offending party.

As Morales has studied, students of color are often tasked with negotiating racial microaggressions—subtle, racialized offenses—at historically White colleges and universities. Therefore, looking to the future, students may utilize four five-point rubrics, as explicated on pages 171 through 172 in this afterword, to foster critical thinking. Students of color may also use the four rubrics to navigate other historically White institutions that are critical to social mobility.

As a key part of the university context, the college classroom has emerged as a dynamic space to effectively learn lessons from discussions on a critical topic, the related DN, and the marginalized counter-narratives.

As instructors leading a classroom discussion on a critical topic such as "the need for social justice" or "strategies to counter racial bias," we always face a classroom conundrum when a student presents a DN, derived from cultural prominence, to challenge marginalized counter-narratives (Asarta et al., 2018). The conundrum is aggravated when the student's DN resonates with the majority of students. Giving equal floor time to the student's DN may legitimize the already unequal power the DN conveys. However, dismissing the student's DN would be considered unfair or biased. Ignoring the DN also fails to address its weight, power, and motivation. We present proven strategies in four five-point rubrics, as explicated on pages 171 through 172, for illuminating and interrogating the DNs to empower students with the skills to critically interrogate DNs themselves.

Engaging Students with Critical Topics, DNs, and Counter-Narratives

Informed by the Scholarship of Teaching and Learning (SoTL), here are five easy steps to engage students by discussing critical topics, evaluating DNs, and assessing marginalized counter-narratives:

1. **Topical relevance:** Informed by student inputs, highlight the critical topic (for example, "the need for social justice" or "strategies to oppose racial bias") and the marginalized counter-narratives that challenge the DN. If a student raised the critical topic, encourage the student to lead the class discussion. If the student is reluctant to do so, you lead or ask another student to volunteer.
2. **Themes of DN:** Request the student to enunciate the DN in response to the critical topic.
3. **Theorize ideas:** Invite other students to discuss, dissent, or deliberate on the critical topic, the DN, and the marginalized counter-narratives.
4. **Thoughtful insights:** Identify agreements and disagreements in assessing the issue.
5. **Teaching lessons:** Informed by this class discussion, prepare a list of lessons learned.

Contextualize and Interrogate the DN with Thoughtful Questions

Use contextual insights to question the DN. Do that with context-focused questions to address and analyze the DN and engage students to counter it. These questions explore contextual insights, as listed here:

1. **Explicate** the relevance of the DN. In what ways might the DN be wrong or right?
2. **Explore** the historical context: How familiar are you with the DN? Identify the source and the context (a peer, professor, professional, people, place, or perspective).
3. **Evaluate** whether the source and context of the DN enhances your understanding of the topic.
4. **Enunciate** who gains from perpetuating the DN. In what ways do they benefit and contribute by furthering the DN?
5. **Enumerate** ten stakeholders with a deep interest in sustaining the DN. Who else might have a stake in this narrative? How are they healed or harmed by it?

Five Questions to Assess and Attribute DN Assumptions

There are five questions to explore problematic or incomplete aspects about the DN as a response to the critical topic. You may also have students divide into breakout groups, discuss ideas, and conceptualize questions about each assumption themselves:

1. **Assumptions:** What assumptions does this DN depend on to hold up as a logical response to the critical perspective? Record and recognize students' responses, for their peers to refer to them later. Help them refine the assumptions to be as specific and thorough as possible.
2. **Aggregate all aspects:** What would evidence aspects for each of these claims look like? Do you expect sufficient evidence supporting these assumptions? Why?
3. **Authenticate:** Assign students to search for the evidence for claims and evaluate the credibility of their sources.
4. **Assess:** Given the lack of credible evidence to support DN assumptions, how do we explain why the DN is so widely accepted as true and reasonable?
5. **Assimilate and analyze** based on all relevant inputs and find out if the DN makes sense.

Using Rigor and Research to Enhance DN Discussions

Review five key steps for students to interrogate the DN with rigor and research:

1. **Identify** the DN and its focus and bias, as you deem fit.
2. **Interrogate** problematic, incomplete, or taken-for-granted assumptions. Explore why.
3. **Infuse** new insights and thinking to reexamine the DN and its counter-narratives. Ask why students think the DN resonates with people. Remind students that their peers are familiar with the DN, and most peers expressed a sympathetic logic to the DN.
4. **Innovate** ways to explicate the DN context (who perpetuates it and why?).
5. **Invigorate, inform, and improvise** ways to identify lessons learned. Based on what we have interrogated about the DN, do you think it adequately responds to the initial critical topic? Why or why not? (*You might choose to define for your students misleading or distracting aspects to explain the futility of some DNs.*)

Afterword

ON NEUTRALITY

On a journalistic level, events such as the January 6, 2021, insurrection highlighted a key lesson. In their quest of the truth, journalists have manifested their news coverage with time-tested values of objectivity, balance, and neutrality. The insurrection motivated news analysts to observe that while "neutrality" is one standard in journalism, it has always been clear that journalists need not be neutral about everything.

As Poynter's Roy Peter Clark (2021) contended, journalists and their news reports "need not be neutral" about violent attacks upon the "institutions that make democracy and self-government possible, a system in which they play a crucial role" (para. 21). Clark urged journalists to establish "the best distance from neutrality," especially in the aftermath of "an administration that propagated attacks on evidence-based enterprises like science and the news industry" (para. 22). Such "distance from neutrality" will have important lessons for the role of journalism in the twenty-first-century racial reckoning.

THE TRIBULATIONS OF DISABUSING STEREOTYPES AND SYSTEMIC RACISM

Teaching diversity connotes myriad challenges in disabusing students of prejudice, stereotypes, and systemic racism (Chronicle Insights, 2018). American political commentator Walter Lippmann famously referred to stereotypes as "pictures in our heads" (Lippmann, 1922, p. 9) and redefined the modern psychological propensity of stereotyping with these words: "In untrained observation, we pick recognizable signs out of the environment. The signs stand for ideas, and these ideas we fill out with our stock of images" (p. 87). These ideas and images contribute to "stored up images, the preconceptions, and prejudices" that "interpret . . . and in their turn powerfully direct the play of our attention, and our vision" (p. 32).

Lippmann's theory of "pictures in our heads" stereotypes was aptly exemplified by noted journalist and renowned educator Charles Sumner "Chuck" Stone Jr. in his humorous depiction "The 24 Politically Unimpeachable Reasons Answering the Question: Why Is Sunday Morning the Best Time to Drive on the Los Angeles Freeway?" To explicate why, "Catholics are at mass. Protestants are still asleep. Jews are playing golf in Palm Springs. Muslims are saying morning prayers," Stone started his now famous letter to Bernie Reeves, the editor and publisher of *Metro Magazine* in Raleigh, North Carolina (Stone, 2002, para. 17).

Media perpetuate prejudices that emerge from widespread reporting of cultural depictions in creative works such as films and news media messages among other nonfiction modes that reflect people's preconceived opinions not based on reason or actual experience.

Lippmann theoretically attributed stereotyping to the lack of "time" and "opportunity for intimate acquaintance" in contemporary life. He observed, in the "hurried and multifarious" state of "modern life," physical distance "separates men who are often in vital contact with each other, such as employer and employee, official and voter" (1922, p. 88). In many ways, Lippmann's perspicuous theorization of stereotypes has inspired several decades of research on how perceptions of stigmatized social groups are represented in the mind (Entman & Rojecki, 2000; Gilman, 1985; Hunt, 1997; Kaplan & Bjørgo, 1998).

However, almost a century after Lippmann's *Public Opinion* was published, Eberhardt (2019) likened his ideas to what psychologists today have dubbed confirmation bias, which essentially says people tend to seek out and attend to information that already confirms their beliefs. Eberhardt also called out Lippmann for his own stereotypical thinking. In *Biased: Uncovering the Hidden Prejudice That Shapes What We See, Think and Do*, Eberhardt noted that in 1919, Lippmann belittled upwardly mobile Blacks who aimed to blend into White America, labeling them the victims of "the peculiar oppressiveness of recently oppressed peoples" (2019, p. 32). Lippmann also advocated for the mass evacuation and mass internment of Japanese Americans in California after the bombing of Pearl Harbor.

INCLUSIVE TEACHING IN THE POSTPANDEMIC CLASSROOM AND BEYOND

Relevant to this book's focus on the struggles, strategies, and scholarship of teaching race in mass communication, this afterword highlights the value and importance of current events in teaching diversity. The COVID-19 pandemic raised awareness of inequities in **inclusion, diversity, equity**, and **accessibility**, also called the **IDEA concept**, in all aspects of our lives. As campus communities quickly pivoted to online teaching and learning in the spring of 2020, SoTL scholars explored how to consider inclusive teaching in online learning spaces (U-M CRLT, 2020; V-U CFT, 2021). They concluded four important points, as listed here.

First is **inclusion**—both in the development of courses (synchronous/ asynchronous, types of course assignments, etc.) and the inclusive generosity extended to students as they shift to a new way of learning and have disparate disruption levels due to the COVID-19 crisis (Campbell, 2019; Leki, 2007).

The second is **diversity**, which is best accomplished by knowing your students (Northwestern University, 2020; Sneed, 2016). If there was ever a time to learn more about your students, this is it (iCivics, 2020). Without knowing them, you may miss some of the important ways they can contribute to the class and assess specific needs better than others (Souza, 2020; Tobin, 2020; Xu & Jaggars, 2014).

Third is **equity**. With a deep significance to equity, the pandemic and the calls for racial justice were significant new events (I-U CITL, 2021). In their commitment to foster equity, prominent news entities compiled key resources to educate, explicate, and enunciate key developments (NYT Learning Network, 2021; facinghistory.org, 2021; WaPoNIE, 2021).

Finally, the fourth is **accessibility** (Cox, 2020; Theisen, 2020; Yang, 2020). COVID-19 has called attention to our students' unequal access to resources (such as computers, Internet access, quiet places to study) that is not always obvious in a face-to-face classroom interaction (Silva et al., 1997).

In teaching race, the collective power of the IDEA concept, as enunciated earlier, ratifies the role and rich heritage of journalism and media to champion social awareness and engagement and social justice.

Even as the pandemic surged unabated worldwide over 2020 summer, the killing of a forty-six-year-old Black man, George Floyd, by a Minneapolis police officer on May 25, 2020 (Memorial Day), sparked calls for racial reckoning and the twin pandemics of racism and coronavirus (Jones, 2020).

The pedagogical relevance of the January 6, 2021, insurrection, historical injustice, and systemic racism highlights the racial reckoning with renewed calls for social justice. For instance, the police shot and killed 989 people in 2020 according to a *Washington Post* (2021) compilation. The *Post* began recording in 2015 every fatal shooting by on-duty U.S. police officers. There have been more than five thousand such shootings comprising a majority of Black people as disproportionate victims of police violence. As educators, we should highlight these current issues to explore theoretical constructs that explicate prejudice, stereotyping, and discrimination to evaluate postracial aspirations in our globalized society and beyond.

The January 6, 2021, insurrection, historical injustice meted to enslaved Black people, and systemic racism of people of color have reinvigorated activism drawing upon the collective power of the IDEA concept in fostering and nurturing diversity. The IDEA concept ratifies the role and rich heritage of journalism and media to champion social awareness and engagement and social justice.

As we look to the future, the ongoing COVID-19 pandemic and the reckoning for racial justice will have sustaining impact on higher education. The postpandemic phase will intensify the need for thoughtful leadership. We continue to do more with less. These challenging times have ratified our resolve to channel the power of communication for the pursuit of a just society.

REFERENCES

Asarta, C. J., Bento, R., Fornaciari, C. J., Lund Dean, K., Arbaugh, J. B., & Hwang, A. (2018). The scholarship of teaching and learning: Changing the dominant narrative about (and in) research institutions. *Journal of Management Education*, 42(6), 731–48.

Biden, J. [@JoeBiden]. (2021, January 7). No one can tell me that if it had been a group of Black Lives Matter protestors yesterday that they wouldn't have been treated very differently than the mob that stormed the Capitol. We all know that's true—and it's unacceptable. [Tweet]. Twitter. https://twitter.com/JoeBiden/status/1347298213422747649.

Campbell, C. (2019, November 21). "The entire system is designed to suppress us": What the Chinese surveillance state means for the rest of the world. *Time*. https://time.com/5735411/china-surveillance-privacy-issues/.

Campbell, C. P. (1995). *Race, myth and the news*. Sage Publications.

Chronicle Insights. (2018, October 22). *Leadership insights: Racial inclusion*. The Chronicle of Higher Education.

Chronicle Report. (2020, September 1). *The post-pandemic college*. The Chronicle of Higher Education.

Clark, R. P. (2021, January 17). Telling it like it is: When writing news requires a distance from neutrality. Poynter. https://www.poynter.org/reporting-editing/2021/telling-it-like-it-is-when-writing-news-requires-distance-from-neutrality/.

Cox, M. (2020, April 1). *Guidance for faculty: Getting & staying connected with int'l students*. Knight Writing Institute at Cornell Arts & Sciences. https://knight.as.cornell.edu/guidance-faculty-getting-staying-connected-intl-students.

Eberhardt, J. L. (2019). *Biased: Uncovering the hidden prejudice that shapes what we see, think, and do*. Viking.

Entman, R. M., & Rojecki, A. (2000). *The Black image in the White mind: Media and race in America*. University of Chicago Press.

facinghistory.org. (2021, January 16). Responding to the insurrection at the US Capitol. Facing history and ourselves. https://www.facinghistory.org/educator-resources/current-events/responding-insurrection-us-capitol.

Gilman, S. L. (1985). *Difference and pathology: Stereotypes of sexuality, race, and madness*. Cornell University Press.

Hunt, D. M. (1997). *Screening the Los Angeles "riots": Race, seeing, and resistance*. Cambridge University Press.

iCivics. (2020, November 17). Tips for keeping control of difficult conversations in virtual classrooms. Bridge Alliance. https://www.bridgealliance.us/tips_for_keeping_control_of_difficult_conversations_in_virtual_classrooms.

I-U CITL. (2021, January 16). Managing difficult classroom discussions: Diversity and Inclusion. Indiana University Bloomington Center for Innovative Teaching and Learning. https://citl.indiana.edu/teaching-resources/diversity-inclusion/managing-difficult-classroom-discussions/index.html.

Jefferson, H. (2021, January 8). Storming the U.S. Capitol was about maintaining White power in America. FiveThirtyEight. https://fivethirtyeight.com/features/storming-the-u-s-capitol-was-about-maintaining-white-power-in-america/.

Jones, A. L. (2020, June 16). The twin pandemics of racism and COVID-19. *Psychology Today*. https://www.psychologytoday.com/us/blog/psychoanalysis-unplugged/202006/the-twin-pandemics-racism-and-covid-19.

Kaplan, J., & Bjørgo, T. (1998). *Nation and race: The developing Euro-American racist subculture*. Northeastern University Press.

Leki, I. (2007). *Undergraduates in a second language: Challenges and complexities of academic literacy development*. Lawrence Erlbaum.

Lippmann, W. (1922). *Public opinion*. Harcourt, Brace and Co.

Morales, E. (2020). "Beasting" at the battleground: Black students responding to racial microaggressions in higher education. *Journal of Diversity in Higher Education*. Advance online publication. https://doi.org/10.1037/dhe0000168.

Northwestern University. (2020, April 1). Inclusive teaching and accessibility online. Digital Learning. https://digitallearning.northwestern.edu/keep-teaching/inclusive-teaching-and-accessibility.

NYT Learning Network. (2021, January 15). Teaching resources to help students make sense of the rampage at the Capitol. *New York Times*. https://www.nytimes.com/2021/01/07/learning/teaching-resources-to-help-students-make-sense-of-the-rampage-at-the-capitol.html.

Silva, T., Leki, I., & Carson, J. (1997). Broadening the perspective of mainstream composition. Some thoughts from the disciplinary margins. *Written Communication, 14*(3), 398–428.

Sneed, O. (2016, January 12). Fostering an inclusive environment when developing online courses. Arizona State University Teach Online. https://teachonline.asu.edu/2016/01/fostering-inclusive-environment-developing-online-courses/.

Souza, T. (2020, June 1). Responding to microaggressions in online learning environments during a pandemic. Academic Impressions. https://www.academicimpressions.com/blog/microaggressions-online-learning/.

Stone, C. (2002, May). Take no prisoners. *Metro Magazine* (Raleigh, NC). https://bit.ly/csUNC.

Theisen, L. (2020, January 22). University of Minnesota student sent to Chinese prison for critical tweets. *New York Daily News*. https://www.nydailynews.com/news/national/ny-minnesota-student-sent-to-chinese-prison-for-tweets-20200123-2syr6takzjcdzek7x3uuacrum4-story.html.

Tobin, T. J. (2020, March 25). Student agency in uncertain times. *Inside Higher Ed*. https://www.insidehighered.com/blogs/university-venus/student-agency-uncertain-times.

U-M CRLT (2020, March 10). COVID-19 and your teaching. University of Michigan Center for Research on Learning and Teaching. https://crlt.umich.edu/blog/covid-19-and-your-teaching.

V-U CFT (2021, January 8). Difficult dialogues. Vanderbilt University Center for Teaching. https://cft.vanderbilt.edu/guides-sub-pages/difficult-dialogues/#tools.

WaPoNIE. (2021, January 17). Curriculum Guides. *The Washington Post* Newspaper in Education. https://nie.washingtonpost.com/.

Washington Post. (2021, January 14). Police shootings database 2015–2021. *Washington Post.* Retrieved February 17, 2021. https://www.washingtonpost.com/graphics/investigations/police-shootings-database/.

Xu, D. & Jaggars, S. S. (2014). Performance gaps between online and face-to-face courses: Differences across types of students and academic subject areas. *The Journal of Higher Education, 85*(5), 633–59.

Yang, W. (2020, February 6). Salting wounds: Accounts of anti-Chinese xenophobia at Cornell and beyond. *Cornell Sun.* https://cornellsun.com/2020/02/06/yang-salting-wounds-accounts-of-anti-chinese-xenophobia-at-cornell-and-beyond/.

Index

#BlackLivesMatter, xvi, xxiii, 4, 126, 130, 175
#CiteBlackWomen, 11
#CommunicationSoWhite, 4
#LoveNotTourism, 102, 126, 136

13th, xx, 88
1619 Project, 8, 11

abolitionist movement, 17
academic culture, 91
accent, 92, 100
Accrediting Council on Education in Journalism and Mass Communication, xiii, xxiii, 10, 41–51, 53, 93, 109, 115, 126, 136, 152
accreditation, xiii, xxiii, 100, 36, 41–51
accreditation standards, xiii, 53, 100, 115, 136
ACEJMC *See* Accrediting Council on Education in Journalism and Mass Communication
Ad Hoc Coordinating Committee on Minority Education, xiii
AEJMC *See* Association for Education in Journalism and Mass Communication

Africa, 93, 96, 113
African Diaspora, xv, 30
African American, xiii, xiv–xv, xix, 21–22, 28–30, 53–56, 60, 70, 86–89, 116, 141–147, 160–163
African American culture, 54
African American culture illiteracy, 53
aggregate all aspects, 178
All Things Considered, 74
Al-Sumalt, Fahed, 103
allyship, 79, 134
American Dream, 26–28, 30, 153
American politics, 175
amplification, 37
anti-blackness, 79
Arab culture, 103
Arasaratnam, Lily, 103
Arbery, Ahmaud, 160
Asia, 22, 93, 96; Asian, 23, 70, 122, 138, 160, 171; Asian American, 17, 39, 137
Associated Press Stylebook, xvi–xviii, 72, 94, 144
Association for Education in Journalism and Mass Communication, x, xii–xiii, xxiv, 46

assumptions, 10, 23, 26, 54, 83, 160, 172, 178
Aunt Jemima, 122–123

Baldwin, James, xix
Barlow, William, xv, 5
Barrow Jr., Lionel, ix, xiii
bias, 9–12, 25, 59–66, 77–83, 89, 97–98, 130, 161, 169–171, 176–180
bicultural, 102
bigotry, 75
BIPOC *See* Black, Indigenous, and People of Color
biracial, 70–74
Black culture, 55
Black, Indigenous, and People of Color, 3–6, 10, 15, 18, 127, 128–129, 131–133, 136, 138–139
Black Public Relations Society, 130
blindnesses, 146
blind spots, 127
Bowe, Brian, 87–88
BPRS *See* Black Public Relations Society
Bramlett-Solomon, Sharon, 127–129
Brookfield, Stephen, xii
Brown, Michael, 130
Brown Kilgo, Danielle, 15, 18, 77
brutality, xxiii; police, 88
Buck, Tamara Z., 136

Caribbean, 22, 28–30, 162
certified diversity facilitator, 53
Chicana/o/x, 17, 22–29
citizenship, 27–29
civic engagement, 111
Civil Rights, 148; Movement, xix, xxiv, 86–88, 109
class, 16, 23–28, 76, 152–154, 171
College Media Association, 136
colonial rule, 22–26
colonialism, 3, 8, 10, 17, 22, 29–30,
coloniality, 22–30
color-blindness, 78, 152–153
Columbia Journalism Review, 131

community: community-centered, 63–64; community partners, 81, 96, 110–112; disenfranchised, 78
competencies, xiii, 10, 43, 46–47, 51, 76, 80, 103, 110, 115, 127, 129
complicity, 5
counter-culture, 30
counter-hegemonic, 29
counteracting performative allyship, 79
COVID-19, 4, 21, 46, 81, 142, 180–181
Creolization, 28
Critical Race Theory, xxiii–xxiv, 22, 24, 35
critical thinking, 11, 21, 48, 114–115, 117, 128, 133, 144, 163, 176
cross-national groups, 157
CRT *See* Critical Race Theory
cultural: barriers, ix; bias, 98; communication, 51; competency, 76, 80; diversity, 21–30; identity, 80, 97, 161; literacy, 53; movements, 29; reflection, 164; resistance, 29; sensitivity, 161–164; taxation, 38; translator, 104; understanding, 109, 121–123; values, xvi
culture courses, 176
curriculum/a, 3–5, 8–11, 16, 17, 30, 42–51, 59, 64, 75–78, 100, 103, 114, 128–129, 133, 144, 146, 150, 152, 160

Dates, Jannette, xv
decoloniality, 22, 35
Deep South, 149, 162
DEI *See* Diversity, equity, and inclusion
dialogue, xxii, xvi, xxiii, 24, 35, 38, 54, 79–80, 89, 99
diaspora/ic, xv, 21, 28, 30
difference, 11, 16, 18, 23, 25, 27, 54, 98–99, 104–105, 121–122, 134, 153–154, 157–164, 169–171
disadvantaged, 5, 86
diversification, 8, 10–12
diversity and media course, xix

diversity: flare-ups, 136–139; diversity standard, xiii, 43, 46–48, 136; plan, 46, 48, 51; statements, 8
Dodd, Julie, 121
dominant narratives, 17, 22, 40, 176
domination, 21, 23, 29
DN *See* dominant narratives
DuVernay, Ava, xx, 88

Elbow Room, 17, 18
empower, 5, 15, 24, 35, 37, 41, 48–49, 128, 133, 136, 155, 170, 177
engagement, 111–118
epistemic, 22–23
epistemology, 24
equity, xii, xxiii, 4, 8–9, 41, 45–51, 76–78, 83, 96, 113, 134, 152, 156, 158, 180–181; Equity and Diversity Award, 46; Equity Unbound, 81
ethnic, xxiii, 27–28, 89, 94, 96, 113–116, 126–127, 154, 157, 160–163; ethnic inequality, 160; ethnicity, xiii, xvi–xviii, 10, 16, 48–51, 76–77, 94, 97, 110, 132, 152, 170–171
Eurocentered, 22, 27
European American, 23, 27–28
evaluate, 129, 170, 177–181
Exhibit A, xx
explicate, 177–181
exploitation, 29–30
explore, 177–181
Eyes on the Prize, 86–88
eyewitness misidentification, xix–xx

first-year experience courses, 15–18
Floyd, George, xiii, 4, 160, 181

Geisler, Jill, 133
gender, 16–18, 23–25, 37–38, 43–49, 76, 86, 94, 103–104, 114–116, 128, 152–155, 171; identity, 66; neutral, 144; orientation, 161; gender-segregated, 102
geopolitical, 29
global diversity, 44–45
Gone with the Wind, 123

Green, Misha, 88
Greenwood, 141–148
Gutierrez, Felix, xv

Hampton, Henry, 86–88
Hannah-Jones, Nikole, 11
HBCU *See* Historically Black College and University
hegemony, 35, 37
higher-education, 76, 78, 91, 104, 114, 116, 158, 160
Hispanic, 21, 45, 70, 162–163
Historically Black College and University, xv, xxiii, 53–56, 86–88, Hutchins Commission of 1947, 5–6

ICC *See* Intercultural Communication Competence
IDEA *See* Inclusion, Diversity, Equity, and Accessibility
identification, xxiii, 27–30
identity, 5
ideology, 27
immersive learning, 109–118
improvise, 178
inclusion, ix, 4–7, 35, 41–51, 59, 76, 94–96, 121, 126–138, 158, 180
inclusion, diversity, equity, and accessibility, 180–181
inclusiveness, 42–51
indicators, 48–51
indigenous, xx, 3, 8, 15, 28, 127, 136
inequality, xvi, 27, 160
inform, 178
infuse, 178
injustice, 7, 12, 27, 146, 149, 181
innovate, 3, 178
institutional, 15, 24, 78, 130, 137
insurrection, xxiii, 175, 179–181
intellectual labor, 59
interactive race beat, 77
intercultural communication competence, 103–104
international, 48–51
interrogate, 177–178
intersectional, 16–18, 23–24, 35–40, 59

invigorate, 178
invisible labor, 38

Jefferson, Atatiana, 160
Jefferson, Hakeem, 160
joteria, 35

K-pop, 95
Kernahan, Cyndi, xii
Kerner Commission, 6, 77, 88, 109
key performance indicator, 46–47, 51
King Jr., Martin Luther, xiii, 18, 87
KPI *See* Key Performance Indicator

Latinx, 17, 21–22, 28, 93–97, 122, 169
leadership, 45, 117, 127–133, 136, 138, 159, 182
lecturer, 59–105
legacy, 8, 30, 149
Lehrman, Sally, xvi
Len-Ríos, María, xvi
lesbian/gay/bisexual people of color, 162
LGB-POC *See* Lesbian/gay/bisexual people of color
LGBTQ, 17, 39, 160–163, 171
Lippmann, Walter, 179–180
Lorde, Audre, 138
Lovecraft Country, 88, 144
Loving v. Virginia, 102

MAC *See* Minorities and Communication Division
majority-minority, 100
Manifest Destiny, 16–17
marginalization, 4
marginalized: communities, 7; groups, xi, 74, 77–82, 96, 162, 176; identities, 35–39; individuals, 169
Martindale, Carolyn, xiii
Maynard Institute, xix, 65
Mentor, xxii, 115, 126
Mentorship, 37, 157, 160, 168
mestizaje, 28
mestizo, 28
microaggression, 60, 78, 138, 160–163, 168, 176

Middle East, 93, 96
migration, 29–30, 160, 170
Minorities and Communication Division, 10
Minorities Task Force, 43
minority: community, 129–133; faculty, 59–74, 92–100, 126; groups, ix, 50; issues, 132; sources, 131; owned, 25
misperceptions, 92, 98
model minority, 17
monocultural, 27
monoracial, 122
multiculturalism, xviii, 27–28, 38
multiplicity, 35
multiracial, 70–74

NAACP *See* National Association for the Advancement of Colored People
NABJ *See* National Association of Black Journalist
Najjar, Jasmina, 81
National Association for the Advancement of Colored People, xiv
National Association of Black Journalist, 45, 60, 74, 158
nationality, 30, 76, 132
Native American, 88–89, 96–97, 137
nepantla, 28
neurodiversity, 104
neutrality, 23, 179
newsroom culture, 128, 129, 133, 134
nonharassing cultures, 133
Noah, Trevor, 73
norms, 4, 8, 12, 64–65, 77, 104

objectivity, 9, 12, 23–26, 179
OneHE, 81
oppressed, 180
ostracism, 6, 36, 154
otherizing, 77–78
Out of the Blocks, 89

pandemic, xxi, 4, 11, 21, 46, 81, 102, 142, 160, 180–181
paradigm, 5, 23–24, 77, 164

Parry, Pam, xii
pedagogy, xxiii–xxiv, 18, 21, 35–40, 59, 64, 76–83, 104–105, 141, 146, 149, 160
performative wokeness, xx, 79
Picking Cotton, xix
political correct, 8
positionality, 23, 37, 39
power, 145, 152, 169–170, 176
pragmatism, 23
predominantly White institutions, 60, 70, 125, 160
prejudice, 92–93, 97–99, 162, 168, 179–181
privilege, 9, 11, 18, 27–28, 35–39, 75–79, 83, 134, 154–156, 162
professional values, 46–51
project for excellence on journalism, xvi
protest movements, 81
PRSSA *See* Public Relations Student Society of America
Public Relations, 6, 79, 93–96, 126–127, 169–170
Public Relations Student Society of America, 127
PWI *See* Predominately White Institutions
Pyle, Ernie, 7

quare, 35

race *See* racial
racial: awakening, 79; barriers, 27; conflict, 25; descriptions, 70–72; divides, 64; domination, 21; fault lines, 65; hierarchy, 170; identity, 61, 70, 80, 89, 96, 161; inequality, 160; justice, 64, 181; language, 148; microaggressions, 176; myths, 59, 65; panic, 136–139; prejudice, 168; pride, 30; reckoning, 4, 130, 179–181; slurs, 104; stratification, 21–26; violence, 142
racism, xii–xix, 5–11, 18, 22–27, 35–39, 75–83, 136–139, 148–149, 179–181
rationality, 23

RAPID *See* Reflect; Amplify; Purposeful; Intersectional inclusive content; Decenter whiteness, privilege, and power
Reflect; Amplify; Purposeful; Intersectional inclusive content; Decenter whiteness, privilege, and power, 35
reflexivity, 39, 62–66, 164
religion, 16, 41, 51, 99, 115, 122, 160
representation, xix, 4–6, 23–27, 38–39, 43–45, 59, 94–98, 122–123, 126–133
Robinson, Jo Ann, 87
Robinson, Sue, 64
Rodriguez, Ilia, 35, 40
Rodriguez, Nathian Shae, 36
Rothschild, Emma, 145

"Save America," 175
scholarship of teaching and learning, xvii, xxiv, 76, 80–81, 105, 177
science, technology, engineering, and mathematics, and education, 161
self-awareness, 63, 105
self-efficacy, 168
service learning, 110–111, 114
slavery, xviii, 8, 16, 29–30
Smoke Signals, 88
social: barriers, 27; construction of reality, 64–66; discourse, 26; identity, 16–18, 98; injustice, xix, 12, 27, 146; justice, 8, 76–79, 123, 148, 176–181; social media, 11, 118, 123; psychology, 163; science, 160–163; stigma, 148
Society of Professional Journalists, xvi, 127
solidarity, 4, 28–29, 39, 79
SoTL *See* scholarship of teaching and learning
STEM *See* science, technology, engineering, and mathematics
stereotyping, xvi, 45, 77, 179–181
Student Press Law Center, 132
symbolic annihilation, 21, 86, 89
systemic racism, xviii, 179–181

Take This Hammer, xix
Tavernier-Almada, Linda, xix
Taylor, Breonna, 160
teaching: innovations, 99–100; lessons, 177; philosophy, 44; race, xii–xiv, 15, 35, 59–65, 80, 92–93, 180–181
textbook, 94, 99
The New Jim Crow, xix
The Confession Tapes, xx
The Innocence Files, xx
Them, 131
theories of the flesh, 35
Thompson, Sherwood, xii
thoughtful insights, 177
topical relevance, 177
transnational, 28–29
trauma, 75, 146–149
Tryzna, Marta, 103
Tulsa Race Massacre, 141–151, 171

U.S. Capitol, xxiii, 175
U.S. Census, 21, 28, 43, 160

Uncle Ben's Rice, 123
underrepresentation, 4–5
universality, 23, 26

Wagner, Venise, xvi, xix
Watchmen, 144
Wesley, John, 113
western epistemology, 24
White: ethnic press, xv, 77; fragility, 136; supremacy, 3–12, 23–26, 75–78, 132; violence, xix
White culture, 53
whiteness, xii, 6, 24–28, 35–38, 59, 76–80
Williams-Myers, A. J., xix
Wilson, Clint, xv
Withers, Ernest, 109
woke, 79
workplace integrity curriculum, 133

xenophobia, xviii

About the Editors and Contributors

EDITORS

Robin Blom is an associate professor and graduate director of journalism at Ball State University. He teaches media theory, media law, media analytics, and sociology of news, as well as honors college courses about pseudoscience, conspiracy theories, eyewitness misidentification, and social injustice. Blom earned his PhD in media and information studies from Michigan State University. He is the director of the Unified Research Lab, where he facilitates eye tracking, virtual reality, psycho-physiology, and gaming studies with more than a dozen faculty and student researchers. His own research is primarily focused on expectancy violations as a mechanism of understanding misinformation and media bias perceptions. He also studies the role of news media outlets in wrongful conviction cases for publishing eyewitness misidentification accounts and the structural violence that this has caused toward the innocent and vulnerable communities.

George L. Daniels is an associate professor of journalism and creative media at the University of Alabama. He is immediate past head of the AEJMC Minorities and Communication Division. Daniels received his PhD in mass communication from the Grady College of Journalism and Mass Communication at the University of Georgia. A former local television news producer, Daniels teaches courses in electronic news reporting, basic newswriting, diversity, media management, and service learning. His research focuses on diversity in the media workplace and in media messages. He has studied media portrayals of African American males and the Black Press. In addition to several book chapters, his research has appeared in *Journalism & Mass Communication Quarterly*, *Journalism & Mass Communication Educator*, and *Journalism: Theory, Practice & Criticism*. Daniels is a nationally certified master journalism educator and the inaugural faculty fellow for diversity and inclusion for the Broadcast Education Association.

CONTRIBUTORS

Gregory Adamo is a professor in the School of Global Journalism and Communication at Morgan State University in Baltimore. He received his PhD in communication from Rutgers University. Dr. Adamo is the author of the book *African Americans in Television: Behind the Scenes* (Peter Lang, 2010) and coeditor of *College Media: Learning in Action* (Peter Lang, 2017). Dr. Adamo was head of the Entertainment Studies Interest Group of AEJMC in 2019–2020. His research interests include media and race, the production of culture, and entertainment television. He has taught at the College of Staten Island/CUNY, Rutgers University, and Richard Stockton College. Dr. Adamo was general manager of WSIA-FM for more than two decades. He is an avid cyclist and hiker and is very proud of his two adult children, Kerian and Colin. His webpage is www.gregory.adamo.com.

Deb Aikat (pronounced *EYE-cut*) is a former journalist and has been a faculty member since 1995 at the Hussman School of Journalism and Media at the University of North Carolina at Chapel Hill. An award-winning scholar, Dr. Aikat theorizes the role of digital media in the global sphere. He coauthored the 2019 book *Agendamelding: News, Social Media, Audiences, and Civic Community* with Dr. Don Shaw, Dr. Milad Minooie, and Dr. Chris Vargo. Dr. Aikat earned a PhD (1995) in media and journalism from Ohio University's Scripps School of Journalism and a Certificate in American Political Culture (1990) from New York University. Dr. Aikat serves as the 2020–2021 vice president and will serve as 2022–2023 president of AEJMC, one of the premier scholarly organizations in our field. Go to https://bit.ly/DebAikat.

Mariam F. Alkazemi is an assistant professor at the Robertson School of Media and Culture at Virginia Commonwealth University. Previously, she served as a professor at Gulf University for Science and Technology, a Carnegie fellow at the University of North Carolina, and a research fellow at the London School of Economics. She has contributed to over thirty peer-reviewed publications on a range of topics. She is a co-editor of a volume on the Arab diaspora, which was published in 2021. She has received a number of awards for her teaching and research, and she has received funding to support her research activities. She holds degrees from the University of Florida (2014, PhD), Michigan State University (2009, MA), and George Washington University (2007, BA).

Cristina L. Azocar is a member of the Upper Mattaponi Tribe. She is a professor of journalism at San Francisco State University. Her research focuses on the intersection of race and journalistic practice, particularly in the area of news coverage of Indigenous people. Dr. Azocar served as a past president of the Native American Journalists Association, directed the Center for Integration and Improvement of Journalism, was a former editor of American Indian Issues for the Media Diversity Forum, and was an inaugural board member of the Women's Media Center. She received her PhD in communication studies from the University of Michigan. Dr. Azocar was the first recipient of AEJMC's Dr. Paula M. Poindexter Research Grant for a research project on news coverage of the tribal federal recognition process that will be published by Lexington Books. Her research is published in *Howard Journal of Communications*, *Health Communication*, *Journal of Communication*, *International Journal of Home Economics*, and *Journal of Broadcasting and Electronic Media*.

Aqsa Bashir is a PhD graduate from the College of Journalism and Communications, University of Florida. Bashir serves as an instructor for the undergraduate courses International Advertising (ADV4400), Digital Insights (ADV3500) Problems, and Ethics in Mass Communication (MMC 3203), being offered at the College of Journalism and Communications, and for the course Introduction to Public Speaking (SPC2608) offered by the Dial Center for Written & Oral Communication at the University of Florida. Bashir has a strong passion for emotional response to marketing and advertising research as well as sharing her knowledge and experience on international advertising with her students. Prior to coming to UF to pursue her master's in Advertising, Bashir worked for Newsweek Pakistan as their marketing executive.

Masudul K. Biswas is an associate professor of communication at Loyola University Maryland. He is a former head of the AEJMC's Minorities and Communication Division. He received his PhD in media and public affairs from the Manship School of Mass Communication at Louisiana State University. A former journalist in Bangladesh and web developer of the Media Diversity Forum, Biswas teaches courses on web development, mobile storytelling, emerging media, digital media capstone, and diversity and the media. His major areas of research focus on diversity in the intersections of public affairs and online news, roles of ethnic news media, and diversity in journalism and communication education. His research is published in *Journalism & Mass Communication Educator*, *Newspaper Research Journal*, and *Teaching Journalism & Mass Communication*. In 2017–2018, he worked on an Ohio University–UNICEF project on communication for development curriculum for the universities in Bangladesh.

Brian J. Bowe is an associate professor of journalism at Western Washington University and an associate professor in the School of Global Affairs and Public Policy at The American University in Cairo. His research interests include media framing, representations of Muslims, and journalism curriculum design and assessment. He received his PhD in media and information studies from Michigan State University, where he also completed the Certification in College Teaching program. Bowe is a veteran journalist, author, and educator whose work examines the interplay of journalism and culture. He has an extensive background in music journalism, writing books and liner notes. Bowe co-edited the book *CREEM: America's Only Rock 'n' Roll Magazine*. He worked as a newspaper journalist in Michigan and New Hampshire.

Danielle Brown Kilgo is the John and Elizabeth Bates Cowles Professor of Journalism, Diversity, and Equality at the University of Minnesota, Twin Cities. She has published dozens of peer-reviewed articles on research that primarily focus on the entanglement of race and gender disparities in visual, digital, and social media communication. Currently, she concentrates on media coverage of issues related to police violence, crisis, and protests in the United States. She teaches classes in diversity and mass communication and visual communication. Brown earned her BA and MA in journalism, public relations, and new media from Baylor University and her PhD in journalism from the University of Texas at Austin. Prior to her research career, Brown worked as a photojournalist and public relations professional. Brown serves as faculty research chair for the AEJMC Minorities and Communication Division.

Tamara Z. Buck is a professor of multimedia journalism and chair of Southeast Missouri State University's Department of Mass Media. She is a 2020–2021 AEJMC Institute for Diversity in Leadership fellow and in 2013 was named to the inaugural class of Kopenhaver Center Fellows. A reporter by trade and lawyer by training, Buck teaches media diversity, media law, and a variety of courses related to multimedia journalism. She earned her juris doctor degree from the University of Memphis. Since 2010, she has served as faculty adviser to the award-winning *Arrow* student newspaper. In January 2021, she was appointed president elect of the College Media Association while serving as the organization's first vice president of member support. She is recognized for her presentations on microaggressions in news content and diversity and inclusion problems in student media.

Meta G. Carstarphen ("Dr. C"), Gaylord family professor, is a faculty member in the strategic communication area of the Gaylord College of Journalism and Communication. Her research interests are to explore the intentional use of mediated communication to create transformative, collaborative, and diversified social change. A former head of the Minorities and Communication Division, Dr. C is nationally accredited in public relations by the Public Relations Society of America. Her books include *Sexual Rhetoric: Media Perspectives on Sexuality, Gender and Identity* (1999), *Writing PR: A Multimedia Approach* (2004), *American Indians and the Mass Media* (2012), and *Race, Gender Class and the Media* (2017). Her awards include the 2020 AEJMC Lionel C. Barrow Award for Distinguished

Achievement in Diversity Research and the 2019 Gaylord College Owen Kulemeka Trailblazer Award in Diversity. She has a PhD in rhetoric from Texas Woman's University.

Angie Chuang is a second-generation Chinese American with roots in Taiwan. She is an associate professor of journalism at the University of Colorado Boulder's College of Media, Communication, and Information. Prior to that appointment, she was on the journalism faculty of American University's School of Communication for a decade. Chuang is a former newspaper reporter who launched one of the first regional race and ethnicity issues beats at *The Oregonian*. She has also been a staff writer at *The Hartford Courant* and the *Los Angeles Times*. Her research on representations of Otherness and American identity has appeared in *Journalism and Mass Communication Quarterly*, *Journalism: Theory, Practice, and Criticism*, and *Communication, Culture & Critique*. She is the secretary of the AEJMC Minorities and Communication Division.

Keonte Coleman serves as an assistant professor in the School of Journalism and Strategic Media at Middle Tennessee State University. He loves sharing his passion for media with students and helping them find their voices as storytellers. While working as a local television news producer, Coleman won two Emmy Awards, an Edward R. Murrow Award, a Peabody Award, and three Walter Cronkite Awards. He previously served as an academic dean, department chair, and assistant professor at Bennett College. Coleman received a PhD in higher education administration from the University of North Carolina–Greensboro. His research interests align with various intersections of diversity, journalism, leadership, media, and higher education. He coauthored a news-producing textbook: *Complete Guide to Television, Field and Digital Producing*. He is married to the love of his life and is the proud father of three beautiful children.

Alfred J. Cotton III is an assistant professor in the Journalism Department at the University of Cincinnati. A media critic and scholar, he runs the New Media and Social Responsibility project out of the Democracy and Culture Lab at the University of Cincinnati. His research covers ethics and social responsibility in journalism. He has written about the coverage of police killings of unarmed Black men, using social media as a reporting tool, as well as news coverage of environmental crises, among other topics. He teaches courses on public affairs reporting, the principles of American journalism, and race and reporting. Before earning a PhD in communication from the University of Kentucky, he worked as a weekly newspaper copy editor and section editor on Long Island, New York.

Maria De Moya is an associate professor of public relations in DePaul University's College of Communication. She also serves as academic director of the MA program in public relations and advertising and director of the Latino media and communication program. She holds a PhD in mass communication from the University of Florida and an MA in business and economic journalism from New York University, where she was a Fulbright scholar. Her research centers on international and ethnic public relations, with a specific focus on questions of community, identity, and advocacy. Her work intersects with the fields of public diplomacy and communication for social change. Dr. De Moya is second vice head and student research chair of the AEJMC Minorities and Communication Division.

Troy Elias is an associate professor in the advertising sequence in the School of Journalism and Communication at the University of Oregon. He received his PhD in communication from Ohio State University. His research interests focus on diversity and equity, media effects, and attitudes and orientations related to climate change. Dr. Elias aims to help climate change organizations, brands, and journalists understand the importance of including and communicating with communities of color. Dr. Elias has received a mentorship award from UO's Black Women of Achievement student group and he is the faculty advisor for UO's National Association of Black Journalists. He has published in the *Journal of Advertising Research, International Journal of Communication, Environmental Values, Howard Journal of Communications, Journal of Interactive Advertising,* and *Journal of Social Media in Society.*

Melody T. Fisher is an associate professor in the Department of Communication at Mississippi State University and was previously the chair of the Mass Communication Department at Tougaloo College. Currently, she is head of the Minorities and Communication Division of the Association for Education in Journalism and Mass Communication and is a member of the President's Commission on the Status of Minorities at Mississippi State University. She was also an educator fellow in the Plank Center for Leadership in Public Relations program. She has written articles and presented papers on diversity-related topics with focuses on activism, image repair, and representation. She earned her PhD in mass communication at the University of Southern Mississippi.

Elliott Lewis is a professor of practice of broadcast and digital journalism at the S. I. Newhouse School of Public Communications at Syracuse University. A former television reporter, he spent ten years in Washington, DC, as a freelance correspondent for BET, Hearst Television, Tribune

Broadcasting, and WJLA-TV and worked as a video content producer for the Associated Press. Before moving to the nation's capital, he was a reporter and fill-in anchor for stations in Reno, San Diego, Portland (Oregon), Cincinnati, and Orlando. He is the author of *Fade: My Journeys in Multiracial America*, published in 2006 by Carroll & Graf. He holds a JD from the University of Akron School of Law and is a member of the New York State Bar Association.

Mia Moody-Ramirez is professor and chair of the Baylor University Department of Journalism, Public Relations, and New Media. She earned her PhD in journalism at the University of Texas at Austin. She joined Baylor in 2001 and has maintained an active research portfolio in addition to her teaching and leadership roles. Her research emphasizes media framing of People of Color, women, and other underrepresented groups. The author or coauthor of four books, Dr. Moody-Ramirez has also been widely published in a variety of academic and industry journals. She was honored with the Outstanding Woman in Journalism award by the Association for Education in Journalism and Mass Communication, and in the summer of 2020 received the organization's Lionel Barrow Jr. Award for Distinguished Achievement in Diversity Research and Education. She is also a 2019 fellow in the AEJMC Institute for Diverse Leadership. She served as head of the AEJMC Minorities and Communication Division from 2017 to 2019.

Robbie R. Morganfield is the Janet Howroyd/News and Record Professor of Journalism and Mass Communication at North Carolina A&T State University in Greensboro. A former award-winning daily newspaper journalist, Morganfield has taught at several other universities and served as executive director of the Freedom Forum Diversity Institute at Vanderbilt University, head of the Department of Mass Communication at Grambling State University, and a senior pastor in the Baltimore Washington Conference of the United Methodist Church. He specializes in news production, research methods, and media representation of race, religion, and culture. Morganfield holds a BA in journalism from the University of Mississippi, an MA in journalism from The Ohio State University, an MDiv from Texas Christian University, and PhD in journalism and public communication from the University of Maryland.

Ilia Rodríguez is an associate professor of journalism and media studies at the University of New Mexico, where she teaches graduate and undergraduate courses in history of media, newswriting, multiculturalism, gender and media, media theories, and research methodologies. She received her PhD in journalism and mass communication from the

University of Minnesota. Her research focuses on the analysis of news discourses on racial relations and cultural difference in mainstream, African American, and Latinx newspapers through the lenses of critical theories, coloniality studies, and Critical Race Theory. Her work has been published in anthologies and journals, including *Black Culture and Experience: Contemporary Issues*, *Howard Journal of Communications*, *Gazette: International Journal for Communication Studies*, *Journalism: Theory, Practice & Criticism*, *Bilingual Review*, *Revista Iberoamericana*, and *Razón y Palabra*, among others. Rodríguez served as head of the AEJMC Minorities and Communication Division in 2010–2011.

Nathian Shae Rodriguez is an associate professor of digital media in the School of Journalism and Media Studies at San Diego State University and core faculty in the Area of Excellence: Digital Humanities and Global Diversity. He specializes in critical cultural and digital media studies, critical communication pedagogy, and pop culture pedagogy. Rodriguez received his PhD in media and communication from Texas Tech University. His research focuses on minority representation in media, specifically LGBTQ and Latinx portrayals and intersectional identity negotiation, as well as pop culture, identity, radio broadcasting, and issues of masculinity/mascing. Dr. Rodriguez has ten years of professional radio experience in on-air talent, sales, promotions, and social media marketing. He is also the creator and host of *Sin Vergüenza: An Unapologetically Queer & Brown Podcast*.

Gabriel B. Tait is an associate professor of diversity and media at Ball State University. He is a member of the AEJMC Professional Freedom and Responsibility Committee and Minorities and Communication Division. He is also a two-term immediate past head of the AEJMC Visual Communication Division. He received his PhD in intercultural studies from Asbury Theological Seminary. His research areas include diversity and media, participatory photography, and the role photography plays in constructing and representing cultural identities. Tait's tenure as a photojournalist spans nearly thirty years, working at the *Detroit Free Press*, *St. Louis Post-Dispatch*, and several other newspapers where he was nominated for the Pulitzer Prize. He is the creator of the visual research methodology "Sight Beyond My Sight" (SBMS). He is also co-editor of *Narratives of Storytelling Across Cultures: The Complexities of Intercultural Communication*.

www.ingramcontent.com/pod-product-compliance
Lightning Source LLC
Chambersburg PA
CBHW052059300426
44117CB00013B/2205